LEARNING
TO EAT

Also by Jeff Weinstein

Life in San Diego

LEARNING TO EAT

TO EAT

EFF WEINSTEIN

© Jeff Weinstein, 1988
Cover: Marsden Hartley, *Handsome Drinks*,
      The Brooklyn Museum
Design: Katie Messborn

Library of Congress Cataloging-in-Publication Data

Weinstein, Jeff
   Learning to Eat

ISBN: 1-55713-015-9   88-043062

---

10 9 8 7 6 5 4 3 2 1

Sun & Moon Press
6148 Wilshire Blvd.
Gertrude Stein Plaza
Los Angeles, California 90048

Acknowledgements

These pieces were first published in *The Village Voice* from 1979 to the end of 1986, most of them culled from my biweekly and then weekly column, Eating Around (the remainder posing as book reviews or features). With the exception of the first two, "What I Do" and "What I Try To Do," they are arranged in chronological order. I have not changed or amended them, although history has: Howard Beach (August 13, 1979) now carries connotations that make my return seem inappropriately sentimental, and the Zwieback infant (November 26, 1985) has been retired again, replaced by a more timely babe.

Since writing for a newspaper entails running a gauntlet of helpfulness, I wish to thank my many colleagues and friends who fielded phone calls, sorted mail, issued checks, edited and proofed copy, checked facts, and designed the pages that carried each piece. My editor, Ross Wetzsteon, found the calm balance between careful assistance and superbly benign neglect; photographer James Hamilton leapt over cliches; editor-in-chief David Schneiderman supported my quiddities without qualms. Also, at Sun & Moon Press, Douglas Messerli had no doubts.

Dozens have braved the unknown with me at table, eating out of curiosity, generosity, and pleasure: I am grateful to you all. But John Perreault has not only downed each dish but has listened to each word, patiently and critically, year after year, and of course I dedicate this book to him.

Contents

What I Do   11
What I Try To Do   16
Howard Hues   21
Waiting on Godot   26
Holiday on Ice   29
Coming Up for Air   33
Mi Utopia   37
'The 25 Greatest Restaurants in America'   40
And Dance the Night Away With Us   42
Table of Content   46
Chop Flop, Nix Chix   50
A la Carte, at Last   54
Table for One   58
Pop Art   62
On Authenticity   67
Victory Garden   74
Surplus Value   78
One Star   82
Here's Looking at You   88
Underground Gourmet   91
Form Follows Biscuit   97
In Which They Serve   102
Suburban Renewal   105
Molly and Me   109
Fission Chips   112
Class Crustacea   115
Cape Maybe   119

Style, Though Your Heart Is Breaking 123
Word Enough and Thyme 127
Flying Down to Rio, or Whatever Happened
  to Carmen Miranda 131
Only Connect 140
Caviar and the Masses 144
Deco on Rye 149
An Ideology of the Sandwich 153
Permanently Fresh 157
The New West 161
Beautiful Soup 179
Why There Are No Great Restaurants on
  the Upper West Side 183
Order in the Court 188
Eating Backward 192
Cooking Backward 196
Eggs for Lunch 199
Ask Not What Your Restaurant Can Do For
  You . . . 202
Local Imperial 206
Apples et Oranges 210
Why They Eat: Deborah 214
Postmodern Meat 218
To Av or Av Not 223
Czardas Memories 226
Bar Salad 229
A Country Full of Italian Restaurants 233
Memories of Things Pasta 238
Artburn? 243
Why They Eat: James 247
Meals on Wheels 251

Tearoom Trad   256
Bring Home the BLT   260
Rich Food   263
Home Sweet Home   267
Why They Eat   271
In Ulster, Among Sconces and Scones   277
Restaurant Row   282
The Semiotics of Zwieback   286
Our Town   290
The Last Cornflake Show   294
Forget the Alamo   302
The Corn Is Blue   307
Yuppie Falls, Hits Bottom   316
Crimes Against Dining   320
Paris, New York   325
Sans Bell-Bottoms   335
Cloy to the World   339

What I Do

You'd think eating at a single restaurant four times in two months would consolidate the big picture. The restaurant in question was terrible, skill-free beyond belief, and I had the notes to prove it. Its ideologically ridden cooking led, without digression, to my thesis for the week's forthcoming piece, why "health food" is synonymous with punishment in our great, gorging city. But a severely negative review—termed, aptly for my field, a "pan"—is an act with serious consequences, so I thought I'd risk one more try.

Those of you who envy me my job, think how it felt to make that fifth reservation, how I had to modulate, over the phone, my tone of disgust to one of bland anticipation. I had hated every eating moment, downing messes the restaurant should pay customers to eat. Of course, I *am* paid to eat, but what some colleagues call professionalism can be nothing more than masochism with a determined face.

We ordered the same two entrees that were, or should have been, signature dishes. The server served, I cringed, she strode away, I peeked at my plate: and it was beautiful, nothing like the dropped brown pile I had been poised to draw. I ate, and it "tasted," which is shorthand for opened up like a flower, or at the very least, like an umbrella. This food did not cauterize my sensorium.

So I sat, stuck. Was a new or different chef responsible for the change or did the old one finally lift the toque out of his or her eyes? If this reprieve was an "accident," what would such haphazard production mean? It seemed to throw the whole project of restaurant reviewing into bleak doubt. None of those eating partners staunch enough to accompany me on the first four trips would come again to reevaluate, I was sure of that. Who would risk eating with me?

Friends and readers ask, kindly and surprisingly often, how I do my work. No one, I must add, inquires about *why* I write about restaurants and public eating, the answer to which may be more revelatory than either party would wish. Part of my work depends on routine and part on chance, even though my assumptions about what I do have retained their basic shapes over 15 or so years of professional immersion in dished-out food. Columns get written as a result of the tension between pleasing a hypothetical reader—dangerous concept—and pleasing myself. The subtle impulse to please the newspaper and its editors is a form of self-censorship—internalizing possible cues of manipulation—I attempt to avoid. It's quite clear, at least, when this writer and some readers are satisfied, and I sleep soundly that night.

I have learned my routine. Only wide-girthed restaurants can afford press releases; I receive a dozen a week, sometimes more before a food holiday such as Thanksgiving. The most helpful of these include menus. Menus obviously provide selections and prices, but if you hold a menu for a while, reading the dishes, so to speak, as they are cooked, the kitchen will appear as a hologram in which you can count how many simmering pots await their pasta—this is a decent kitchen—or how many cooks are standing around, ready to spoil the broth. The plangent redundancy of "Shrimp Scampi" demands the circular file (although I save every menu, valuing it as record of otherwise despised cultural history). So does "Stuffed Sole," especially on First Avenue and sixty-something street, although I try to keep my mouth's ear open for corrections on too early a dismissal.

I get letters from readers with suggestions about their favorite eating loci. I can smell, however, the missive generated by the restaurant itself: underfunded ethnic eateries, for example, find a dissimilarly ethnic client with an M.D. attached who then types a single-spaced two-pager about how exquisite is the Chicken Tandoori. Sometimes there is evidence that the restaurant writes the letter and invents the signator, an act whose implied desperation makes me sad.

I read trade mags. Word of a big opening, like Joe Baum's Aurora on 49th Street, usually gets around. Friends give me tips. The tip that's simply notice of an opening is remarkably helpful, like having a centapod appetite walk the city for you. The tip that's opinion of the food is less to the point, unless I get to know the tipper: one couple always touts places I can't abide, so their discoveries are as good as opposite gold. In case it isn't clear, the most difficult *routine* part of my work is finding a restaurant that, through its novelty, merit, pretension, tenure, or embodiment of idea, is worth writing about. This assumes I write only "about restaurants"; there are other ways to consider the job.

I eat at least three times in the same restaurant over a

month or two for a full review. The paper pays, by reimbursing me after I tote up my receipts. (I spend from $100 to—rarely—$500 a week.) I now brandish a credit card with a *nom de plastic,* to disable a canny cashier from fingering me, but waiters are the real danger because they move so often from restaurant to restaurant: they spot me at art openings and department stores, where I foolishly thought I had not needed anonymity.

The first time I try a place I go with my long-suffering spousal equivalent—as he is designated in our union health plan. We choose (I choose) what my intuition tells me will be either most disastrous—restaurant syntax allows "most disastrous"—or most pleasurable, saving the category of typical for the optional future. Can we enjoy ourselves, are we tempted to return of our own free will, would we buy this grilled snark with our own money? Try as I might to recapture the innocence of these questions, the gray aura of work denatures them. Once in a while I pay my own way to remind myself how quickly money can dribble out of a wallet—once in a great while. During these initial meals, John and I eat a great deal of bad or mediocre food.

One restaurant in five will tempt me to return, with a party of curious friends. I always explain that they must choose their fate from a menu of my needs (I pick last, sweeping up) and that we might have a ghastly meal. They say it makes no difference, we have a horrendous meal, and I don't see them for half a year. When it's good, they gorge; I try to nibble. One fried, one broiled, one roasted, one sauteed, one grilled; two repeats; weekends plus weekdays; early and late. "Forget about what we're doing," I ask, "are you having fun?" Masters of the modal, they answer that they "could." Someone says the name of the newspaper as loud as possible and then apologizes to me by name even louder. One colleague even wore a *Voice* T-shirt, which is ugly enough as it is.

When I get home I take notes on every dish, and ruminate. Sometimes I read books or articles connected to the cuisine on the stand. Finally, on deadline day, I rip up my notes, try to forget them, and write.

(1/28/1986)

What I Try To Do

On the one hand you have Rian "Bicarbonate" James, born the last year of the last century, who says his "weaknesses are airplanes, Coca Colas, and headwaiters named George" and who in 1930 wrote a reader's guide called *Dining in New York*. Rian James dressed for dinner, in the black-and-white sense; that was no doubt him holding the door for Carole Lombard as she swept by in tulle, looking to complete her scavenger hunt by finding a Forgotten Man. Rian James ate at Trotzky's, the restaurant owned by Leon's kosher brother; at the Rajah, a Turkish place "about as big as a medium-sized clothes-press, and not nearly so sanitary"; and at the primordial Beefsteak Charlie's. For slumming James preferred Harlem—"where the banker rubs shoulders with his elevator operator"—to the Village. Apparently the Village was not what it used to be:

The interesting people who once frequented the better-known Village favorites have been supplanted by long-haired men and short-haired women; by fiery-eyed politicians, who'd rather rave than work; by messy maidens, who believe in free love, free passion and free food, and messier swains who live on what they can borrow, rather than on what they can make; by giants who dabble in tenth-rate water-colors, and pygmies who sculpt; by wide-eyed little ladies from the middle-west, but newly arrived, who don't as yet quite know what to make of it all; and by pallid failures who hide their inabilities under the

16

all-embracing term of Art."

He was referring to what we now call the *West* Village, in case that isn't clear. On the other hand you have Primo Levi, a prisoner at Monowitz (a part of Auschwitz) 15 years after the publication of Bicarbonate James's book. In an article called "Last Christmas of the War" (*New York Review of Books*) Levi remembers the arrival of a gift of food sent by his sister and mother from Italy:

The package contained ersatz chocolate, cookies, and powdered milk, but to describe its real value, the impact it had on me and my friend Alberto, is beyond the powers of ordinary language. In the Camp, the terms eating, food, hunger had meanings totally different from their usual ones. That unexpected, improbable, impossible package was like a meteorite, a heavenly object, charged with symbols, immensely precious, and with an enormous momentum.

We were no longer alone: a link with the outside world had been established, and there were delicious things to eat for days and days.

I was once scorned in print by a journalist who measured the foolishness of this newspaper by my attempt, he thought, to join "politics" with restaurant reviews. One is always upset by attacks from folks who shake your hand at parties, but later I understood his devaluation as a deadly misunderstanding of the role of criticism. I have already written about why I mistrust the trap of expertise and objectivity—not the same as knowledge or experience—set by the test-tube restaurant reviewer; why I hate "best" lists and the passivity they engender; why I attempt to avoid adjectival description that does little more than provoke saliva. I have also acknowledged the interest I, and I hope my readers, have in the novelty and excitement of new restaurants, new food, and eating out. What I may not have done, however, is illuminate how restaurant reviewing can be simultaneously ridiculous and important, an act of critical balance.

Anything that involves necessity as well as pleasure creates an apparent double bind, mostly because "pleasure," especially as quantified through commercial media, is thought to be base and frivolous. Ethiopia on 1985's front page will have soured the blackened redfish on its back, unless you managed to leap guiltless into the discontinuous fray. But I can't divorce pleasure from responsibility, as I am supposed to. Rian James's utilitarian exercise is bloated with the assumptions one reading and eating class had of itself and of the rest of its city. Even so, I am attracted to him. He is drawn to see people eat, to eat with them, to make his impressions stick to his circumscribed world by writing them down. And, even though the word "Depression" appears nowhere, it's written all over the book. *Dining in New York* can be pried apart and it will give up a great deal, if you happen not to ignore photographs of breadlines and fur coats: the outside.

I take some of this lesson from Primo Levi because he uses the word "delicious" in describing his bounty. It stuck out. He could have said any number of things about why the food was important, how it gave him strength by alleviating hunger, how it provided him with power to bribe his guards, how it filled him with security. With all that, he chose a pointed word of pleasure, a word one could despise—what if the cookies were not technically well-baked?—in his situation. This can only mean that flavor itself gave him some happiness, security, strength. He did not hate its pleasure, or think it frivolous.

What my critic called politics has nothing to do with parties or agendas: he couldn't fathom that the restaurant reviewing slot needn't come with world-wide blinders. Restaurants—or movies, or books, or city councilmembers—become absurd and somewhat nauseating objects of study if one does nothing but scout, list, and rate. Restaurant reviewing as it is generally practiced has reduced, I think, the eating pleasure of its readers by narrowing our lust for invention, history, and public life to a dull and crass treadmill of comparisons.

There's no mechanism that enables a writer to measure success, but if readers can be influenced one way, perhaps they can be influenced in, or at least shown, another. That is my program. If it is interrupted by the demands of newspaper format, by my own conformity, or by accidents of writing—*its* pleasure—then I apologize in advance. Readers are usually generous about such things.

(2/11/1986)

Thomas Wolfe never heard of Howard Beach.

Howard Hues

The new MTA subway map is clearly better than the one it replaces. It looks old-fashioned, but that's because the lines and shapes attempt to indicate dependable relationships, unlike the knotted schema we were offered before. Colors have reverted to simple symbolism. The waterways of the new map—Jamaica Bay, for instance— are not the former ridiculous gray but a lovely graded blue, though in the case of Jamaica Bay the gray is more realistic.

I mention Jamaica Bay for two reasons. There aren't many places within city limits where you can sit outdoors at a restaurant table and watch boats rock in their docks, and a finger of Jamaica Bay sticking into Howard Beach is the site of some of this rare waterside eating. The other reason is personal—I was a teenager, happy and unhappy, in Howard Beach, and it may be time to go home again.

If you have the new map in front of you, Howard Beach is located at coordinates 9H, part of South Queens (though suspiciously close to Brooklyn) and adjacent to JFK airport. The area usually gets bad press: "Residents Complain: Howard Beach Is City Dump," or "SST Won't Land Here, Civic Group Swears." In the early '60s, when JFK was Idlewild and the new 707s were not yet muffled and routed over water, jet noise was the distinction of our neighborhood. We adapted well to the regular 60-second interruptions of conversation or television—amazing how little difference it made to the latter—but never accustomed ourselves to falling statuary and rattling walls. We lived in one of the new "developments" built on fortified swamp, and would joke about our second-story apartment ultimately becoming ground floor. But Old Howard Beach was well established on solid foundations, an economic mix of tree-lined streets and unpaved roads, though it intrigued me at the time (and to some extent still does) that some of the houses scattered on channels of water in an overlapping area called Hamilton Beach are built on stilts.

If you drive south along Cross Bay Boulevard, toward Broad Channel and the bridge to Rockaway, you will see gas stations and pizza parlors and a hot dog palace called The Big Bow Wow—an ugly two-dimensional Venturi vista—but you won't see Old Howard Beach. You're going too fast. The town—and it is like a small town—is almost entirely isolated from general traffic, surrounded by marshland, the channel, and the bay. There is a small bay-shore strolling-park on its southernmost end (with the only vacant tennis courts in the city), but the wooden bridge that connected it to the boulevard collapsed three years ago and was never rebuilt. So the park remains quiet, almost "town property."

Young people can champ at the bit of small-town life, even in New York City, and I was glad to leave. But I will defend Howard Beach against detractors. I've certainly had practice. A smirking college acquaintance kept referring to my address as Howard's End, forcing me, as yet un-Forstered, to correct him again and again. I was puzzled—why couldn't he remember the proper name?—but after all, the joke's on him. The Bronx, his home, is only the Bronx, and he's never eaten clams in the sunset on Jamaica Bay.

These clams, I found out, don't come from the bay but from further out on the South Shore. "All that's here is mud," or so the experienced fisherman at the fish stand said. (I can't tell you what this stand is called. The sign reads T E L O   S H D. The Lobster Shed? Theo's Lox and Shad?) Some folks did seem to be lucky crabbing and fishing in this mud, off the bridge going to Broad Channel. Different people have been throwing lines here for years, but since the Nixon administration made this flat expanse a bird and wildlife sanctuary—The Gateway National Park—perhaps their catches have improved. Or maybe not. Many of Bob's Clam Bar patrons come from that bridge, ordering a dozen to go.

Clam bars are the best reason to visit Howard Beach, and I don't know why so many along the boulevard have closed. Bob's, attached to his Shellbank Restaurant (164-01 Cross Bay Boulevard) draws people from the Surfside Motel next door (I stayed there once, very nice, but my bath water was Easter-egg green), and Sonny's Clam Bar (163-35 Cross Bay Boulevard) is thriving, but these are all we saw. Bob's (for example) will shuck a dozen cold, sea-watery cherrystones—oceanic pleasure—for $3.75, and will deep fry a gangly soft-shelled crab and bed it in Italian bread for about $4. The crab will squirt as you break its puff.

Fish and meat are evenly divided by Cross Bay Boulevard. McDonald's and the like are on the even-numbered west side of the street, while fishish places take their spots on the channel side. The semantically shaky Blue Fountain Diner—we sighted a couple in evening dress on its portico—is an odd number (160-31), boats visible from its rear window. A Lenny's Clam Bar—the flagship restaurant of the chain, I think—is on the water side but takes no advantage of that; somebody's Venice is reproduced indoors.

Lenny's is fun. Customers are families unless proven otherwise. All sorts of nicely handled seafood—clams, scallops, squid, scungilli (which is sliced conch, delicious, smells like sweaty feet), mussels—are smothered in homogenous tomato sauce. This red blanket is offered in three grades of hot, and the result is spicy and flat at the same time. Meals cost about $10 per person, depending on cannoli.

There is a smaller Lenny's Pizza down the road (at 159-49 Cross Bay Boulevard), which I'm told is family. And speaking of Lenny, he has become the object of neighborhood goodwill by presenting life-sized statues of patron saints—he brought them back from Italy—to Our Lady of Grace in the old part of Howard Beach and to Saint Helen's, in the new. Now, every Labor Day, these churches combine their bazaars into one inclusive ecumenical function.

I leave the Shellbank Restaurant for last, because even my sneering Bronx friend would agree with my mother that it's romantic to sit on the many-tabled rear porch and eat lobster fra diavolo as the sunset widens the bay. She waits for the channel streetlamps to light, to see their flicker on the opalescent water.

We also hear the zap of a giant bug-electrocutor hung dead center from the canvas ceiling. Jamaica Bay, so close to the City, is wonderful. But the narrow channel's opalescence is partly oil slick, from boats picturesquely docked because gas costs so much.

It's not too difficult to get to Howard Beach from Manhattan without a car. It's a long ride by bus, but the A or CC train—even the JFK Special—will drop you right in the center of town, at the Howard Beach Station, and you can walk around or hail a friendly black Checker of the Howard Cab Company. And if you take the train, try to find the poster that advertises mustard by picturing supposedly exemplary New York-neighborhood sandwiches. I was so proud when I saw the "Howard Beach Hero"— something I never was.

(8/13/1979)

Waiting on Godot

Howard hasn't voluntarily eaten out in 15 years, which I could not understand until he called last week, when he grudgingly acknowledged my work: "It's readable, but how can you support an institution where people *wait* on you?" I didn't know what dream of collectivity he had in mind—Howard doesn't work easily with anyone—but I hung up full of guilt.

Howard, I agree with the writing on the soda straw: Eating Out Is Fun. Your discomfort reflects this country's confusion of service jobs with servitude, as well as an inability to think of waiter-work as skillful labor, which indeed it is.

If you ask friends to recall the worst waiter or waitress they've "had" during the last month, you will probably hear surprisingly detailed versions of rudeness, slothfulness, wrong orders—"we're at their mercy" sort of stuff. But ask for stories of the best and it's like no one's ever eaten out. Unless you find a regular customer who has personalized (or "Aliced") somebody, a pleasing waiter or waitress is usually invisible or, at most, "cute." Unobtrusiveness is thought to be part of a servant's skill, and any deep embarrassment one may have about "ordering" is usually overcome by his or her smile, your smile, and the fact that this is what we're here for. Not to mention the tip.

For however blithely it's handled, the tip turns whatever relationship you think you have with the waiter or waitress into a master-servant one. It's a job interview at every table. You may vow never to reduce your 18 percent—and notice that it takes just as much work to serve a hamburger (rare, please) as a filet—but the waiter or waitress cannot know that. If she scowls, her tips may drop. Even if they don't, her position is still based on her ability to please. As any waitress (or waiter) who has been pinched in the ass will tell you, "ability to please" is not always the same as doing a good job.

She gets "stiffed." He has a rotten station. It's a nice day, so no one comes in. It's rainy, so no one comes in. Waiting on tables is anxious work. Most restaurants pay a guaranteed hourly, but usually well below minimum wage. (And some restaurant owners keep some or all of the tips if they can get away with it.) So although we know stories of $400-a-night plums, these are few, far between, and white male.

The institution of tipping—and the economic relations it reflects—is immoral. Restaurants should pay good wages. Those waiters and waitresses who defend tipping do so either because this immediate-award system appeals to something childishly Skinnerian in their—our?—natures, or because they manage not to declare their tips as taxable income. Sufficient salaries and more corporate, less personal, taxation should compensate for the latter. Hotel & Restaurant Employees and Bartenders International Union please note.

A restaurant runs on the feet of its waiters. (And waitresses. Perhaps now is the time to ask for a single word that embraces both sexes. It's more than awkward not to have one—and don't tell me it's picturesque the way it is. Such water-closet distinctions not only reflect inequality, they help to perpetuate it. I suggest waiter for everyone, like sculptor or actor.) Waiters know all the dirt about a place because they are interlocutors between backstage and front. Watch the way their smiles drop as they head toward the kitchen, and come on again as they hit the "out" door. The cook just threw a knife, and there are things on the kitchen floor you wouldn't believe, but that smile is ever-fresh. Equity should collect dues.

Waiters who are proud of their work are angry when management cuts butter with margarine (common), mixes olive oil with vegetable oil, uses frozen crab meat when the menu says fresh (still no truth-in-menu law in N.Y.), or peddles instant mashed potatoes as vichyssoise. (These are examples from a popular and expensive SoHo restaurant.) Asking if the scallops are bay may work, but waiters are sometimes "trained" to lie—they will lose their jobs if they don't.

Howard, many waiters are proud of their work, and are conscious of the manipulations and the range of details that make the job so difficult to do and so enlightening to watch. The images of success are complex: speed without hurry, grace under pressure, some sense of work enjoyed. It's admirable when you see it, and I see it often.

I have always depended on the kindness of waiters.

(10/8/1979)

Holiday on Ice

One Sunday before Thanksgiving—I was about nine years old—my mother looked hard at my father and said, "I am not cooking a turkey, I don't care what you say. We are going out."

I knew from her granite eyes that we would have a lovely time; and in fact the event was everything I had feared. Perhaps the House of Wong, our neighborhood Chinese restaurant, was not the most convincing place to celebrate national ideals, but at that time I wasn't sure what place would be. I still don't know.

Many of us dread the holidays we are supposed to enjoy. Loneliness takes heightened forms, and suicides increase. This may be because the original ritual value of Thanksgiving—a community thanks itself and God for survival—has disappeared, the grammar-school picture of an Indian-Pilgrim handshake over mutual succotash undercut by more accurate history and guilt. A cornucopian, pagan aspect remains—people tell me they can't wait to "pig out" on the holidays—but Thanksgiving now is mostly an affirmation of the successful family, and this is a difficult notion to maintain.

It is not that "happy" families don't exist—I see them on television all the time—but not everyone is a member, and those who are sustain unexpected attacks. The economic argument is that late capitalism, which depends on the family as a production/maintenance/consumer unit—

the raison d'etre of washers and dryers—is not providing enough benefits or services to keep it going smoothly. The Thanksgiving table, a particular altar of family happiness, becomes the scene of its sacrifice, another kind of groaning board. So many pressures and disappointments are projected onto the poor Swift's Butterball that it can't possibly satisfy. Thanksgiving dinner comes with its own knife.

When alternatives to the nuclear family were sought actively in the early '70s, so were alternatives to the nuclear-family holiday table. I remember one dinner, a Thanksgiving potluck (unfortunate choice of words) that brought together 50 or so feminists, antiwar activists, gay liberationists, assorted parents and children, with almost as many bowls of green salad. We were thrilled and excited that we could overcome tradition by incorporating it—and Nancy did have an enormous turkey in the oven. At 8 p.m. someone noticed that the oven wasn't turned on. During the evening I snapped at Elizabeth, a nine-year-old I liked very much. Someone else burst into tears.

This year I'm going to a restaurant for Thanksgiving dinner. Many people in this city do, and not only because it's less work for mother. You may be solitary in a restaurant, but you're not alone. A roomful of people buzzing about a prix fixe dinner of turkey galantine can feel, if you shut your eyes, something like an extended family.

At their best, restaurants enhance a sense of community, of festivity. They are not necessarily inimical to family pleasures, either; so-called family restaurants do quite a turkey business with their nuclear clientele. Even my mother recounted an earlier, happier Thanksgiving, when she, my father, the Schwartzes, and the Bells would wheel all their infants into the welcoming doors of Lundy's, the cavernous seafood restaurant on Sheepshead Bay, and be treated to the best of both worlds—family and community—with balloons for the kids and mince pie for everyone.

It's not always like this, of course. I wouldn't want to be alone in a Horn & Hardart's automat on Thanksgiving, though the food could be fine. I hope it is possible to survive Thanksgiving in a restaurant, surrounded by family or not.

(11/26/1979)

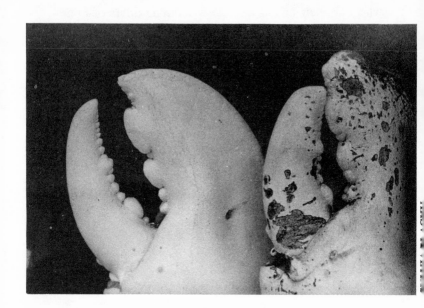

Coming Up for Air

It is wrong to assume that eating in a restaurant, judging its food, writing the review, is an entirely objective process. You cannot trust the claims of the test-tube mouth.

Three weeks ago, right after my last column was filed, I visited a restaurant I knew well and ordered Old Faithful. Overworked and annoyed by Christmas prodding, I sought comfort in food that was indistinguishable from my memory of its flavor, food that would not deck itself in red and green surprises. But . . . was the bread stale? And why were the lights so dim? Soup was a blank, I couldn't taste it. The spicy entree was dust.

For a restaurant reviewer, stomach flu is a sobering thing. Illness is built into restaurant reviewing, because through your stomach pass the city's best-fed germs. (However clean, a kitchen has its own profile of yeast and bacteria.) There is something of the king's ritual taster left in this envied job. Those who think of restaurant reviewing as a salivating romp forget that you have to have a mouth that can't say no.

So losing your appetite is dangerous: it affects your wages. And I had suspicions that "flu" wasn't the only reason. As December marched toward its department-store apotheosis, as general consumption became more indiscriminate and prescribed, my consumption of food became less connected to hunger, to pleasure, to the integrity of the restaurant. "Loss of appetite" is an existential state, or can be, whatever the state of one's bowels. The question is what to do about it, if a course of yogurt or avoiding news of Kampuchea doesn't change the queasy condition.

Would Camus have gone to Provincetown? Not in the summer, not if he was gay—the crowds can be nasty then—but the town is quiet in the winter, the light is white and strong, and the wind blows around you from all directions. This wondrous land's end air is so clean that it almost has a flavor. I began to taste it, and other tastes followed.

Is walking good for the appetite? Provincetown's few streets are studded with urban, cosmopolitan restaurants, most of them ostentatiously boarded up for the winter. The ones that stay open have deeper roots. Provincetown's Portuguese fishing and business community is reflected in the kale soup and red linguica sausage that are found even in the excellent gay-run omelette luncheonettes. Perhaps I should have moved more slowly, but Cookie's kale soup was the kiss that awakened my hunger. Winter tonic, city relief: green, acidic vegetable, diced potato, salty linguica to drive the warmth home. You may call it simple food, but simple food has been impossible for me to taste in New York.

There was a blackboard in (Wilbur and Joe's) Cookie's Restaurant that, for the convenience of fishermen customers, listed dragger's market prices for dabs, sand dabs, cod, blackback, yellowtail, haddock, pollock, and scallops. Some of this haddock was marinated and fried at Cookie's, Portuguese style. So were pork chops. Flatulent, cold fava beans were soaked in the same marinade.

When the Pilgrims first landed at Cape Cod, before settling on Plymouth Rock, they ate so many quahogs—thick-shelled sea clams—that they got sick. Cookie's sea clam pie is a reminder of this, so much of the sea in front of you that you can eat too many. But there were no Portuguese fish cakes and clam cakes because "Wilbur's mother makes them only when she feels like it" (said our waiter) and she hadn't felt like it yet this winter.

Provincetown offered another successful treatment, in the form of "American Food." Most Provincetown restaurants feature steak/chops/chicken—Waverly Inn fare in New York City—but the Red Inn's bedside manner was superior: harbor views, copious linen, spitting fireplaces, all the comforts of imaginary home. Take one velvety Gibson—is it really so much better here?—and follow with sweet corn relish or fruit relish, as directed. Some prime ribs of beef and a few more mashed turnips and you'll be yourself in no time.

But oysters are my talisman for resurrected appetite. How did they gleam so in Provincetown? Things they called oysters in Manhattan restaurants reflected the same candlelight; why did they go down like disappointment, like lumps in one's throat? The Red Inn's plateful were not the prized jewels of nearby Wellfleet but came from Cotuit, because the Wellfleet oystermen are an independent lot and sometimes (we were told) want to stay home in bed. "But these are the plumpest and freshest that can be found." I agreed, with no doubt. My taste was coming back.

Recuperation and regeneration are part of the transition to a new year. A job may require that you can't acknowledge your variation and fallibility, but an honest writer has no place in a job like that. I'll cook fish cakes if I must and gather my oysters while I may, but if I have to stay in bed once in a while, I will.

(1/14/1980)

Mi Utopia

It is possible to feel alone, isolated, anywhere and at any season, but the blues become more and more likely in these cold, isolationist, anti-community times. If money is tight, so probably is the spirit. Even the struggle to do meaningful work becomes futile if you can't find any work at all.

One reason I like to spend so much time in restaurants—meaningful work for me—is that once or twice I've felt breezes of pure communal happiness among the tables and plates. This is different from the solid, we-against-the-world pleasure that is sometimes available at the family table, nuclear or extended. Eating from a common pot has always required some measure of trust, but the old ritual of public meal-taking, however diluted and privatized, still has the power to bring us close in mutual enjoyment.

Utopia, however, is not around every corner. The "good" restaurant treats you special, as if you were the only credit card in town. "Romantic" restaurants shelter the two of you with alcohol and dim banquettes, to protect a fragile possibility and prepare you both for a life of us-and-them. "Family" restaurants—I have never understood that term—do take a more group-nurturing stance, but I have seen clans battle each other to victory for penultimate shrimp at the never-ending salad bar.

Perhaps the furred couple who walk into Mi Chinita announcing, "This is supposed to be the hottest place in town," as if no one could hear them, doesn't belong here. What would Sir Thomas More do with them? Ship them off the island? But, you know, they fit right in and add to the *misch* or mise-en-scene that makes this otherwise typical Cuban-Chinese restaurant such a delight to the humanistic appetite.

This couple certainly has plenty to look at. *Every*body in Chelsea must be here—as they are every night the place is open—many of the men in the tightest Levis this stretch of Eighth Avenue has to offer. "I'm sure," Harry says, "that cute guy took the stool instead of the table just to swivel it around." There is tentative eyeballing over the pork yat kamein, a big, salty bowl of soup that heats a mop of thin noodles, topped with slices of roast pork spread like playing cards. Handsome mustaches are checked periodically for dangling noodles.

"Where are all the women?" ask Batya and Bonnie, but when their eyes adjust they see all kinds of women, all ages, and children, and colors, and hands in the air in the midst of important conversations: How long will it run before it closes? How can you not support Taxi Rank and File? Does Sharon need braces? Did you eat in Little Afghanistan? Don't, I say, pay any attention to the Chinese food.

The waiter brings out some Chinese food to people who look like they'll enjoy it no matter what I say, which is fine. But I do recommend the popular, sweetish shredded beef with rice and black beans, or the roast pork Cuban style, or the chicharron de pollo—pieces of spicy chicken fried, I think, in lard. They are greasy. But as Tina Turner used to say, ain't nothin' good without grease.

Oh, an extra order of french fried potatoes, which I want and no sharing allowed (everybody takes, of course—they taste non-frozen). John? Why don't you try the fried chick peas with hard chunks of sausage (turns out delicious, with crunchy bits of raw onion). I'm told the squid in its own ink is good—had that in Tijuana once—but we'll experiment next time. Five more Heinekens, please. No, the beans go on the rice—you've heard of complementary proteins—and that pot roast at the next table looks good. These fried bananas go fast. I like the pouch of fatty cornmeal called a Cuban tamal as an appetizer—Harry doesn't, but then Harry is picky. None of us can stand the paella, which sticks out like the $8 sore thumb it is. Also, stay away from shrimp.

Harry is staring at every other male who walks in, but he's smiling. So are they. Mi Chinita used to be a breakfast diner, wide, with curves instead of corners. It still is a diner in spirit. Diners are forever. This one feels expansive, like the mood it engenders and the state of our waists. The check is slim.

Flan? No, we're full. How about cafe con leche? And maybe we will have a little dessert. Five flans. Can't wait to go home and write.

(2/25/1980)

'The 25 Greatest Restaurants in America'

I've had it with these restaurant lists. There's been a lot of them lately, some amazing in their arrogance and disdain for readers' abilities. But don't we depend on restaurant .rundowns? Isn't there something satisfying about curling up in bed with a good list? Not for me. If anything can kill the possibility of spirited and serious food writing, it's the list. Because:

1) Summarizing and rating are the Scylla and Charybdis of the restaurant list, and each has its perils. Most lists are nothing but menu information and prices, with a few adjectives like "silky" or "pungent" tossed in as camouflage. Not only is this an impoverished way to describe experience, it presupposes that *all* experience is available to this predigestion.

2) Rating is usually a search for the best. The best is unattainable, a lie. The best hot dog doesn't exist, and if it did, you wouldn't get to it in time, before it was ruined by all the attention.

3) Lists lead us to expect perfection. Lists don't have moods, memories, ambivalences. They won't refund for disappointment.

4) Lists have a deep, structural connection to fads; lists help create them; they are subject to them. The same editors lick their chops at both.

5) Lists give the illusion of cornucopia.

6) Go to any of the restaurants in the "$50 Excellent"

category; there are still six others we have to try. ("Why, Ollie?" "Because they may be *better,* Stan.")

7) And how come it wasn't as excellent as she said it would be?

8) You can't have a restaurant list without an expert, and anyone not an expert is a schlemiel. Other kinds of media games can reinforce feelings of inadequacy, but the list does it without even trying.

9) A list is a fundamentally lazy way for a newspaper or magazine to fill space and woo as many advertisers as possible. Modern restaurant reviewing was born as advertising copy that snuck onto the other side of the page. It may die there.

10) *Ships* list—before they sink.

(6/25/1980)

And Dance the Night Away With Us

I can't write musical notation, but if I were to hum the seven notes—da da da DA duh da duh—and wiggle a little, chances are you would recognize it. People all over the city recognize it, we who stay up to three in the morning to watch Mary Tyler Moore reruns—two of them, back to back—every night except Friday and Saturday, when they're not scheduled and the disappointment gives an extra push to our insomnia.

One does not expect company in one's obsessions. I never watched the thing first-run; the idea made me sick, and Judy—who is usually right—told me that her normally sensible colleagues at Upstate U. would drop their quenelles and conversation and run from the dinner party to switch on the next installment of the Early '70s. "Like clockwork," Judy said, "and the next morning all they would jabber about was how wonderful Mary was not to make coffee for Mr. Grant or how nobody suspected Phyllis's brother was *gay!*"

The show's time was ripe then, but it may be riper now, and the question is why. When I shyly told Barbara about my nightly habit, she admitted that she fantasized more about putting her head on Mary's shoulder than on those of any living friends. Without warning, Mike did a frightening imitation ("Gee, guys") of Ted Baxter, the white-haired seven-year-old newscaster with a makeup bib (these capsule descriptions are for the uninitiated—

42

habitues bear with me). I can telephone most of my friends at 2:45 a.m. and they will be up, though annoyed at the interruption.

Joe knows why he feels at home in either of the show's usual sets, Mary's studio apartment or her television-studio workplace: his life is divided the same way. *Mary Tyler Moore* is about mostly single people trying to tolerate (Ted) or support each other in the office and at home through friendship. How *nice* to be padded by Minneapolis, to—as Flo Kennedy said—work with one's friends, to know that whatever happens, Ted will be a fool, Rhoda will wisecrack, and Mary, every hair in place, will have some cheap Scotch in her kitchen cabinet just for you. *Mary Hartman* is dead; long live *Mary Tyler Moore*.

A contract for commercial time must be dirt-cheap at 2 a.m., and the price of our extended-family sustenance is watching the same medieval hucksters wear holes through videotape two to four times an hour each night. As of this writing, that makes up to 560 times (since January 1) I've seen and heard certain people try to sell uncertain things. But one commerical hits me where I live just the way *Mary Tyler Moore* does—because it is *my* workplace.

Da da da DA duh da duh . . . 560 times . . . do places like Chateau Madrid still exist? Did they ever? Can the commercial's quick switching—between Ricky Ricardo chorines with Zapata sombreros, bandoliers, and bare bottoms; cut to rare beef sliced on a wooden board; cut to two customer-couples of unlikely glamour; cut to a splash of urine-colored wine that will not adjust no matter what I do to the hue knob—can this giddy arrangement reflect

what is real? After trying to explain half-a-city's attach-
ment to a simpy, decade-old situation comedy, such a fic-
tion/reality question is not absurd. IS THAT BEEF ANY
GOOD?

My fantasy was that if there were any clients at Chateau
Madrid they would all be bleary-eyed over their paellas,
talking about Mary and Mr. Grant. But not so: the Chateau
has been around since 1937 (as the Havana Madrid) and
packs in happy-to-sour tourists in search of New York's famous nightlife. They find it in the Hotel Lexington.

I know they're tourists because the star of the floor
show—"direct from Spain"—did a marvelous run around
the audience between costume changes and the elaborate
flamenco tableaux. "Do you speak English?" (she sidles
up a la Charo to a confused table). "Ohhhh, Hebrew!"
And to everyone's delight she starts to wail something in
Hebrew that the adjustable band picks up immediately.
"Are you from Japan?" and she tosses a Japanese bon mot
to four men. But the economy has shifted—they're from
China. ("So sorry.") Others hail from New Jersey ("I hear
there're no *mosquitoes* there, no?"), France, and Queens
("Nice place Queens").

I loved the floor show (sorry, a different show—no bandoliers) and the quiet way it is approached: lights dim, the
few exhibitionistic couples leave the dance floor whether
they've finished dancing the night away or not, and segue
to a male vocal warm-up that reminded me of a nightclub
experience in Brooklyn at age eight—Johnny Valentine
singing "My Funny Valentine" on Valentine's Day. I
glowed, but my mother was unmoved, and my father admitted that the food wasn't any good. But, he said, you

don't come to a nightclub for food.

Father knows best. The two couples of unlikely glamour at our table (the "spacious one" by the kitchen door—remember to tip the maitre d' *before* you are seated) tried to reproduce the rich and elegant site of the commercial with Chateau Madrid Chateaubriand on a wooden board and two other uncommittal "Dishes from the Spanish Heritage."

Reality does not disappoint fantasy. The asparagus accompanying the beef was identical to that on TV—the same batch, probably. I don't know if that's hyperbole or synecdoche, but it is accurate. When my friend John writes his forthcoming *Eat Out and Lose Weight Diet Book,* Chateau Madrid gets three stars.

The Chateau Madrid commercial looks different now: I am no longer hypnotized. In fact I'm embarrassed when I hear those seven notes, and have to turn away. I even think twice about watching the reruns of reruns, and might have to look elsewhere for affection and support, because Mary's time is about up. It's like what Mary's nemesis Sue Ann, the Happy Homemaker—she was good last night—predicts will happen to her Veal Prince Orloff if left in the oven one minute too long: "He *dies.*"

(7/9/1980)

Table of Content

Last year a friend handed me a button that says "Question Authority," which I wore. Some people gave it the intended anarchist reading, and that made them feel good (unless they had authority). Others, though, wanted to know what questions I specialized in. They weren't kidding. Questioning authority is not the same as denying intelligence. The two nouns are hardly synonyms; in government, for example, they are especially antonymic. I would like to use the opportunity of a new year to throw a Hostess Snoball, because it's time again to assert that no matter which authority tells us what the best this, that, or the other thing is, people who trust themselves will go where they want and eat what they like.

What might a "good" restaurant be? Try these definitions for a change: any restaurant you can't afford; any restaurant that makes you feel like you're wasting its time. Note that we haven't mentioned the finish of the sauce, which is supposed to be why a restaurant is good. When critics shine the hot light of their authority on restaurants in order to rate them, they taste the individual dishes, remark on the atmosphere and service, and set restaurants of each class into a line—in what schoolteachers call size place. There's always some little fight about who's taller this year, always some pinching and squirming—but teacher has the ruler. Why anyone would *choose* to eat at a "shrimp" is beyond me. It's incredible, but millions do.

I want to praise a bad restaurant. We know its food will not stand up to scrutiny, to comparison with X or Y up the street, but the year should begin with something other than a report card and disappointment. How can a bad restaurant be good? Have you ever eaten at Emilio's?

Chances are you have. It's been in the Village on Sixth Avenue long before the street Avenue of Americaed. I've eaten pizza at Emilio's with thin, hard crust, drunk wattery draft, finished every oil-soaked green at the bottom of that plastic wooden bowl and could not have been more pleased. Usually I prefer the meatball hero, or the veal chops with a side of soggy escarole—but J. likes his pizza. After years of eating in Emilio's when we are tired, or butter-and-creamed out, or just (just?) romantic and need a table's distance between our eyes, we finally noticed that we head for the same booth in the back room to the right, the room with the fireplace, each time. That booth is always empty, even if the restaurant's full.

Amy says Emilio's was a meeting place for cinema avant-gardists in the '50s. John says he spent most of his first Village time—he ran screaming from New Jersey—eating alone cheaply, and later trying out the booths with different people. One summer my political group adjourned after each meeting to Emilio's backyard garden—where 20 could practice collectivity at one table—and tortured waiters with attempted separate checks.

There's a whole world at the long bar we pass to get to the back. What are those gridded numbers on the blackboard? It's a comfortable bar, but I have no desire to stop. And who are the folks, couples mostly, who choose to eat in the windowed terrace out front, where people can stare at their shopping bags and their food? What are they talking about?

Perhaps I risk beginning my own deromanticization, but I do have some ideas about why Emilio's works.

It's dependable. Emilio's won't be a Waldenbooks the next time you go. The food never varies, nor does it intrude. Some locations—this may sound crazy but I believe it—are particularly suited to cooking and eating; the ground has the right "sink," the right air, the right alignment. This is not a question of foot traffic; some plots, in otherwise "good" locations, never make it as restaurants.

Emilio's fulfills popular expectations of what a restaurant should be. We get these ideas, I expect, from *Mildred Pierce,* from our parents, from the many *imitations* of restaurants we see all over town, in which we pay overmuch and have to extrapolate to the real checkered tablecloths of our imagined past, when things were cheap and tasty and young. Emilio's allows for such idealistic projection because it has just enough cues—red-and-white checked oilcloth, old wooden booths, waitresses who look like they've seen life but smile nonetheless—to set off your restaurant fantasies, and no details to deny them.

You cannot have a conversation in Emilio's about whether or not this veal cutlet is better than the one uptown. It simply doesn't apply. What a relief. You can eat out and talk about something other than food.

There is nothing wrong with evaluating food—many do it involuntarily. But it takes something more than a best-dressed list to explain a salad, something more than a reviewer to anatomize the nature of enjoyment.

Most of us have an Emilio's. Watch out. There are those who would talk you out of yours. Thank goodness they can't make a list of them.

(1/7/1981)

Chop Flop, Nix Chix

It may not pay to generalize from Emilio's; not all bad restaurants are good. The ones on West 46th Street between Broadway and Ninth Avenue are known as "theatre restaurants." This label carries a certain something with it: these eateries can entertain, and theatre people—you know who *they* are—sit in permanent bloom around the bars, which are terrific.

And the food is wonderful dahling.

I don't think people care about the food in theatre restaurants. We have spent $30 per on *Amadeus* and will have a good time—who can blame us for trying? Since the preparation for a Broadway outing includes a shelving of critical faculties, an almost hysterical immunity to disappointment, a sodden leg of poultry should not stand in anybody's way.

Mildred Pierce is a new theatre restaurant, a perfectly charming one at that, and no threat to the genre. The bar's congenial, and the hosts gifted—they know *everybody*—and, without mirrors, I saw not one unhappy face. We did, however, shine a critical light into the food, just for a moment. A moment was quite enough.

A pan of a restaurant like Mildred Pierce is usually not necessary, but I have two reasons. One is hortatory—I think the unambitious food can be easily improved. The other is angry—Mildred Pierce is an inspired name for a restaurant, and this place fails to live up to its responsibility.

In spite of social realism and Upton Sinclair, modern American literature is not known for its accurate descriptions of how to teach, how to make steel, how to make a living. James M. Cain, though he mucked around in opera and the subconscious in most of his melodramatic novels, made extraordinary use of the details of work and business in books like *Double Indemnity* (selling insurance), *The Postman Always Rings Twice* (short-order roadside cookery), and *Mildred Pierce* (how to be a waitress, bake pies, and open a successful chain of restaurants). These books made popular films, and if we know the character Mildred Pierce it's probably through Ranald MacDougall's screenplay—six others, including William Faulkner, tried to adapt *MP*—and through Joan Crawford's determined face. Although MacDougall and director Michael Curtiz limit the actual hash-slinging to only a few lines and some quick-dissolve montage, the examples are pungent:

MILDRED (reaching the cook): Two chicken dinners, one without gravy.

IDA (Eve Arden, intruding): Two chickens, hold the gravy. (To Mildred.) You can't say "without." You got to say "hold."

Dissolve to plates being cleaned off table with uneaten (pre-Mildred) pies.

MILDRED (voice-over): I learned the restaurant business. I learned it the hard way. In three weeks I was a good waitress.

Shot of Mildred rushing to kitchen to order.

MILDRED (shouting): One chicken. Hold veg. Club

sandwich. Roast beef. Hold one. Club and salad.

MILDRED (voice-over): In six weeks I felt as though I'd worked in a restaurant all my life.

Ultimately *Mildred Pierce* develops a misogynist and antifeminist edge—it's a cautionary tale about kicking out your husband—but the I'll-do-it cut of the Crawford/Pierce cheekbone is more convincing than the moral. Crawford won an Academy Award—as the Oscar who holds a hamburger and a glass of wine, pictured on the menu of the film's "Academy Award Winning" progeny, makes clear.

Mildred jumps from waitress to restaurant via her irresistible pies. Mildred's—the restaurant in the film—is sparkling and prosperous, because all the food in it looks delicious:

MILDRED (to a waitress): Dorothy, don't ever go in like that. Put some more potatoes on. (She puts more potatoes on her plate.)

DOROTHY: You'll never make any money that way.

MILDRED: It's all right, as long as the customers are satisfied.

LOTTIE (Butterfly McQueen, with excitement): This is just like my wedding night. So exciting!

Any restaurant that takes the name should not send out broiled chicken that's burnt without, raw within; or "spicy Bar-B-Cue chicken wings" with no flavor of any kind; or crunchy undercooked potatoes; or burnt-dry baby back ribs; or flaccid and mushy steamed mussels; or overcooked, undrained tortellini with a therefore-watery Gorgonzola (!) cheese sauce; or, perhaps the dumbest offering on any menu, "broiled stuffed olives wrapped in bacon" ($4.35!!). Rumaki is pushing it, but this is a new variation on salt-on-salt, with oil/fat overtones. Even the pies—average—are made somewhere on Columbus Avenue.

It is not enough to enmenu a "Mildred's Roast Chicken" or call the chili "Veda's Revenge" (Veda is Mildred's selfish daughter). One can't blame a place for missed possibilities, but if camp would do, Mildred Pierce the restaurant hasn't even scratched the surface: how about Joan crawfish, padded shoulder of veal, gingham flounces? *The Village Voice's* female film critic was told, "You look like you get the Eve Arden table," but that was the height of our evening.

I wouldn't can it yet, though. The bar *is* good, and so was the Key Lime pie, whoever made it. There are silly paintings of Crawford in the bar room, a few fake-captioned stills over the kitchen porthole, and execrable "art" on the teak-painted paneling of the comfortable dining room in the back, which manages to look more like the *noir* hideaway in *Laura* than like anything in *Mildred Pierce.*

The restaurant is on theatre-restaurant row; it should have been named after a play; East Lime, the Carrots of Wimpole Street, My Fair Ladle, or even Peter Pan.

(1/21/1981)

A la Carte, at Last

If we eat out, menus are our main experience of food in writing. They have always fascinated me, because they allow me to imagine food without seeing or eating it. Menus offer a promise, and one way to evaluate a restaurant is to compare the writing with the food, the art with the life, to see if the promise is kept, or even acknowledged.

I learned to read menus just after I learned to watch television—very early in life. Usually, a child's experience of choosing food—if indeed there is a choice—is an oral one. "You want carrots?" Or, "You're having carrots," and you the child have the limited option to spit them up or, as I heard last night from someone who used to hate canned peas, to patiently ring the vegetable under the rim of the plate into a necklace of green pearls (she's now an artist).

The menu was my introduction to an important process of anxious self-definition. As a five-year-old, the first restaurant demand on my self-image was: Would the waiter give me my own menu? Would the waiter think I could read it—of course I could—or treat me as invisible? If I did get a menu all to myself, it started a chain of power and self-sufficiency that stopped, abruptly and with some guilt, only when I realized that I couldn't pay for my wishes—and neither could my father. It was through menus, very early, that I realized we were not rich and sometimes had to be careful. So a bargaining balance was set up (this one in the recently closed Lundy's restaurant in Brooklyn): Could I have lobster? You can have some of mine; try the broiled fish. I was always gently warned off anything a la carte. And sometimes my father would have to drag out the story that when he was a kid he was so poor he went into restaurants like this, asked for a cup of hot water, and made tomato soup out of catsup. I assumed this was true—he *was* poor—until I heard the same story from many former kids about their fathers. Was there a book fathers read, with catsup stories to handle difficult situations?

Some of this bargaining was unspoken; after a while I understood the price limits, internalized them, and could displace my annoyance with gratitude for the fact that we were eating out at all. It turned out that the fish was good at Lundy's, sometimes better than the lobster.

It's possible that credit cards are used because they privatize this embarrassment and delay it till later, at home.

Not all menus provide choices, and the old rich, who expect all their food, even at home, to take some previous written form, may have been unaccustomed to the vulgarity of mix-and-match eating. M.F.K. Fisher, if I remember correctly, writes about a large English matron at her first meal aboard a transatlantic liner. She's offered a menu of the shipboard type—many choices, no prices—scans it carefully, looks up at the waiter, and says simply, "Yes."

I enjoyed reading this, but had never seen a ship's menu myself until I bought a set of glowing airbrush-prints at a flea market in Escondido, California. Only when I took them home did I see that they opened and became dinner menus, of the *S.S. Matsonia* en route in 1946 from Honolulu to San Francisco or L.A., I can't tell which.

Reading these menus may not be as exciting as uncovering olive stones in Pompeii, but it does communicate a sense of time transfixed: there's a day and date on top of each one. I can eat my way through a voyage taken before I was born. My only comparable experience was flipping through a dated mimeographed sheaf of elementary-school lunches in Laramie, Wyoming, fish sticks every single Friday.

The postwar food on the *Matsonia* was more various than it probably was in most postwar restaurants in England or Germany, but these American menus are remarkably stolid and unadventurous by our present standards (though the raw materials might have been much better than their counterparts now). I have imagined many times the difference between the *best* possible "Roast Aylesbury Duckling, Sage Dressing, Gooseberry Sauce" (Saturday, June 15, 1946), or "Cold Essence of Chicken" (Sunday, June 16), or "Melton Mowbray Pie with Fruit Salad" from Saturday's cold buffet—and the worst. What leftovers did they throw into the "Matsonia Delight," one of only two desserts on the final Aloha Wednesday? Or was it a special, good-bye surprise? Did they run out of Tuesday's "Petaluma Fed Chicken"? Did anyone crave something—anything—spicy? Who was too seasick to eat at all?

I don't even know what "class" these discreet menus served. I assume, because of the dates, that they also served as attractive favors after they were used, and were not stolen.

I have stolen menus, slipping them in my briefcase or sleeve. I don't do it anymore, both because I can call a restaurant and request one, and because of the new New York shoplifting law. In the course of my work I have tried to photograph menus with a miniature camera (a 35mm Gravlox), and once I attempted to tape-record selections and their actualizations at the table. (Loudly, at my lapel: "Isn't this a *wonderful* reduced raspberry-vinegar sauce with chives, cloves and a touch of marshmallow?") I am told another restaurant critic has used this method; did people laugh at her too?

So now I have a menu collection. The increase in prices it shows from year to year is frightful. I do not believe that the proposed minuscule tax cut—do the unemployed pay taxes?—will be thrown into savings accounts, according to Reaganomic predictions, and pull this country out of inflation. When I see the change for the better on my menus, and enough people can afford to order what they want from them, then I'll be happy to eat my words.

Did I become a restaurant critic 10 years ago in order to order a la carte? Maybe it backfired. Now I not only *can* eat any food I read—I have to.

(3/4/1981)

Table for One

The word had spread around the office that poor K.'s hospital menu offered "egg cutlet" and something called a "cheese sandwich loaf," a word-cluster impossible, the copy editors tell me, to hyphenate without knowing what it is. K. had not been brave enough to underline either of these ("PLEASE UNDERLINE EACH ITEM DE-SIRED"), so we never found out what they were, or who underlined them. Can we assume, in a large hospital, that everything is chosen at least once? The recipe for cheese sandwich loaf seems inevitable:

10 slices Velveeta cheese food
20 slices Wonder Bread
1/2 cup industrial tomato sauce
  Alternate vertically, in a loaf pan: bread, cheese, bread; bread, cheese, bread; bread, cheese, bread—until well packed. Drizzle with sauce, and bake.

My editor admitted it was short notice, but could I run up to the hospital before K.—much better now, by the way—gets released, in order to eat her last supper? Maybe she could stay an extra day.

The energy of the request confused me. One understands the abstract attraction of predictably bad food, or the humor of such dietary poetry as "egg cutlet," but haven't these people ever eaten in a hospital before? (No, they hadn't.) We've read plenty of glossy lists about hospital cuisine—which Manhattan beds offer caviar, or bagels and lox, or booze. Hospital food is only one example of various, usually boring and often unnutritious, institutional food; we could just as well try breakfast in Congress, lunch in the army, dinner in prison, for a laugh.

From her bed K. could see trees, the East River, and the Roosevelt Island tram. (K.—"so that's what that is.") The breeze was lovely, and she had a tiny Sony color set suspended on counterweighted rods, like a dentist's drill, that delivered the best picture we'd ever seen. K. looked flouncy and relaxed, and after a few minutes of chat I realized that during her stay she had become obsessed with television, and with her meals.

Before I left for the hospital I had asked people in the office if they knew any hospital-food stories, because everyone does. A former nurse's aide reported, in puzzled detail, that one of her charges "broke a tooth on the fish." It wasn't frozen or anything, she went on, and it didn't have any bones. A former patient in a South Jersey hospital said that she couldn't stand the food, it made her sick, but so did the food in South Jersey restaurants. (Toward the end of a long stay in an unaccountably ritzy hospital in Southern California, one that served lamb chops and rosé almost every night, I still became so bored with tray messes that I got dressed, drove to a friend's house, and had dinner with him. No one knew I was gone.)

K. didn't know why she was so fascinated and upset by hospital food. She had saved the paper menus, because some of this stuff she said, isn't so bad; sauteed liver for lunch was excellent, so was the Daffodil Cake (angel food with yellow and white icing-petals), and beautiful too. Tonight's dinner (5:50) was chicken. "Oh!" she said. "Chicken will be good. At least I think it's all right. Perhaps I've lost my taste."

I sampled everything from the tray. The chicken was neither dry nor bloody at the bone, and the gravy had some life to it. The "chicken consomme" should have been served in an Erlenmeyer flask; the nearest it had come to chicken was the plate next door. The rest was canned wax beans, a heavy, sugary roll, steamed rice, and a sickening pseudo-chocolate pudding. This was a typically bland (a word with emollient connotations in a hospital), salty, carbo-ridden institutional meal, not bad, not good, just—soft.

K. was afraid that she had lost her taste because a few days earlier someone had the bad sense to bring her a cup of deli shrimp salad from the outside. K. looked at me full-face, wide-eyed: "It had . . . flavor." This shrimp salad had begun to stand for everything she could not do, for all the cosmopolitan choices, all the physical insensitivity that a load of foreign spice requires. It brought K. out of her hospital body, which was unfair because she couldn't leave yet. Sex in the hospital would have been equally teasing; how could you go back to Daffodil Cake?

Nurses and flight attendants know that a meal, in times of stress, boredom, or healing, is the center of their charges' existence. With the exception of excretion, eating is the only primary, regular sensual act available. At mealtime you balance your basic helplessness with some kind of power; you underline egg cutlet, you get egg cutlet, and heaven help the lackey who thwarts you here. This observation is not new, but for the first time, in K.'s quarter of the room, I realized that the passive-aggressive structure of the institutional feed is not really different from that of the usual meal in a restaurant.

The restaurant diner is also the immobile victim, starved by evil, sluggish fiends for just a little white wine and bread. The waiter is a nurse to his or her customers, a god and a devil simultaneously. But the customer is an imperious prisoner, demanding and open-mawed as a young bird . . .

This is a horrible vision of a restaurant's hospitality, seen in the common glare of bed sheets and white tablecloths. It has sources in Freudian assumptions about how children deify parents but is also implicit in any situation where children of all biological ages must be served. K.'s ward was outwardly placid and pleasant, hushed just the way tony restaurants are. K. wondered how long it would take before she could exercise her independent palate. Would there be any scars? I assured her I've voluntarily eaten comparable—and worse—chocolate pudding in restaurants, "good" restaurants, but optimistically she didn't believe me, and was content to wait and be fed for herself.

(6/10/1981)

Pop Art

In 1885, Charles Cretors of Chicago invented a steam-powered popcorn machine, engravings of which show a silvery wet-popper (using oil) that looks just like the one suspended within glass bins in movie theaters.

During the 1930s, the popcorn industry pushed its way into recalcitrant movie houses, sometimes employing teams of vendors, or "plants," who sold the stuff to patrons as they bought tickets. Theater owners, when they realized the buying capacity of a captive audience, made the most of it and started to sell their own. However, there were still artistic objections: according to an article in *In Cinema,* the freebie magazine that's often used as a popcorn placemat, David O. Selznick sent a memo to the theaters that booked his *Gone with the Wind,* asking them to ensure that the popcorn they served wasn't too noisy for the film. ("Frankly, Scarlett . . . CRUNCH!")

In 1948, ears of popcorn 5600 years old were found in a New Mexico cave, the so-called Bat Cave.

When TV bit into the movie market, the convenience-food and home-popcorn markets combined to produce E-Z Pop, a disposable foil pan that was supposed to expand to a Sputnik shape with the stovetop popping. Many children of the '50s were seriously disappointed when the flat foil would simply rattle and steam even after 10 minutes of frantic shaking and higher heat, by which time anything in the pan, popped or not, was burnt black, the kitchen smelled awful, and *Ozzie and Harriet* was over. We learned later that those impotent specks at the bottom, those forever-latent kernels, had been given a name by the sexist and ageist popcorn industry: "old maids" or "grannies."

At present the only forward development in movie popcorn is its rising price, which helps keep otherwise doomed theaters afloat. Why velveted nabes that charge $5 for the right to walk in—giving you the right to walk out—need popcorn as flotation is answered by the economics of the monopolistic movie industry, cauterized elsewhere on these pages. Prices have so far inflated beyond the real value of popcorn—a substance rightly loved for its worthless frivolity and lack of concentration—that the cardboard Lily Nestrite cups and portable tubs themselves take on symbolic value. And sometimes more than symbolic value in theaters where the concession's receipts are tallied against the number of popcorn cups used (for who would bother measuring the *popcorn?*), some underpaid ecologically minded employees run through the aisles between screenings, collect used cups, and recycle them, pocketing the difference.

Aside from price, movie popcorn is well within its historical tradition: most of it is Bat Cave brand, and tastes all of its 5600 years. When popcorn isn't just-popped, it might as well be fossilized. Unbuttered popcorn, by the way, has been and still may be used as a packing material; as a child, I sampled some from a wooden crate of dishes, before I had it correctively slapped from my hand. Last week I bought some popcorn ($1.25) in an East Side theater. Its glass popper-bin was shiny and empty of everything but a chewed pencil; my purchase was scooped from a five-pound (very large) poly bag behind the counter. Ungreased, the popcorn's smell, texture, and flavor transported me back in time, to my childhood and that packing case. Organic styrofoam.

Have you ever smelled fresh popcorn in a theater that didn't have a working popper? There's a useful class of chemicals called "industrial fragrance"; some auto dealers, to refurbish models that are only slightly used, employ an aerosol that mimics the "new car smell"— vinyl upholstery plus nylon carpet—that customers have learned to expect. It is just as easy to reproduce the aroma of popping corn, especially when so few of us have contact with the original. We also know, of course, that the optional liquid dispensed with such unction isn't butter, and if it were it would have to be clarified butter so it wouldn't solidify. No. Sniff your fingers after movie-buttered popcorn. This particular rancidity is not natural, but probably an alembic result of coconut oil and whatever preservatives and artificial flavors—sometimes one in the same— are used both to move the product and preserve its shelf life.

The Chicago-based Popcorn Institute, an association of popcorn processors, reminds us that popcorn need not be eaten only in movie houses, need not be simply "buttered" and salted, need not be, actually, eaten at all. This reminds me of my friend Carol, also in Chicago, who found other uses for popcorn when she was a youngster in Brooklyn. Carol and her friends would first soak their versatile popcorn at the water fountain, then run to the first row of the balcony (remember balconies?), make vomit noises, and dump the stuff over the edge onto people like me. Anyway, the Popcorn Institute suggests that you soak your whole or ground popcorn in hot water, and then add milk and strawberries for an appealing—if disorienting—breakfast treat. Or how about a Popcorn Roast? ("As satisfying as the real thing. Enjoy it with your favorite sauce or gravy," says *Popcorn Cooking.*)

My editors maintain that movie theaters sell food other than popcorn, but I tell them that the only change in candy is the size of the box; there's certainly no change from your dollar bill. Everyone already knows that the slightly bitter-sweet chocolate on the outside of Goldenberg's Peanut Chews is unbeatable, that much-mourned Bonomo's Turkish Taffy (crack!) was invented by dentists, that the vision of oil-slick hot dogs relentlessly turned between hot metal rollers, perpetually underdone or eternally shriveled, is a more convincing picture of hell than any offered inside, on the screen.

A hot dog may be the most complicated food one can manage in the dark. Ice cream cones proved difficult; hence the rigid, simple bonbon in its protective wrap, though its list of ingredients is hardly elementary ("Ice cream center contains: milk, cream, sugar, corn sweeteners, buttermilk, whey, nonfat milk, guar gum, mono- and diglycerides, cellulose gum, Polysorbate 80, carrageenan, sodium caseinate, salt, vanilla extract and artificial color." Note that this is a premium bonbon—real milk—and that the list doesn't cover the "chocolate flavored coating.") Bonbons get soft, warm even, but they never, ever melt.

Theaters that serve more ambitious food, like the

french-bread pizza of the 8th Street Playhouse or the quiche, Perrier and gummy cheesecake assortment of the mock-beret cafe of the Carnegie Hall Cinema, do this to dissuade you from carrying your food inside. In the Carnegie Hall Cinema this makes sense: I don't see how you can really savor a Toblerone when a Marguerite Duras film is going on about "leprosy of the heart."

But perhaps the management is aware of the major question in cinema eating: how can you eat and watch at once? One group of theorists, the *prosynesthetics,* believes that the use of taste, smell, and the active enhancement of hearing (crunch, crackle, "shhh") heightens the otherwise passive and voyeuristic sense network involved in viewing a film. The resulting experience is more complex, more integrated and much more satisfying, according to this theory, which is exactly opposed to that of the purists, the *antisynesthetics,* who assert that although eating and watching do affect each other, it is to their detriment, diluting and averaging individual senses and ultimately reducing the possibility of careful or intense pleasure in either food or film. According to the antis, eating popcorn during a movie is partly responsible for lowering the standards of both, i.e., stale popcorn helps one tolerate a stale film, and vice versa. I don't wish to agree with the antisynesthetics, who seem to be basically antifun and anti-American, but, considering the data we have, can there be any other conclusion?

(8/19/1981)

On Authenticity

Are these native ingredients? What's the original recipe? How can you tell if it's a fake dish or wrong flavor? I've cooked it this way all my life, the way my father taught me, but how could his father, from the Ukraine, have made it? Could it possibly be authentic?

The anxiety in these questions is modern, even though cooks of the past, those who bothered to pass along recipes, may also have concerned themselves with a dish's genealogy or a raw material's proper native soil. Why should they have worried or, for that matter, even have taken the trouble to teach or write down what they knew? Curiosity, personal or national pride, local conservation, a wish for immortality—there is evidence for all these motives. However, recorded recipes are accidents of individuality when compared to the evolution of large cuisines. Evolution seems like the right word in this case, because Darwinism is still a persuasive model for slow changes in large groups. The fear here would be of cataclysm, of extinction. Have whole cuisines become dinosaurs, suddenly wiped out by earthquake or influenza, without leaving an influence or aroma behind?

Even if we had records of Atlantis dinners, or came as close to the past as a dish of petrified beans from Pompeii, we would still not know if our reconstructions of these would be authentic. We could backbreed Colonial corn, as some are now attempting to do, grind the new old corn, and bake it according to something like Susannah Carter's *The Frugal Housewife or Complete Woman Cook,* published in 1772. But there is no mention of corn or maize in Carter's cookbook! And how could we be certain our result would be anything like its namesake? Flavor has no verifying language, no standard, no life past a generation. Novels, letters, diaries—metaphors—are the closest we can get. Those Pompeiian favas may have been prepared by visiting Africans; history is sometimes a nightmare.

Contemporary fear about authenticity is downhill-ism: that the good and the pure are being replaced by the bad, the diluted, the inauthentic, and there is nothing we can do to stop this because we have so little control over who grows our food, who processes it, and sometimes even who cooks it. The motive for these commercial activities is profit.

This anxiety—justified, I think—takes daily consumer forms. Peaches are mushier again this year and will never be good again. I can't find fresh cream. We are being cheated out of authentic restaurant cooking.

Food critics, when not flacks for progress, are supposed to be watchdogs of the authentic. I would like to be, but last month's eating does not make it entirely clear what authentic really is.

●

We were staring into the scum on the top of experimental "cappuccino" offered by American Airlines. Bruce, Ira, and I were treated to this after-dinner surprise as part of a general campaign to calm the nerves of those passengers who imagined they would die because of the incompetent old managers who are filling in as air controllers during the PATCO strike. On the first leg of my return trip, from San Diego to Dallas, the pilot volunteered a fascinating commentary on every puddle and hill beneath us. On the next shaky leg, a different pilot thrilled us with his geographic harmonica, "Deep in the Heart of Texas" as we took off and "Give My Regards . . ." as we landed, thank God. This to calm our nerves.

Bruce and Ira, who had seats next to me, were a friendly and cynical art director and copywriter for a well-known ad agency. They had spent a long day shooting Cybil Shepherd, who was "very nice." According to Bruce and Ira, all the people in Dallas were promoters. "They didn't do anything except promote someone or something else." I mention this because it approaches an absolute definition of authentic, but from the back door.

We asked a flight attendant what was in the cups. Oddly enough, she seemed to know: "Coffee, chocolate, something like cream, and brandy." It was revolting. The something like cream diffracted the overhead light the way an oil slick turns sunlight into colors on the street. Any abstaining alcoholic would fall off the wagon without knowing, which infuriates me. But perhaps the alcoholic, like us, could not get past the first sip. It was the perfect end to a perfect meal. The plastic cups were never even warm.

Bruce and Ira, of course, wanted to know if I knew any good, cheap restaurants, the authentic New York kind. I did, and do, but instead of a list I offered the complaint that I was apprehensive about the coming restaurant season, apprehensive most of all about the "cheap." It is my job, I explained, to concentrate on what frugal *Village Voice* readers are supposed to be able to afford (though when *Voice* ad people want to sell ads, they concentrate on how *upscale* the readers are). But this year I may be stuck for good, inexpensive restaurants. My last five tryouts were flops, and I don't usually review flops because other critics have that review-everything beat. Would you like to hear, I asked them, about authentic food in Southern California?

"Whenever people ask me—and they do ask, believe it or not—what's good in San Diego, I automatically advise them to go for what's local: fresh and special sea food, like abalone and totuava, and Mexican cooking. (I do not tell them that my favorite cheap restaurant in Tijuana is Basque, not Mexican.) It isn't, however, so easy to recommend any one restaurant that illustrates authentic localism. Anthony's Fish Grotto in La Jolla, one of a small, popular chain, serves whatever is just caught—shark fillet, all kinds of snapper and yellowtail, and that oily, indigenous totuava—but though Anthony's fries beautifully, it broils dry. Also, its large crab salad is the same size as its small crab salad, but served on a larger plate. As for authenticity, native San Diegans go there mostly to see the tourists—they are sometimes permanent tourists—from Iowa. But the cost of a drink, clam appetizer, fish dinner, and coffee is less than $10. Low price is the authentic mark of a San Diego meal; because of woefully underpaid, mostly Chicano labor, the average restaurant check is only two-thirds that in old New York. Why don't people in San Diego know it's a bargain?

"The authentic Mexican restaurants? If you are eating out, Mexican-food authenticity comes from a long impression over time, not from one meal. And the inauthentic may be pleasing. Take Garcia's of Scottsdale, in San Diego, a new restaurant in a new shopping center near the Marine base. Its architecture is stucco-bunker steakhouse, rather handsome actually, but why would San Diego import a branch of Mexicana from a ritzy suburb of its sunbelt rival, Phoenix? See the matchbook? A Mexican bourgeois Mom and Pop, like Roy Rogers and Dale Evans, and the Mexican national flower: a rose. (A rose uses more water than any other cultivated flower, and is particularly unsuited to arid climates, like those of Scottsdale or San Diego. La Jolla, the richest, whitest part of San Diego, is known for its roses.)

"We were led to a waiting area and seated in Boston Colonial chairs. We stared at floral curtains of fake chintz, Mexican tiles, and various European plates. We were beyond the pretense of authentic here: this was historical delirium, our every swoon met by the blondest, collegest, minimum-wagers imaginable.

"But the food was . . . delicious. We truly enjoyed an authentic Ariz-Mex specialty, the deep-fried burrito or chimichanga, while our pigmentless waiter told us how fine the surf would be manana. It just occurs to me that he may not have been a real surfer.

"This same shopping center offered a quietly waiting Moroccan restaurant and—a special surprise—a futuristic, frozen-yogurt emporium designed and run by a former curator at both the La Jolla and San Diego museums of art. He was smartly dressed like *Star Trek's* Mr. Spock, and wanly complained from behind the counter that people had no respect for his carefully wrought high-tech tables. One end of the room, we saw, was dramatically occupied by a form that floated, apparently, in a field of light, casting beautiful shadows on the cordoned-off wall. Was it art? (It looked like an early Robert Irwin, and I think it was.) Is it usable art? Would it sell yogurt?

"So what is authenticity? Does 'local' grant the seal of approval? In New York I recently tried a new Thai restaurant, praised because someone from Thailand 'ate there and loved it.' So what? If you transplanted a New Yorker to Thailand and asked that person if such-and-such a place served a good steak, would you automatically expect that person to know a good steak? An authentic steak?

"Authentic Los Angeles is Hollywood, is fake. On this trip I pulled at a tired artichoke in a French 'bistro' on Melrose Avenue, sitting in a hedged patio under a sea of Ricard umbrellas. *Tres* atmospheric, except the place was built on a busy intersection, and even at midnight exhaust fumes spewed through the facade. Perhaps it's like that in Paris, too.

"Theatricality is not inauthentic; the need to entertain and be entertained is serious. It's lying, or packaging the truth, that I hate. It's the new 'diet wine' made from unripe grapes, or the kangaroo meat in hamburgers. Jack-in-the-Boxes, the California subjects of the Australian kangaroo meat scandal, were empty. If they were honest they'd have played it up as a new taste sensation: the Jumping Jack."

The harmonica played "Moonlight on the Wabash."

Back in New York a week later, a friend told me that, according to the *Times*, dietician-bureaucrats classify ketchup as a *vegetable* when computing school lunches. "Can you guess why?" he asked. He told me that he rarely cries, but after reading this he felt like crying.

(9/30/1981)

Victory Garden

Who hath not seen thee oft amid thy store?
Sometimes whoever seeks abroad may find
Thee sitting careless on a granary floor,
Thy hair soft-lifted by the winnowing wind;
                                    —John Keats, "To Autumn"

In 1981 there is some danger in personifying the seasons. Even when Keats did so, he was accused of sentimental Druidism and sloppy Hellenism all at once, though his Autumn has outlived the season of his critics. A personification of contemporary fall promises change, in terms of new clothes and fresh products, just as it did to 19th century England, but it no longer offers plentiful harvest and presages renewal. Or so it is feared.

We drove to Coventry, 40 minutes east of Hartford, Connecticut, ostensibly to visit Adelma Grenier Simmons's 18th century farmhouse and 28 herb gardens, together called Caprilands, but really to see if the possibility of seasonal recharging is still with us. I know you are not required to leave this city in order to sample autumn, but I still notice the Plaza Hotel from almost every vantage in Central Park. Caprilands (which means goatlands), on 50 acres of woods and old dairy pasturage, offers herb lectures and a garden walk, a luncheon, and a Sunday tea to "the greatest number of selective, garden-oriented people," which is about 85 a day. The ever-changing luncheon was my column's hook, but I am sorry to note that, although graciously served and a very pleasant opportunity to meet some of the other diners, the Ritz cracker canapes, peanut butter soup, lamb curry, and tossed salad we sampled did not illustrate the use and power of herbs in ways that would impress ethnicky eaters already used to the lemon grass and basil of Thai cooking or even the few herbs of a straightforward Julia Child meal.

I say this in the quietest and most well meant of tones, because it should not dissuade anyone from visiting Caprilands or even from eating there. It may be that a peanut butter soup is adventurous for the majority of those who visit from unurban garden clubs, but that sounds awfully condescending. People knew what they were eating; "Scarsdale is going to hell today," yelled one happy and not unsophisticated eater. It may be that I could not judge from just one meal, or was disappointed because there were no flowers in my salad, as earlier spring accounts had promised. You cannot expect spring in fall at an honest herb garden. Caprilands, I remember, is not a restaurant. The punch, which Mrs. Simmons called autumn wine, is composed of sweet cider, cinnamon, cloves, grated nutmeg, and sliced oranges, all boiled, then allowed to sit for a while until it's kicked with a quantity of sherry. I usually hate these cloying holiday exercises, but this one tasted as wonderful as the lunch's herb bread and airy honey loaf. Sunday tea, I imagine, could be a delight.

The lecture and garden walks that precede lunch are open to all, and free. Of course the lectures, held in the barn, change seasonally; October was witches and wreaths; "a wreath is only as good as its foundation." Mrs. Simmons's determined voice, direct and full of little practiced jokes with a slightly selling tone, wound around the heads of the seated women (and the few men) in the barn and wafted up to the lofts, getting lost amid inverted sheaths of drying herbs. Herbal fragrance, powerful, rich, and no accident, deadened all the words, or at least softened them, and began what was for me a rebalancing of senses.

Herbs have a history along a continuum of practical eating on one end and magic and healing on the other. But what is impractical about healing? And why isn't necessary eating connected more closely to the spirit? Perhaps this is a fake continuum, or so I began to think as we strolled behind our lecturer to the autumn gardens that had not yet given up. The Silver Garden, for instance, lasts through December. "Lavender bloomed *three times* for us this year," she said, as if it were doing us a favor. How practical, too, the gallon jugs of cheap vinegar sitting near the plants, labels still on, with tarragon, basil, or mixed herbs steeping in whatever sun is left. "Some people use rose-geranium vinegar for headaches." A few women murmured and wrote this down. Mrs. Simmons spoke almost as if we were someday going to take her place, to grow and understand herbs.

"Herb gardens are a puzzle, because they don't look like much unless you know what they are." She was obviously dealing in metaphor as well. Then she walked to the little bookstore, to inscribe *Herb Gardening in the Five Seasons* (the fifth is Christmas) and her many other books at her captain's chair, with a fine flourish and comments both businesslike and completely warm and sincere. Guests were also invited to visit the gift shop, in part of the old barn.

How is a garden a metaphor? In the past, gardens have stood for an orderly, even creative, relationship to nature. "Where man is not, nature is barren," at least according to William Blake. Caprilands also suggests another kind of metaphor, more of an example, in the person of Mrs. Simmons. In her books, her lectures, her house, her clear, patient manner with 85 people a day from April to December, and especially in her and her staff's gardens, you see that she thrives as a proselytizing herbalist. To allow her vegetable love to grow, she had to root it in the dirty world by opening gift shops, selling Crabtree and Evelyn soaps, making money. She may, in fact, enjoy this too.

Adelma Simmons and her garden plots illustrate a way to survive and flourish, fighting to do only what one loves to do. She has made her profession private and public at once, so that old skills are renewed and even—can it be said?—improved. Her exemplary "garden" is not a retreat; it seems hard-won over her many years, and gives me more hope in the revivification of all things we fear will disappear than any unpruned natural wilderness ever could.

(11/11/1981)

Surplus Value

Dear Restaurant Review Critic:

We are requesting a moment of your time to explain our situation. We are workers who came to this restaurant 14 years ago. The man we used to work for lost this restaurant because of tax problems. The restaurant closed. Eventually we, the workers, got together and bought it.

While the old owner was in charge, the restaurant was dirty; but because of the cook's skills (now one of the owners), it did well. After we bought the restaurant, we fixed and cleaned it up and improved the quality of the food. For instance, we buy the finest and freshest meat and vegetables available, while taking extra care to ensure that everything served has a home-cooked flavor.

However, the restaurant is not doing too well as of yet. We don't know why. We suspect that it may be because the restaurant was closed for some time between the last owner and ourselves. We are working very hard and have invested a great deal of our own money, but the truth is none of us have any more money left to put into the business.

We know this is really not your problem, but nine families depend on this restaurant for their income. If things don't improve soon, we're afraid it will be nine more families on the unemployment rolls. This is why we feel we must contact you immediately. All we would like is a chance. We know our food is good; the customers we have come back again and again. We are asking for a little attention and an honest evaluation. Our food can speak for itself.

Sincerely,
Nine Struggling Workers

If food could speak for itself there'd be no need for reviews. Vladimir Estragon and I literally collided, running to show each other our copy of this plaintive missive. We may be sentimental fools, but we didn't doubt its sincerity. We do question almost all our other food mail; press releases may be sincere (EAT HERE!!!) but they require translation from the hype; it's gotten so that we can almost predict a dud from the tone of a press agent's praise. But I have never heard of an agency called "Nine Struggling Workers."

Vladimir and I agreed that if the food is "at least edible" I should make every effort. This may sound like random selection, but unless one eats in and reviews every eatery in New York, there will be a John Cage element of chance to the process. I can only exhibit the procedure. And it's not like there's a glut of edible food. I can't begin to tell you how many awful meals I've committed myself to lately in order to scare up a cheap restaurant. Over-$25 places can dish out garbage too, but as good raw materials become both more scarce and more expensive, a cheap restaurant that strives to retain quality is usually the first to suffer and close.

After three dinners we found the New Acropolis letter to be 100 percent sincere and about 75 percent accurate, hooray. You may be familiar with moussaka or fried cheese from sturdy places like the Delphi in lower Manhattan or coffee-shop restaurants in Astoria, but the New Acropolis offerings are generally better. Filo pastry of the two spinach-cheese pies they call an appetizer was browned tawny, not burned, not oily, and held a creamy, almost moussey, filling. The bekri-meze (which has many spellings), here a mini-mix of sauteed calf's liver, fatty Greek sausage, sweetbreads, and chips of fried cheese, sits in a salty, smoky puddle comprising, among other things, tomato ketchup. It is surprisingly satisfying to taste the soft white sweetbreads or rare liver in conjunction with such a wicked sauce. Other appetizers, like whipped tara-masalata, eggplant salad, minty stuffed grape leaves, are simply and freshly prepared, with less oil and salt in toto than we are used to expect.

The New Acropolis has linen, actually and metaphorically, on its tables. When one of our eating partners asked for pita bread to mop her fish-roe cream, she was politely but definitely told that the substantial Italian loaf in front of her is better than any pita, which is properly employed "down on the docks." New Acropolis, you see, is attempting to reform the reputation of honest dishes that have taken to the street. The fish entrees best prove good intentions: a whole porgy was rubbed with olive oil, perfectly broiled—perfect is a word you can use about broiling fish—and served immediately and in concert with the other entrees. The chef knows his business. I chewed the bones of about 10 fried smelts, toothbrush size with a tempura-like batter, dipping them in a side bowl of a pillowy-light "garlic sauce," not mayonnaise and not aioli, that I would buy by the gallon if available. Chips of well-fried zucchini also accompany this sauce. Marvelous food.

A lamb shish kebab was ordered medium-rare, appeared in great chunks medium-rare, and I've had racks of lamb less tender; other lamb entrees just passed muster. Of the dishes we tried, only the relatively expensive, tired shrimp should be avoided. We all wished the kitchen would replace the side of frozen peas with any fresh vegetable, though we appreciated the gesture of its bulk and the pan-roasted potato next to it that accompanied each main dish. Homemade egg custard in filo piecrust was an outstanding dessert.

Another eating partner enjoyed the place but wondered if it would appeal to *The Village Voice's* fussy readers. Would tweedy theatergoers go? Could you impress a business buddy here?

Why not? With a filling dinner for under $10 per, and a superb four-courser (if you choose carefully) for under $15? But Greek food this cheap must be "working class." Or so it is oddly assumed.

So instead of "cheap," let's call it "inexpensive." No one will know the difference. Collective restaurant efforts like this, if they please the individual, are worth the support of any pretension.

(11/25/1981)

One Star

If you plan to visit Manhattan for a month and want some restaurant advice, you probably couldn't do better right now than Seymour Britchky's *The Restaurants of New York*. There isn't much else. Stained copies of *The Underground Gourmet* that grace the bins of used bookstores are useless, unless, for the few restaurants that survive, you move the decimal point of estimated price one place to the right. Most of the other books and pamphlets that pretend to restaurant knowledge are either valentines to advertising or self-promotion, sometimes both, and heaven help those of us who take a 1971 *Cue* or 1981 WABC-TV decal seriously. Instinct is a greater guarantee.

But the wandering stomach needs its Vergil. In strange cities I have used the Yellow Pages, where a careful, cynical reading can sometimes yield the lay of the restaurant land. This strange city, however, and its 29 pages of telephone-book listings do not give up their secrets without help. The best aid *Restaurants of New York* can offer the stranger is to exhibit a cluster of plausible restaurants, those that through their merit, tenure, or recent debut are reviewable. In some cities, even large ones, such a book would by necessity include most of the available restaurants; in New York a wieldy book requires some discrimination. The real merit of *Restaurants of New York* is, oddly enough, tautological: here are 202 restaurants that a serious reviewer has chosen to review.

This is not a bad start, but New Yorkers who eat out often or read restaurant reviews regularly must look beyond the selection to the utility of the reviews themselves. Here there are difficulties. And those who look beyond even questionable utility to the meaning, the ideology carried by the act of reviewing in Britchky's manner, use his collection with some peril.

What is it like to eat with Seymour Britchky? In print the reviewer seems either to ignore his companions or eat alone. I have always assumed his dinner partners, if any, would be female, because the male narrator is apparently fascinated with eavesdropping on heterosexual dinners *a deux,* on the "dolls" and "girls" that frequent his choices. He takes his one cautious step into a restaurant with some gay men in it (the Paris Commune) gingerly, as if it were an effete gymnasium, though he never mentions the forbidden word and is reasonably kind to the food. No gay men exist, apparently, anywhere else, and lesbians, if they exist, should know better. People of color are also invisible at table, though they turn up as "swarthy" (Mitali) and "professionally black" (Gloucester House) waiters. But since he's sarcastic to everybody the ol' curmudgeon must be all right, right? He's properly acerbic, anyway, about haughty maitre d's or waiters who try to separate you from your table. His introduction's "Ten Sensible Rules" are sensible and caustic at once, and I have read the formula for "Departure" many times: "Leave when you are good and ready. It is your right to eat at your own pace, including lingering over a second cup of coffee. Enjoy possession of a table that others are waiting in line for. Later they will." This is good advice, though the strength of the

Hobbesian imperative is depressing. I can't enjoy a table *because* others want it.

The book's persona is fond of good beef and veal, of almost any cheese board, of "sweets"; he does not hover over vegetables except as garnish or in sauces. Salads are rare, as is a meal without wine. Britchky's concentration of attention at the table is on Brillat-Savarin's primary taste-sensations, the simple chewing-perception of flavor. Anticipation, usually the disappointed anticipation of others, is dealt with, but contemplation on the satisfaction of eating, a possible humanizing step, is nowhere to be found.

Such a narrowing prospect requires skills specific to the description of food isolated from experience, and at this difficult job Britchky is adept. He belongs to the adjective school, and he trots out clear and apt modifiers in combinations that belie their rare repetitions. Metaphors and similes are used as seasoning, sparingly but with drama: "Garlic at Grotta Azzurra is used the way sand is used at the beach."

The question most often asked about books like this—is it accurate?—isn't easy to answer. My judgment of food in a number of the restaurants reviewed is similar to Britchky's, though my description of the experience would often be, and has often been, different. About some places we completely disagree, but this is not unusual in most critical fields. Compare Britchky's tour de force pan of the Coach House to the praise this Village eatery has received over and over again from the reviewer at *The New York Times*. Can these be the same restaurants, the same chefs? Does the difference of opinion mean that one expert is more expert than the other? Does either reviewer display standards, the first step in allowing a reader to decide?

The usual assumption about the "expertise" of a reviewer is that there is a science to reviewing that goes beyond the cumulative experience of eating out. "Where did you learn to review restaurants?" people ask, and it's a good question, but there is no school for restaurant reviewing. A chef, a writer of cookbooks, a nutritionist, even a waiter can be a restaurant reviewer, but one need not be any of these. A restaurant critic, like almost any other critic, must at some point demonstrate expertise if he or she chooses to be an expert at all. That two reviewers can differ so intently about the same data means either that the kitchen is unstable, that one (or both) of the critics is wrong, or that what a reader is trained to assume is test-tube truth is not a quantity guaranteed by a respectable byline. Expertise may exist, but if it does it should be verifiable. I prefer the instructor to the expert, for the paradoxical goal of reviewing should be to enable readers happily to evaluate on their own. Expert opinions are welcome, but they must be perceived as opinions. In the case of the Coach House, it might be remembered that a feud, however honest, is good journalistic business.

The stars that festoon most reviews, also good business, appeal to the basest need to be told what to do. Who in a right mind would go to a one-star restaurant when four-star restaurants exist, unless four-star "excellent" places can only be expensive and French, as they are here? Britchky has developed an amazing paragraph of persiflage in his introduction to defend the fact that, in previous editions of this book, readers complained that "the ratings

did not invariably conform to the particulars of the text."
Ratings are, apparently, subjective. Minds boggle; because various publishers want ratings (they sell), he is including them even though he can't compose descriptions
that will conform. And so to bed. Stars, both rating and
media, pretend they are utilitarian, but they most certainly
are not.

Finally, any collection of previously published reviews
has utility problems. Britchky garners reviews in this an-
nually expanded and partially updated collection from the
modules of his monthly restaurant newsletter, from similar packages in *New York* magazine, and from his brief output at the *Soho News*. Although we can assume that the
author revisits important restaurants, reviews as old as 1971
will probably not stand up without complete revision, because restaurants change very quickly. The Raoul's review, for example, however agreeable or not a few years
ago, is now clearly dated overpraise, and others are
equally chancy. Also, descriptions of mood and fashion,
the Frye boots and tank watches that provided color in reviews when they first appeared, do not wear well year after year. Even the first phrase of the introduction, "It is
now just ten years since the day when . . . " has read that
way too long.

It is not that the present is unimportant to the perception
of a restaurant and its food. On the contrary. But little else
in these reviews is concerned with immediacy, change, or
the rest of the world at the time of the author's meal. You
can't have it both ways: a timely, accurate, colorful review,
and a permanent evaluation. You either acknowledge the
moment, or you don't. But such an acknowledgement

would throw this whole project into disarray, for it would admit the possibility of doubt, memory, and complex pleasure, things that make eating out worth anybody's while or money. These are also qualities that would make one want to read a book more than once, something most readers will not be tempted to here.

(11/25/1981)

Here's Looking at You

I think we had an apple-brandy sidecar to begin with. It did not seem this was only the second time we had met. All at once a whole lot of things were moving and mixing, as though they had always been there.

—Kenneth Fearing
The Big Clock

Maybe it's coincidence, but in every old and new movie I've seen this week, in every novel and story, someone's drinking booze. A few of these, like Fearing's *The Big Clock,* measure out their plots by the jigger. This may be an author-conscious act or perhaps just below consciousness and the better for it, I don't know. But alcohol is all over, and most of the time it's meant not to be noticed because it starts out as a neutral, natural fact, like talking, eating, or going to sleep. Every culture—assuming the fantasy of tribal pluralism—drinks if given the opportunity or the need. Alcohol makes some people—alcoholics—ill, and does the same kind of things to children that it does to adults, but sooner.

"Drink" has always been as great a temptation to moralizing as sex, but that does not make the two even generically equal.

Since I write about food throughout the year and once in a while dip testing fingers into the house wine, I suppose I must consider drinking part of eating out. Alcohol is the margin of profit for many a restaurant. An interviewer of food critics once asked if I thought that booze dulled the senses. I assume she meant "taste buds" for "senses," those that in food experts are supposed to be honed finer than usual, like the eyesight of film critics. Did I drink? Enough to enjoy the food, sometimes enough to enjoy the drink, and more rarely, both. No, I don't know if it dulls perception. I do know it lubricates my tongue, may raise the feeling that we had a "good time," but that depends on how much, with whom, and of course I am speaking for myself. One local restaurant reviewer regularly begins his column with "drinks were large and excellent" or some such barroom expertise; others are known vineal indulgers. Some writers write only when drunk, and write beautifully, so I assume it could be the same for those who eat out.

Putting aside commercial motives, arguments, hangovers, and all the other holiday wrappings that become garbage almost immediately after, it's still the year's end that brings this subject up. If you are among friends, even if you are by yourself, you can toast the Christian-Western renewal, in wassail ritual for those who need history as excuse, or just in the modern manner. Cheers, here's mud in your eye, down the hatch, let's drink to the New Year.

It demonstrates, this toast, a great deal of faith, first in the solo flush of warmth and comfort that things will get better and here's how, but also in the knowledge that we who lift our glasses do so in shared spirit and similar results: the world is high together. Facts may intrude—for the poor, the sarcastic, the lonely—but all in all our toast is a hopeful sign. Some may think that the moment of toasting is itself the height of communality, the most we can reach; but they are maudlin. Others know the toast to be only a respite from the usual discord and fear.

Why not for a moment *not* be afraid? I am often afraid: of my own and anyone's poverty, of war, of bad health, of selfishness, and the shrinking returns of individuality. My apprehension has increased this past year and I—and others I think—expect the next one to be worse. How can we toast such a year?

It depends on our drink. Some may drink to forget, but who will *toast* to forget? Very few. I will toast my lover, my friends, my family, and drink to whatever we can work for and whomever we can work with, alone and together. Perhaps I should say "I will have toasted," for though I write this before the holiday, you are reading it a week after. So I also toast you, reader, and stretch my wishes over this slightly longer period, that we can drink, and at the same time get on to work in order that the "moving and mixing" is no inebriate illusion, but real.

(1/6/1982)

Underground Gourmet

Levi-Strauss based his now-unfashionable structuralism on the premise that the world and its language, as far as he was concerned, are either-or. You're either a structuralist or you're not.

When we passed out of the restaurant door, we saw to our right a short, burnished, camel-coated woman carrying on a lively conversation with herself while standing in and facing a corner. She didn't look mad, and there wasn't room enough for a pay phone. But my dinner partner, exclaiming that *she* used to do that when she was a kid, stood me in the corner when the other speaker left and walked to another corner about 20 feet away. Then lo and behold, her voice dropped from the ceiling like an angel, so intimately, and began to taunt: *woo-oo, Jeffrey, here I am, woo-oo.* An architectural trick. When I told my friend Andrea, she said that 25 years ago she used to stand in that corner, wait till some businessman hit the right spot, and whisper "Your fly is open." It drove them crazy, those gullible men.

So the world is black and white: those who know about the oral corners outside the Oyster Bar, and those who don't. Those who know about the Oyster Bar, and those who will. Clams, mussels, and oysters themselves are divided in two, with only a muscle to keep them closed and whole. But that bared muscle has moved many men and women beyond their unhappy dualism, some of them right here in the lower level of Grand Central Station.

The Grand Central Oyster Bar and Restaurant

If you already know about this place, don't bother to read on, unless you want your pleasure verified—which seems unnecessary to me. You who mob the place at lunch already know how quickly the waiters, the older, gruffer ones especially, turn over the tables. I think I can generalize that everything is better at lunch, the soups hotter, the cold seafood platter (a bad choice in any case) not quite so limp, the shellfish just a bit more shocked about newly leaving home. We will therefore concentrate on dinner, an early, leisurely dinner, when the grand, groined, Romanesque dining room has some empty tables, the bar and counters have gaps, and the brown saloon is—no, it's still packed. This intimate giant is a wonderful place to eat.

For food, the red-checkered whole is greater than most of its parts. You can probably get the commoner reciped offering better-done, singly, elsewhere. This whale of a menu is unfashionable, and the bearnaise and mousseline are indispensable. But even though icy-fingered fishmongers on the outside complain that there is no X or Y in cold winter waters, the Oyster Bar will broil or sometimes pan- or deep-fry a dictionary of extraordinary fishes and friends. I could list their names for novelty, but let me tell you of a few we ate: steamed fillet of Point Judith Ray, which splits into delicate, scallop-tasting strands, in a brown butter sauce shot with zippy capers. It was not fancy, just a rare combo of straightforward chiffon. Or butter-fried filleted shad—superb—with bacon and its liverlike roe, dry and chewed into flavor. A slightly over-broiled whole Chincoteague sea bass—this is geography— with snippets of aromatic fennel. No almonds on woody broccoli, no julienned zucchini, but a side of luscious individualistic cole slaw and some tired new potatoes. And when was the last time you ate biscuits where you could taste the baking soda?

We tried to prove that one could get away with a three-course fish dinner for under $20, but we kept adding up to $25 or $30, more with wine. The wine list on the back of the handwritten menu (some would say that the menu is on the back of the list) offends francophile conformists because only a few American cabernets and one pinot noir are stuck on the end of 118 alphabetically ordered California whites—a terrific glossary of slight and major variations that range from $8.25 to $39. "The" waiter, if you leave it to him, will choose the most inoffensive and undistinguished, so do it yourself.

Anyway, the only way to climb out of a hot meal under $20 is to pare down to essentials: chowders, stews, pan roasts, slaw, beer. The pan roasts, shellfish and toast soaking in the bottom of paprika-rashed cream broth, are a bit heavy for me. The $8.95 fish fry, cheap, is assorted, bready, and squirmy. However, the pale New England and orange Manhattan clam chowders can satisfy generations: not a wet collation of crisp youngster-ingredients that haven't yet let go of themselves, but a thickened amalgam, a real soup.

For dessert, you can have strong coffee and one of the brighter specials, like rhubarb trifle, or maybe the two-buck chocolate truffle cake—or you can have rice pudding. The pudding pushes me out into meditative superlatives. Only in a large, successful city, where business and distribution bring together so many farflung foods and eaters, can such a restaurant be found. It is right that these are the bowels of Grand Central. When you get depressed about the stupid filth and Gotterdammerung of the subways or the sidewalks over them, just come here and look around. Who says commerce has no spirit? The protean sweet pudding and whipped cream commingle to make the most beautiful placid yellow I've ever eaten.

OR . . .

You can go to the bar and request a blue point in exchange for a subway token, a salty Wellfleet or chickeny Maine belon for a little more, or five or six other kinds. You can have oysters, and the world is yours.

(2/3/1982)

"Gainsborough" (1902), by Huntley and Palmers, commemorates the rediscovery of the artist's portrait of the Duchess of Devonshire, stolen from its gallery 25 years before. Art, along with everything else, can be assimilated in the bowels of commerce.

Form Follows Biscuit

What some modestly call the "capability" of the museum system is really its power. Museums collect, store, restore, catalogue, and show art, and if you think these are neutral activities, you're forgetting about who decides what's accepted or bought, how it's written into history, and whether or not something is shown. A museum's selective power is more than just a particular curator quietly increasing the market value of art owned by the same museum's board of directors—though such partisan backscratching is not unheard of. The power is general, for museums, in grand tautology, *validate* what they show. What an institution chooses to exhibit becomes more precious, becomes more art, by the showing.

"Isn't it precious!" a guard said. "Isn't is gorgeous!" echoed a viewer. The objects of gushing were neither Byzantine icons nor someone's new baby, but 19th and 20th century British biscuit tins, under glass until March 7 at New Haven's Yale Center for British Art. Biscuit-tin collectors must be thrilled; how much more interesting are their collections now, and how much more valuable. I agree with onlookers: this is a beautiful and curious show, but its beauty lies in the paradox of displaying, as rare, objects that are prototypes of modern commercial packaging. Biscuit tins wouldn't be in a museum today if there weren't, at one time, so many of them.

An English biscuit is not the steaming, buttered item

Americans extrude in prebaked form from cardboard tubes. It is, rather, an unrisen, hard cracker (or, with sweetener, cookie) that will not easily mold or dry out because it is already bone-dry ("biscuit" is from Old French and means, like the German zweiback, twice-baked). A biscuit is the wheat-and-water version of salt pork, beef jerky, or pemmican, and without it sea trade and imperialism would have been even more difficult. The British biscuit is, in fact, a simulacrum of Empire: it goes anywhere, and anywhere that servants can brew tea and proffer biscuits is England, is home.

Since the biscuit, when baked, can take an impressed image, it is something like art—edible canvas. Since it can be trademarked, it becomes food that is also property—a sacramental wafer of ownership. The biscuit's simplicity, convenience, and ability to hold a brand name may have set the stage for its mass production and mass packaging, though this causality could be reversed. (Does food lead to appetite, or appetite to food?) According to package-historian Alec Davis, in the early 1830s biscuit-baker Thomas Huntley of Reading sent trays of his wares to the stagecoach stop for sale to passengers. The biscuits must have satisfied, for their reputation spread at least as far as the travelers, who wrote for more. To solve the problem of shipping, Thomas asked his brother Joseph, an ironmonger and tinsmith, to supply him with tin-plated iron boxes; these were practical, and caught on. Identifying the container with a "brand" was first accomplished by embossing the metal or pasting on paper labels; the tin surface itself could be enhanced texturally with a crackly finish called *moire metallique*. This early example of package-over-product was taken to its 19th century peak by multi-color printing directly on tin and the development, to best accomplish this, of offset lithography—a major printing method invented to sell biscuits.

Biscuits remained substantially the same while tins metamorphosed and flowered, taking on a currency and desirability of their own. The messenger became the product, which proved an important lesson to entrepreneurs of market culture: not only can you sell a book by its cover, the book may *become* its cover. Our consumer satisfaction can be displaced, "alienated," from our immediate needs. So let's buy a tin—with biscuits in it. Tins were advertised in 1887 as "not spoiled in opening," so they could be re-used, though the advertiser may not have imagined that objects of containment would ultimately include jewelry, bullets, paper clips, or the ashes of cremated friends.

It is difficult to tell whether or not the 51 tins on display, dating from 1868 to 1937, are average examples; in their showcase context and in comparison to present tins they appear elaborate and special. Certainly those shown are carefully and extravagantly designed. As designed objects they fall into two categories: passive boxes to which scenes and geometric designs are applied, and containers that are themselves decoratively shaped, some to resemble other objects—a box camera (1913) with handle, a wall telephone (1907) with a message printed on the receiver ("Everybody is asking for Macfarlane, Lang and Co. biscuits"), or an eggstand (1928) apparently intended to function as a utilitarian utensil, though it does not appear to be a particularly utilitarian biscuit tin because there's no room for biscuits. A tiny "Nile" tin (1886), large enough for two Fig Newtons, was a promotional sampler; Greek, Roman, and Egyptian details are combined on some "historical" tins in a style that can best be called Heterogeneous Antique. And the 1936 issue by Peek, Frean and Company of a tin commemorating the upcoming coronation of Edward III strikes a note of popular melancholy, of treats forever untasted, though one viewer wondered aloud if present-day biscuits would fake the likeness of the royal biscuit-tin baby "so they're ready when Diana has hers."

Robin Cembalest and Leslie Picot, the two Yale undergraduates(!) who organized this exhibition under the direction of Joan M. Friedman, have reason to be proud. However, their inexpensively produced catalogue is wrong-headed in what it includes. It does not say what biscuits looked like, what they were made of, and what they cost. It does not discuss the designing process: what printing method was used for each tin; were designs determined by one person or a committee: were sales a factor in choice of design; did some themes "flop"? Instead we are offered extensively, almost absurdly, detailed descriptions of the "art" on the tins: the clothing and rank of the Japanese women of one, the type of binding of the trompe l'oeil books of another, as if the authors were puffing up lots at a Christie's auction.

Their message, and the museum's, is that biscuit tins are neither industrial milestones nor cultural spoors but are instead collectible objects of fine art. Such a conservative curatorial stance explains why none of the tins is displayed open, to remind us of their homely function. I wonder if this precious-object type of validation has anything to do with the catalogue's statement that "the inspiration for an exhibition on British biscuit tins came from the private collectors whose objects are on view."

If objects possess their own "validating" power, they may be able to resist a museum's skewed presentation. One of the strengths of art is its ability to transform the way we perceive the nonart world. Perhaps, though, such alchemy is not limited to art. In this case, after viewing the Yale show, I was struck with how the museum could be a biscuit tin, and all its artworks biscuits. The paradigm of consumer culture has persuasive power of its own; the Supermarket will give any Museum a run for its money.

(3/9/1982)

In Which They Serve

You who have been there or have read about it know that you don't eat at Tavern on the Green for the food. The food is a hurdle, but if I were a visitor to this city, or needed a fix of gloss, I might risk the menu for the Tavern's flowered tablecloths, its mood of detached festivity, and the promise of service. He will open the door for us. He will greet us proudly. He will usher us. He will smile.

I was part of a party of 10 at Tavern on the Green last night, and the service rubbed a bad meal into our faces. We came in bubbling with celebration, adults who usually know what we are doing; we left as chastened and diminished children, wondering what we had done wrong. Nothing, of course, except to have chosen this restaurant in the first place. When we, the objects of service, can only be objects of derision, the servants are their masters' betters.

This is how it went. They overbooked and could not find the large table to honor our reservation, so they covered their embarrassment with supercilious tolerance. The penguin waiters know what a sham the kitchen is, and so treated us like the fools we must be; only half a smile need drop to become a sneer. A waiter in this situation has two choices so as not to lose the tip: either intimidate his captives, or commiserate with their collective disappointment. Neither pose looks good in full waiter dress.

The problem at Tavern on the Green isn't just one of a bad restaurant or rude waiters; rudeness is really a term of relative perception. This kind of dishonesty of presentation and mutual letdown is unavoidable when the concept of service has lagged so far behind the society it serves, no longer reflecting the rigid divisions that even tepid democracies have struggled to reject. Yet restaurants proposed an out-of-date service ritual from their very inception in post-Revolutionary France, where royal cooks, suddenly out of work, opened up bourgeois public dining rooms to anyone who could dress and pay. To keep up appearances and pride, an aristocratic superstructure was established: Maitre d', sommelier, chef, etc. These knew their places, even if their clientele didn't. This inauthentic profession of restaurant service has been assaulted by cafeterias, fast food, even by its own costliness, but though our modern, cheerful, tip-hungry Alice has one historical foot in Tom Jones's tavern, her other foot has never left Versailles.

Why don't restaurant reviewers write more about being waited on? How can service not be conflict, a bittersweet pleasure if a pleasure at all? Most everyone likes to be cooked for, likes to be served; that's one reason many of us eat out so often (and part of the reason some of us—men—get married). Have you ever been a waiter? Do you know how it feels to be spoken to like a thing, then pinched, rushed, and stiffed? Someone told me that a Seven Sisters college used to require its students to wait tables for a few hours a month, like little Katharine Hepburns, in a character-building penance of noblesse oblige. Sounds good, the tables turned, but the richer kids *bought* the services of the less rich, to do their dirty work for them.

Is there a way to run restaurants without servants? Cuba and the People's Republic keep the waiters but eliminate the inequities of tipping, assuming that a living wage should not depend on the whim of a drunk. (The Chinese Embassy in Toronto requires that its diplomats regularly perform the building's "menial" jobs, including waitering and cooking. I don't think it goes the other way, however, with chefs as ambassadors.) Most progressive solutions to the "servant problem" involve upgrading and dignifying the job: waitering is a special skill. When waiters, with a restaurant's support, can reject stupid demands, when customers need not resurrect the idiotic trappings of dead aristocracy in order to feel important . . . but this is utopia.

It is tempting to sink back into history. I learned this recently at a small inn in Barbados, at which breakfast and dinner were announced and served with a deference and formality—the habits of servitude and English butlering— that I did not understand. The servants thanked *me* for the plates they brought; they expected commands I was unprepared to give. In the kitchen they laughed, chopped, and talked. I would have loved to go in with them, but that was forbidden, and, to them, wrong. The point is that it took only a couple of days to learn the language of mutually agreed-upon inequality, and soon we all gave orders as if born to rule. This in Barbados, the oldest democracy in the Western world.

(4/6/1982)

Suburban Renewal

What are the results of becoming immune to change? I am thinking of the accelerating reflux of neighorhoods, the razing, erection, gutting, razing that is this culture's tradition, our Rock of Gibraltar. You are in danger if you choose to remain steady while "your" neighborhood leaves you in the dust. Yet, if you incorporate the flux, you risk rootlessness and chaos, no matter what you gain by frantic climbing in place.

Fascination with urban archaeology—the science of reading, like tea leaves, successive layers of human walls and garbage—has melancholy and fear of nonbeing at its core. At least, two or three centuries ago, there were distinct strata to poke through. Could anyone distinguish us in the quick, slim rubble accreting now? This doubt is the source of much present anomie, topped only by the horrible possibility that these spoors, however bland, may be our last.

Oh, the fantasies of going back a hundred years! It isn't so long ago. Little sections of the city shake themselves free of recent facades and sandblast their way to the past—look, for instance, at the Broadway Corridor. This is the name realtors have given the part of lower Broadway that's converting its factories and sweaty places to upper-income co-ops and lofts. Sounds evil or lovely, depending, but those sweatshops were themselves conversions from the likes of the Olympic Theater and the Grand Central Hotel, the fanciest places in town for brief spans of time. Fashion rolled uptown on Broadway at the unbelievable rate of a block or two a year, so perhaps we shouldn't feel uniquely unanchored; even 19th century layers are thin.

And there are still plenty of sweatshops on Broadway.

The Broadway-Mercer conversions between 3rd and 4th streets never looked so new, but what fascinate me are the businesses which rent the ground level. My spoors: Fayva Shoes, Swensen's Ice Cream, Plymouth! (as in Rock!) women's clothing, a large, clean drugstore, and two restaurants. Demographies take time, but I bet the new Broadway Corridorians who live in these apartments hail from Merrick, and before that, Brooklyn, and before that, the Lower East Side, a few blocks away. These nomads are also known as Suburban Returnees, and their money is supposed to save our city, whatever "our city" may be.

The only explanation for the concurrent appearance of Fayva-Swensen's-Plymouth! is that consumers are expected to move their shopping-center habits with them. It works both ways, of course, for chains (an apt word) will propagate the appetite for locationless culture as well as satisfy it. I do not blame Returnees for this; I assume they didn't choose these stores. But if we can imagine a free-market Darwinism, then we should be able to see if Returnees will keep the faceless units alive.

Ice cream will flourish anywhere; it's the cockroach of foods. Swensen's, in all its plastic glory, sits catty-corner from the Bottom Line, and music lovers who have braved the LIE to stand on line for tickets flip out at the familiar sight. "Where am I?" one stoned teenager asked no one in particular, thinking for a second that he hadn't really left home.

The Cactus Cafe on 3rd Street borrows some of its Mexican menu—chimichangas and eggplant casserole in particular—from Broadway's popular El Coyote farther uptown, but the Cactus's ferns, processed tortilla chips, and watery margaritas are not so specifically sourced. There is no use expecting Mexican restaurants in New York City to be authentic, but this one is so far from the ostensible original that it succeeds in giving its Manhattan rivals some sort of identity by contrast. When flavors don't blend in Mexican food you don't have Mexican food, you have contemporary Atomic Mexican, what a Mexican friend of mine calls One-Dimensional Flan. Atomic Mexican was invented all at once, in many places. In it, you are not in Mexico, you are not in Mexico-in-Manhattan, you are in the United States of America, everywhere and nowhere.

This block's only attempt at restaurant Manhattanization serves—with shaky, untutored hands—reasonably lusty spaghettini alla puttanesca (olives, tomatoes, oil, anchovies), reasonably creamy sauces over decent meats, unreasonably hard liver, madly peppery marinated Cornish hen, and bad bread next to tin-foiled butter. How will Buca di Bacco (683 Broadway) survive its linen-and-Levolor image unless it manages to appeal to the adventurous Corridor faction willing to try Manhattan as long as Manhattan shares a ceiling and landlord with territory it already knows? I wish Buca di Bacco luck, but two parties celebrated birthdays with candles and song the last night we were there. It could go either way.

If you believe in ghosts, or rather in spirits, as I do, perhaps we can look to the influence of Ada Isaacs Menken, Lola Montez, and Walt Whitman, who ate a few doors down, at Pfaff's. I'd be surprised if they didn't celebrate birthdays, and know that Whitman, at least, could celebrate change.

(5/18/1982)

Molly and Me

Park Slope contains a designated historical district, but realtors trying to plump their wares have been known to push Park Slope all the way to Red Hook. The American Institute of Architects Guide lists Gowanus, Park Slope's real border, as "a shabby, dull, and monotonous part of Brooklyn," but they overlook a noteworthy Victorian manse at 225 9th Street. It sits exactly between the two labeled neighborhoods, and, as we know, quantities often lose themselves at an edge. Who would anticipate that this fenced-in ghost is a restaurant called "Villa Storica"?

We had to be told, and are telling you. Right off, to cut suspense, "the food" is not the reason to visit. It's not bad, because if it were I could not tempt you to Brooklyn, but it's not of superseding interest. This is spring; spring overrides pasta. Spring will burn off in a week, so before it does, while our saps still rise, before you-know-who plans your chicken-salad picnic-elegances in the other magazines, let us hie ourselves to a curtain-romantic last stand in Gowanus.

I'll pretend I'm Molly. Molly came along with her parents and us to roughen out a complacent party of four. It does not pay to romanticize children, but if the metal gates loomed for me, how would they seem to Molly? Could she push them open by herself? She waited impatiently on the horsehair for us—the subway made us late—and watched nicely while we poured ourselves sticky-sweet vermouth from a houseguest decanter. Are we guests? A party of 16 upstairs! And we are seated in one of many rooms, insulated from everything, with only three other tables.

Sconces, filigree, tatty engravings, a pipe organ, fine chipped paint: Gowanus restoration, in stubborn continuity with what it was restored from ("an old-ladies home," our maitre d' said). This is no polished-Brooklyn Hubert's—which is no longer in Brooklyn in any case, but in high-priced Manhattan.

"How ya doin' kid?" The maitre d' had Gowanus charm.

"Mom," Molly whispers, "why did he call me 'kid'?"

Semiprivacy goes far for elegance. Are there really single-table rooms upstairs? (Who read, sewed, in them?) Molly's confusion about the food resulted from not knowing whether she was in someone's house or in someone's restaurant. The daily-changing menu was set, but we could choose between marinated fish salad or steamed mussels as appetizers, and among stolid red-sauced sea trout, aggressively inoffensive spinach-stuffed veal rollatine, or chicken pieces they called "scallopine," which Molly ordered. Savory, the best dish, if she says so herself. A pasta course (Molly—"Courses?") earlier, fruit afterwards, dessert, coffee. I (J.W.) will not consider a tray of sorry apples in spring "fruit," for shame, but the wonderful pastry from Alba bakery almost made it up. But *half* a cannoli? Half? Please, sir . . .

Our new waiter, no sir, obviously had better things to do than wait, and went far to mar an absurdly enjoyable time.

The chef took me—Molly—up to the top story, to show me a walkway where wives could look for their captain-husbands as they sailed in. Jeffrey took me out to the almost-finished garden, and we placed the cracked monkey-head that was lying on the ground back on its neck. He told me why the Gowanus Canal was once known as "Lavender Lake," but I didn't care. I'd rather know about the ship in the yellowed picture under the stairs, where the label reads "Andrea Doria."

(6/1/1982)

Fission Chips

If an emergency strikes I'll pack a picnic lunch. We'll have ham sandwiches, carrot sticks for strong eyes, my own peanut butter cookies, and this big jug of lemonade. An all-day picnic, a permanent picnic, won't it be fun? It'll be the camping trip Dad is always too busy to take. Don't be a sissy, only little sissies don't want to rough it, only sissies aren't prepared!

This is one nuclear dream, and we have a slew of them. I don't know what else you could expect but dreams. The restaurants that will escape even a small blast are few, and those that do will probably be shorthanded. No rare meat, all well done. A great deal of tarragon chicken will spoil.

We shall pack our baskets and go to the country, and the only thing I can suggest is to try and remember what our favorite meals tasted and felt like, remember whose eyes you fell into and loved through the courses. Sissy or not, keep your memories for strength, they will be in short supply. We don't know yet how many roentgens will kill them.

I'll tell you what some persons think. They believe now is the perfect time to provide information about how to build a bucket-stove with an adjustable damper, or how to pound soybeans and wheat to meal in order to fully assimilate their nutrients while avoiding the diarrhea so unpleasant in a crowded shelter. *Nuclear War Survival Skills,* by Cresson H. Kearny (retired), a U.S. Department of Commerce publication, confides to believers that "for most people food would not be essential for survival during the first two or three weeks following a nuclear attack." This is a definition of survival I am not familiar with. "Exceptions would be infants, small children, the aged and sick, some of whom might die within a week without proper nourishment." The syntax of expertise is so dependable, especially the "some" and "might."

We are prepared to pound, aren't we? Prepared to mash, prepared to dole out water? In a fortnight we'll emerge from our homes away from home and see if McDonald's, our best emergency distribution system yet, has arranged something for the kiddies, like an Egg McMushroom. The Teamsters on the McDonald's trucks will have contract problems, though, because:

The reader should realize that to do essential work after a massive nuclear attack, many survivors must be willing to receive much larger radiation doses than are normally permissible. . . . For example, if the great majority of truckers were so fearful of receiving even non-incapacitating radiation doses that they would refuse to transport food, additional millions would die from starvation alone.

Kearny urges future truckers to emulate the "heroic Russians who drove food trucks to starving Leningrad through bursting Nazi bombs and shells." After all, he did *his* bit by writing the book. I wonder if he thinks those Russians are still heroic.

We are supposed to eat what's stored and not worry about future vegetable growth, for we have no Department of Ecology. Growth is a passive, sissy thing. I won't tell you what Cresson says about eating postfallout meat, or about rural hunting and gathering, except that attempting either can cause cancer. Breathe easy, however, for this would be nothing compared to the cancer rate resulting from external radiation. "Cancer deaths would be one of the tragic, delayed costs of a nuclear war, but all together would not be numerous enough to endanger the long-term survival of the population." Delayed costs are, my accountant tells me, amortizable, an interesting word when applied to people.

Enough. What good is undamaged food without undamaged mouths to eat it? The nightmare of annihilation, that sissy dream, takes many forms, and one of them is NO MORE FOOD, NO ARUGULA, NO ARTICHOKES, NO ALMONDS, NO ABALONE, NO APPLE BROWN BETTY, NO MORE, NONE.

So before I slip into a more comfortable scenario, I will woo you to accept the challenge to survive. Among other things this means don't stop going to restaurants, to good restaurants, especially now. Don't blind yourself to the pleasure such a basically human activity—eating voluntarily together—can give. Because when you see most clearly what you will lose, when you know that someone wants to grab the fork out of your hand forever, you will hold firm. Are we cowards who enjoy living? No, of course not. It is more cowardly to prepare quietly for war than to fight for happy peace. It is the sissies who are brave.

(6/15/1982)

Class Crustacea

. . . As far as crabs are concerned, my mind is addicted to them, my mouth enjoys the taste of them, and not a single day in my life have I ever forgotten about them.

Li Yu's 1730 dissertation on crabs is sometimes cited to illustrate one criterion, the psychological, used to measure cultural preoccupation with food. It's no accident that these are crabs he can't get out of his head; substitute cucumbers and the result is merely doddering or quirky.

Crabs are serious. In the melodrama of crabs you run toward or away, eat all or nothing at all, love them or leave them. I have seen sophisticated consumers literally petrified by a basketful of dying crabs, incapacitated by a knot of slowly waving claws. This was pre-*Alien*—though post-Medusa—and it's not as if they had never opened an Alaskan can filled with the muscles of king crabs larger than the span of a fisher's arms. Or employed a staff to stuff the handpicked gold back into a hollowed shell and serve the robot up, disintegrated, denatured, and civilized. Why do we eat them at all, if nothing will finally allay our insect fears?

There is one moment in a crab's life when a human can face its music head on. In the bayous of Louisiana, the bays of Maryland, or the shoals of Long Island, blue or green "hardshells" are herded into boxes the moment they show colorish signs of becoming "peelers." Watch them, for peelers turn quickly to "busters," and then all of a sudden, they drop their shells entirely to star in a limited run as the famous "soft-shell crab."

A sympathetic biologist reminds us that "molting is, of course, an exhausting and dangerous process . . . molting is the price these animals pay for their protective armor"—which sounds to me like a particularly Protestant notion of physical development. It takes only 48 hours for the pliable virgin carapace to stiffen up, and within this span is the crabber's interlude, to ship fresh or to freeze. The softies, if unhampered, will ingest their former shells, which provide some of the lime salts needed to harden themselves first into "buckrams," and then back to the solid norm. Is there something metaphysical about this doppelganger shell game, in which the reborn baby body must eat its own ghost?

The soft-shell crab is a pun, a Freudian dream-reversal. Alone on the plate its image is one of porcelain resistance, but dare to bite into it and it breaks away under your teeth. It's like chewing cellophane, a two-dimensional practical joke. Imagine a soft-shell lobster. The infamous crab shell, once a nightmare and a hindrance to food, *becomes* the food, as if your Daddy said, "Don't worry, darling, I'll make a candy-crab just for you."

If this isn't pleasure enough, the crab flavor, almost as an afterthought to surprise, rinses fish-juicy through your mouth as a reward. Take that, you crab, you're not so tough. I bite the hand that bit me.

Poor crab.

Americans have loved our vulnerable soft-shells. During the 1939 World's Fair the demand for deep-fried soft-shell crab was too great for Long Island waters to satisfy. Coney Island fried-crab sandwiches, once a cheap, popular fixture, are just about gone. Soft-shell crabs have metamorphosed again, for they now profess an affinity for painted tin ceilings and African flowers. Appetites follow dutifully, to obliging restaurants like Pesca.

I have not reviewed this much praised, busy Pesca because it offers too little for the $25 to $30 check each customer is heir to. Its run of broiled fish and bouillabaisse specials is okay, nothing terrific. In spite of a charming maitre d' and excellent bartender, the waitering is all smiles and perfunctory, often inept. No one table in the long, high-ceilinged room sufficiently creates its own space, so you feel as if you impinge on someone else no matter where you are seated. The clientele, affluent enough to dress well, hasn't decided what it wants to conform to, though conformity is obviously the goal. The house wine argues easily for the wine list.

On the other hand, it took a leap into imaginative space to use soft-shell crabs as a momentary raison d'etre. Since the temptation to simply saute is overwhelming, what fortitude it requires to hold back with:

—two sauteed crabs in puckering pesto
—two crabs deep-fried in fancy beer batter
—two crabs bubbling in a tomato-based sauce alongside boatlike shrimp
—two curry-flavored (James Beard style) crabs with orzo and string beans
—two crabs wrapped in parchment with "spring

vegetables"—tomatoes, fennel, zucchini, but since
when are mushrooms spring vegetables?—all sitting
in lemony juices

—one crab sauteed, plopped in a salad of butter lettuce,
and dressed with mustardy creme fraiche

—one crab (supposedly) in a salty corn chowder,
though I had to take their word that crab was in there,
and that it was soft-shelled

We missed a bunch of other crab costumes but can assume, because success resides in the attempt almost as
much as in the result, that all were successful. Actually,
though the straightforward beer-battered crabs were most
pleasing, all entrees proved that this kitchen can do much
better than usual if given the chance to shed its skin.

A last note: if you buy crabs these last few weeks of
molting and want to prepare them at home, should you believe the cookbooks that say no cleaning is necessary, just
wash and fry, or should you listen to the authors of *Joy of
Cooking,* who blithely ask you to "cut out the face"?

(6/29/1982)

Cape Maybe

Colonel Henry Sawyer, a Civil War prisoner released in exchange for Robert E. Lee's son, built the Chalfonte hotel in 1876. Cape May, at the southeast tip of New Jersey, is now a landmark district because of its concentration of wood-frame Victorian buildings. A local index classifies the Chalfonte as "Italian Victorian," with which irresolute term the authors mean to lighten the dowdy image of Victorian Gothic and simplify the gewgaw collage of Queen Anne. Anyway, Sawyer had the awful opportunity to spot first, from his fourth-floor tower, the 1878 fire that destroyed every other dainty elephant in the city. But Cape May built, burned, and built again, and whatever the shorefront resort is now—a mess, I think, of spruced-up claustrophobic charmers, nightmarish bungalows, and Las Vegas remainders—the Chalfonte sits where it always has, partially restored and as pretty an old hotel as you'd ever want to see.

No tours of Cape May from me, though. It sports some oddities, to be sure: inns with phallic gingerbread, concrete video arcades. Emlen Physick, a rich bachelor doctor who never practiced, in the last century built himself a gorgeous Stick Style home that holds an autographed photo of Karl Marx on his bedroom wall. But bad planning caused the broad beach to wash virtually away, so Cape May is now a beach town without a beach. Henry Ford almost built his first auto factory here; Cape May could have been Detroit.

There is one fine reason to visit this town; and her name is Helen Dickerson. She's 73, born and raised in Virginia, and reasonably well known, because with her daughter Dorothy Burton she prepares a kind of unfashionable institutional Southern food at the Chalfonte that is rare as a . . . well there isn't much that's rarer than this. Notice I am not saying anything gourmet, but I feel about her spoonbread and rolls the way Darwin did about the lovely things he knew would no longer flourish on this earth.

The Chalfonte's long dining room was once its ballroom, for the time when balls were socially second-nature. Its china is heavy and has seen use, service springs from the feet and good nature of "college girls," and the result is elegance plus summer camp. Here's the dinner bill of fare, whose regularity could drive one either crazy with comfort, or just crazy:

Monday: herbed roast leg of lamb, or fish of the day
Tuesday: roast beef seasoned au jus, or fish
Wednesday: Southern broiled or fried chicken, or fish
Thursday: Virginia country ham or roast turkey with baked apples, or fish
Friday: deviled crab a la Chalfonte, or roast leg of lamb, or fish
Saturday: roast beef, or fish
Sunday: chicken, or fish
Sunday breakfast: kidney stew

We wanted it all, though we stayed only one day (Monday). But let me tell you, the tomato-based vegetable soup, thin certainly, had a well-cooked pig somewhere involved. Who anywhere makes hundreds of yeast-risen shortening rolls, fist-size, that smell like the sun? Though our lamb tasted good, and savory lemoned bluefish even better, some would find them overdone because the last 20 years have pushed eating assumptions toward the rare and raw. I treated as my main course the platter of eggplant fritters that accompanied the entrees, cut poker-chip thin, with sweet and peppery batter. Nutmeg-lemon-butter carrots gave the lie to the prevalent vegetable ideal. Carrot flavor changes as it's cooked; carrot is an ingredient, not a crisp absolute. So are boiled potatoes. For dessert we did not understand the combo of chocolate ice cream and wonderfully cakey grain-tasting rice pudding, but I'll try anything once, or more than once.

I want you to envy our breakfast. Beaten biscuits (speaking of rare), nicely fried eggs, thick bacon, buttered corn bread, weakfish morsels fried in that same batter, and an emerald crock of spoonbread. Northerner, have you never had spoonbread? Ground yellow cornmeal here, shortening, evaporated milk, beaten eggs, butter, baking powder, baked. Steamy when you break the surface, hot, bright yellow, a physical state hovering between vapor and souffle. We found it easy to eat too much: for when will we visit again?

After this meal I met a man on the street who told me that if I wanted to take a picture of the Chalfonte I should stand "over there."

"I stayed at the Chalfonte in 1917," he said, "and for years after. Whatda they charge now?"

I told him.

"Is the food any good?"

I described my breakfast.

"Sounds unhealthy," and he said that I needed more fiber, green vegetables, and fewer fats. We chatted about Adelle Davis and her likes. I asked him what the Chalfonte was like then, the people, the fun.

He said it was quiet, a lot of old people rocking on the porch, same as now.

(8/24/1982)

Style, Though Your Heart
Is Breaking

If I had to be a culture nowadays, I'd be Japan's. I'd especially be Japan's economy, forgetting for a moment about more ethical possibilities—like socialism. I mean, Japan figures that two percent of its population (two, that's 2) is out of work and immediately declares a national emergency. But this is supposed to be small potatoes; we have bigger and better emergencies over here.

One way to measure Japanese culture is through its style, but not everyone likes that word. I just read a self-righteous review in *The Nation* of a now-California cookbook. I must say, I sympathize with some of the reviewer's involuntary shudders at the words "feeling" and "involvement" as applied to the construction of Berkeley dinners, but his distaste at seriousness being applied to food, or to pleasure in it, disgusts me. It is as if one has only so much passion or commitment to go around, and "politics" requires it all. The reviewer, a puritan in sheep's clothing, is therefore not a man to trust politically. I would keep him as far away from art and from the fight for integrated, happy lives—frivolous things—as I possibly could.

Style is not easy to pin down. I am certain that the style of Chiaki, this restaurant on the singles strip of Third Avenue, makes it worth eating in. The food is good, just good enough not to let you feel that the style compensates for it. But what's the style? Chiaki's canvas marquee, the kind that looks like a squat cookie-box, is the most typical new awning in town. You walk in, and . . .

Maybe I can describe the style better if I allow it to work on me, so what I'll do is take my yellow pad and continue writing this at the table. (*In Chiaki.*) We do have a problem with light, for the track spots are focused on the center of the black, wire-gridded, glass tables. When he puts down the steamed mussel appetizer (flicked with a puckering, relishy sauce—they call it Cantonese) it blooms up the light, as if the waiter pressed a foot-switch. Plates just emptied reflect the most light, and we achieve this state fastest with the marinated and fried chicken strips served on giant toothpicks, and with the steamed, cut dumplings of pork, shrimp, or crab. Fried eggplant or tofu with a ginger sauce is a mite oily but fresh; sauteed broccoli in black bean sauce should be hacked down from tree-trunk size. Broccoli also appears everywhere else. This is not a Chinese restaurant, and you see it's not Japanese, exactly.

The long walls of the storefront room are stacked floor to ceiling with horizontal pipes, the large kind that should be holding water or something industrial. But they're cardboard, painted a lacquer blend of beef liver and Chinese red. A dead platform at the end of the space holds a tableau over your head; a giant Japanese fan, an over-stuffed American chair, an ice bucket, a spread kimono. The waiters, this one right here for example, wear T-shirts faced with a punked-up Kwan Yin. The waiters are all extremely efficient, and—we're not done yet please—the busboy almost always jumps the gun.

We began with crudites, including white radish, surrounding a bowl of tasty garlic-laden dip of the kind that magazine recipes refer to as "secret." The $2 hot and sour soup buoys plenty of vegetables and tofu in a vinegary broth—an excellent choice. Then we have hefty tempuras, sautéed shrimp (good raw material) with avocado in too-sweet surroundings, a soy-sauced whole steak. (A *whole* steak? For those frightened of cut—Japanese—meat?) A porgy is fried into armour (nutlike meat underneath) and served upright, "sizzling." So many of these and other auditory entrées are marched self-evident out of the kitchen that the urge to stand up and applaud—or just make a matching noise—grows great. Broiled salmon, breaded cutlets—you get the picture. Entrées pair rice or oily (good oily) sautéed noodles.

Opposite the tableau stands a real sushi bar, and the other side of the menu enumerates sunomono (sashimi vinaigrette of octopus, conch, fish), nori rolls (one called "California," of crab and avocado, fine) and sushi and/or sashimi assortments. These are presented not on aesthetic little tables but in flat, white, glazed bowls, like Victorian wash basins without their pitchers. The nori rolls we are eating now taste marvelous, fluke and plum paste, but I have never seen sushi so chunky and colorful, particolored colorful.

Are you beginning to see the style? It may sound vulgar, but Chiaki is based on discontinuity, on the disintegration and recombination of national and period styles. Every now and then the background music flares up to a Callas aria, then segues to the *1812 Overture,* then to heartbeat disco. They put as much money in the audio equipment as in the kitchen, maybe more.

Chiaki is popular at night with families, couples, and otherwise assorted units, folks who make me wonder who lives where and how they earn their dough. (Chiaki is not too expensive if you order carefully.) I am enjoying myself, and those around me are too. There's kibitzing galore between tables, especially if one of them orders the ice cream tempura flambe. John says you forget you're on Third Avenue, which is true, and not easy to pull off.

Chiaki is not a "serious" restaurant, qua food, but its style is serious. Chiaki emphasizes eating as entertainment, and entertainment as melange. Of the small restaurants that do this, it is among the most delightful.

I also wanted to suggest that when you open the door and walk in, you can identify the style at once. "Gay." I certainly don't mean that the owners, waiters, or customers are gay, necessarily. Or that all gay people are alike, or have style—this or any. And I'd be in great trouble if I set about to prove my assertion. The Heisenberg Uncertainty Principle would smack me down; I'd get close to the meaning and genesis of the T-shirts, those red pipes, that crazy sushi, and they would retreat into discrete parts, with no sex left at all.

(10/5/1982)

Word Enough and Thyme

We have few words for flavor, just as we have few words for desire. This does not mean we do not wish to talk about them. Some of us are afraid that speaking about lust or taste will destroy their delicate alembic. Words, being frigid things, condense fragrance into a cold sweat. We are supposed to light our cigarettes and discuss it later; we write afterwards, in order to remember and recommend, but writing is a distant average of the event. The beef I had last night was "good," "bad," "bland," "spicy." Can't we do better than that? Think closely about the flavors of that boeuf en daube, its dirty-russet color, the confetti of its market herbs. What words help us? Any hint of flavor, just a hint, leads through a tunnel back to a light: my best memory of my favorite stew. I never had words for it in the first place, although, when I am inebriated with memory, emotions about the ghostly meal rattle around.

How can anything live up to a memory? Strong memories can't be repeated and are rarely surpassed. They even change, to prevent their disappearance. In the case of flavor or desire, memories can barely be described.

Yet that is my job, to wring essential oils from some pretty inadequate flowers. This is a new year, and it's an opportunity to think about the quixotic notion that flavor can be successfully trapped in words. Yes. I know there is a science of flavors. Open any cheap wine book, the kind that trains by lists and intimidation, and read off the dozens of exact, responsive words that qualify a glass of cabernet. Its bouquet can be *corky, heady, must.* The taste, which comes after the bouquet, can have *size,* be *firm, clean,* and possess a *finish* (or aftertaste) which should be *long.* Wine can also be *noble.* This is a science.

Tea, chocolate, apples, they all have their guardians at the gates, and guardians have their Rosinante-languages to hold them. I am grateful for the words the tasters use. At least they clue us in to complexity we might not otherwise apprehend. What do we know about wine when we are born? No matter that *big,* when applied to wine, confounds description with evaluation; it's a trick, this agreed-upon, absolute-relative scale, but all words trick like this. Language is like money; agreed-upon value is the best it can offer.

Beowulf's contemporaries drank mead—ate it actually, for it was food and drink—and said it was good. Have you had mead? Most people spit it out. It may not be the same stuff now as then, but how different could it be? Our *taste* is different, we conclude. Our taste is not the same.

Science is much more comforting than the nightmare of relative experience. Essential oils are not only wrung, they are invented. Oil of wintergreen, peppermint, amyl-banana: flavors become chemicals and chemicals can be isolated first, synthesized later. This is not a crime; plants and animals, they tell me, are just laboratories with roots and feet. Biologists have recently bred a mild Vera Cruz jalapeño pepper. It is mild because it contains less capsaicin, the compound which, the inventor said, "makes peppers hot." I want to taste this profitable, virus-resistant pepper. It is supposed to appeal to our growing taste for

Mexican food in a form that we Americans will like. However, many items other than capsaicin compose the bag of chemical soup that is a jalapeño pepper. We also know that proportions as well as quantities determine flavor. Will one-third less capsaicin affect the rest of the taste? Our professors at Texas A&M must not think so. They know that pepper comes in three flavors: mild, medium, and hot. It's written on the bottle. They want mild. "We're helping Mother Nature," bragged the man responsible. Does he eat Mexican food? I can guess how he'd describe it if he did.

My favorite gift this holiday season came from my mother—a stocking stuffer called "Country Baker Apple Pie Room Scent," by Avon. "Scent the air with the scrumptuous aroma of freshly baked apple pie. Bring back the delicious memories of Mother's kitchen. SHAKE CAN WELL."

It smells precisely like the real thing, if the real thing is that apple pielet wrapped in plastic paper, "flavoring added," sold almost everywhere. This concoction was the first apple pie my neighbor's daughter ever ate. It may have been my first as well. It's sad, and you've heard all this before. The only difference between the little girl and me is that she has no pleasure in, or even consciousness of, the magical imitation. She agrees, we all agree, that real apple pie smells like this. The spray became the word for apple pie.

Flavor is a communicant between material and spirit. Metaphysical poetry, the best of religion, the sexual act, and even isolated words themselves are go-betweens in this way. If I remember this, I should not have trouble writing about flavor: I can compare, I can invent. When words fail, as they do so often in politics, salesmanship, or the worst of religion, it is because they are not grounded honestly in either material or spirit. Lying language may pretend to *body,* but it never will attain a *finish.*

(1/11/1983)

Flying Down to Rio, or Whatever Happened to Carmen Miranda

Coffee Time

On November 22, 1982, *The New York Times* published a map of Ronald Reagan's South American itinerary. This map placed Sao Paolo, South America's most populous city, larger than any city in the United States, in the middle of the Amazon jungle, where it is not.

Reagan promised Brazil a short-term loan of $1.2 billion, to help the country with its gigantic international debt. Much of this $80 to $90 billion debt, initiated by flash industrialization, is interest on previous loans, high interest kept high by U.S policy. The International Monetary Fund will be called on to "bail out" Brazil, but the IMF will "roll over" the debt only if Brazil plays along: by ceasing to bind wages to inflation—a rate of almost 100 percent a year—and by allowing foreign investors to buy natural resources and carry profits out of the country. This is called "stripping Brazil." It was once, wisely, forbidden.

The already embattled middle class can't survive this, to say nothing of the half of Brazil's population that makes under $100 a month—the official poor. Brazil's first elections in 16 years were held in November; they helped morale, but the national military leadership will probably keep its demonstrably corrupt control.

Knowing this, Carrie, John, and I were still flying down

to Rio, Rio by the sea-oh. We couldn't get that song out of our heads. We wanted to experience the liberal political "opening" or *abertura;* we wanted to smell Dolores Del Rio's orchids in the moonlight.

Flight and Arrival

Our cheap flight and hotel were offered by the ACLU, through a charter group called International Weekends. We expected a DC-10 full of Nat Hentoffs, but instead got a random bunch, one of whom, a muscular young fellow seated behind us, desired nothing more than to "meet Carmen Miranda" (dead these 30 years).

Charters aren't cheap for nothing. After 16 hours on or near the plane, we arrived at Rio at six in the morning. The hotel rooms wouldn't be ready till noon, so they pushed us onto a bus and gave us our first tour of the city. Those awake were eager tourists. The *favelas* (hillside slum cities) were brightly painted, the industrial areas smelled diesely and looked "like the Bronx," according to the drained man next to me. Our fine young guide from Rio was deeply embarrassed at our exhaustion and imprisonment. IF YOU GO: take a cab to the hotel, ready or not, and wait it out.

Intimations

To ease us into our beachfront Copacabana hotel, the modest, bronze-fixtured, mahogany-paneled, bidet-bathroomed Excelsior, we were handed fruit juices or coconut milk spiked with *cachaça,* a sugarcane distillate that goes down like razor blades. (It's 11 a.m., no sleep.) These appeared with platters of *freshly fried* potato chips from the hotel kitchen. Their vegetable heat pierced the backs of our heads. "Potato," we cooed, "gooood."

Our head guide, call him Bruce, was lecturing his chicks in a series of apologies, warnings, and threats. He had recently arrived from a stint in Hong Kong, where it was likely that he knew as little about that city as he did of this one. "Don't use the buses, kids will rip the jewelry from your necks, and no one will help," he advised. This was followed by a welcome from a representative of H. Stern, a giant gem and jewelry chain based in this city. Did Bruce know which hotel was in *Flying Down to Rio?*

We learned fast by ourselves and picked up the language of hotel, taxis, and restaurants. *Quanto custará?* How much will it cost? *Muito obrigado*. Many thanks. And definitely, *não groupo,* no group, not with the group.

The Beach

Rio is trapped between mountains and beaches. The beaches are free; the only way to have a revolution in Brazil, one Carioca told us, would be to charge admission to the beach. Most of the pastel high-rises along the Copacabana crescent are apartments; only a few are hotels. Etiolated tourists are swamped by Cariocas. One weekday, the newspapers said, there were a million people—a tenth of Rio's population—at the beach. At the risk of committing sexual imperialism with my eyes, I must find a way to say that I have never seen such large numbers of beautiful people. Skin shades ranged from well-tanned olive, through rich coffee, to deep, deep black. The Brazilian melanin bouquet is a smack in the face to U.S. assumptions of all-or-nothing race.

Those at the beach worship the body, as well they might. Lithe women have no bellies and shiny hair; lithe men wear Speed-O suits—chic from the States—to declare themselves entries, front and rear, in the Rio beefcake sweepstakes.

Bruce warned us about theft of cameras and wallets at the beach, but no one told us how the Cariocas would plunder our physical self-esteem.

At the end of the week we had sunk, or risen, into the swim and felt terrific.

Snapshots of Shopping

Plastic shoes for women in dozens of colors and leather-mocking styles: hot pinks and turquoise, wing-tip eyelets, ballet slippers, high-heeled pumps (in shiny red), from $2 to $6, not all sizes available. Brazil exports its leather. Men's shoes, in fact all men's clothing but beach and soccer wear, are drab as mud. Sex roles are severely polarized; men lead women across the streets as if they were blind.

Cotton in a yardage store: a pattern of 19th century workers pasting up posters which read (in English!) THE DREAM IS OVER, HUMOR IS OUR POLITIC, NEW YORK IS TODAY'S ROME, A KING IS KILLED BY HIS COURTESANS. What Carioca would buy this (in pink, green or blue), and why?

As we left the tiny backstage bathroom in Rio Sul, Rio's

giant indoor shopping center, we collided with the Hulk, Spiderman, and Wonder Woman, themselves pursued by streams of screaming kids. Couldn't get my camera out in the crush.

At the Movies

Carrie said we should see a movie. It costs 800 cruzeiros, or about $2, apiece. We were treated to 10 minutes of newsreel (mostly balletic *futeból*), 15 minutes of coming attractions, and a short on beekeeping, in the middle of which the young student apiarist was lifted from the ground and passionately hugged and kissed by his grandfatherly instructor.

Each segment was introduced by a raggy slip of paper from some film board of approval. Brazil has so much of this red tape that it has created a Minister of Debureaucratization. These slips serve as true titles, for a great roar went up from the impatient audience when it saw, in typed letters within the appropriate blanks, JOHN HUSTON and "ANNIE." During the film, men slept, mothers and children cried, and some sang along with "Tomorrow."

The Party

John's gracious Rio friend, Esther Emílio Carlos, threw a late cocktail party for us in her penthouse apartment, which overlooks Sugar Loaf (absolutely breathtaking, everything San Francisco should be). She had shopped all the day before for pita bread, and served a 1959 white wine that had "turned" into a kind of delectable dry sherry. We met artists, actors, a famous TV soap opera star, and one of Brazil's few harpsichordists, who introduced herself as "Marshall Brickman's cousin." When we told her we intended to take a day trip into the mountains, the harpsichordist described our goal, the city of Petrópolis, as the "Scarsdale of Rio."

We also met Virginia Munson, who admitted she was the only female head chef in Rio, and I think Brazil. Esther (pronounced "Astaire," as in Fred) phoned us the next day to say that "we" had made the gossip column of one of Rio's major dailies, *O Globo*. Carrie and I were not mentioned, in respect to our modesty, we think. We were very proud of this anyway, and showed it to anyone who seemed interested.

Food

We winged the first few days, cross-referring guidebooks, newspaper clippings, and advice. The American dollar is strong in Brazil, and we felt as if we were stealing food. Raw materials are extraordinary, and Brazilians know—they told us—that U.S. agriculturists breed size in, flavor out. Tiny Brazilian bananas tasted twice banana. However, Brazil has replaced its black bean crop with profitable soybeans and now must import their luscious staple. Beef butchering is apparently haphazard, and meat is lean. Rio, like New York, seems to possess no cuisine of its own, but gathers from African Bahia to the north, from Brazilian pampas to the south, from manioc Indian and sundry European. The result is a jolly lack of focus known as cosmopolitan. The international rich do not know where to dine; French restaurants and even one example of "Italian medieval nouvelle"—to use Virginia's fanciful description—are overwhelmed by native and ethnic fats and vitality.

I Cannot Forget . . .

A roasted peanut. Boys throw one miniature peanut onto your plate as you drink at open-air restaurants, or onto your face as you sleep on the beach, for you to sample and buy. Imagine the earthiest, most concentrated peanut unfurling inside your mouth.

Cajú fruit juice. "Cajú" means cashew-apple. Fruit-juice stands blend ice, fruit, and sugar for less than 50 cents. Dozens of otherworldly varieties are stacked and named for you to choose, including cactus pear (white pulp, grainy), fig, and this cajú, which puckered our membranes with acid, sweetness, and nut aroma. Some stands will add *vitaminas* to these, gilding their lilies.

A roast chicken sandwich with mayonnaise on white toast at Maxim's, the open-air eatery next to your hotel. Sometimes flavors you think you know, when sampled out-of-doors, near a beach, and accompanied by a full-bodied, icy *chope* (Brazilian draft), take you completely by surprise. Also, all over the city, squab-size spring chickens called *galetos* are split, basted with brine, grilled over charcoal, and served with french fries, or farofa (a fluffy manioc-meal scrapple) and bananas, or a simple heart of palm salad and *chope,* for maybe $1.50 to $2 altogether. I could cry.

Codfish pieces in a bouffant of potato and egg at a

gorgeous Portuguese restaurant in Ipanema. Also here, bottle-cap-sized local oysters, unbelievably shiny and electric.

Squid and smelly rice, marinated pork chops with collards, cod and green pepper casserole, at an ancient, breezy lunch place businessmen love called Aurore. It would have had sawdust on its floors, if they had sawdust. Thank you, Virginia. They knew her and liked her, serving us thin Brazilian wine in thick ceramic coffee mugs. Around the corner was a plastic surgeon; they are big in Brazil. The Catholic cemetery in this area marks its graves with tall, white, winged angels, baroque sentiment calmed down in a soft, green grid.

The Carmen Miranda Museum and Other Fantasies

Our ostensible reason for flying down to Rio was to discover which old hotel served as the "Hotel Atlantico," the cube saved from evil bankers by peroxides strapped on biplane wings. I suggested the sprawling Hotel Gloria, now distinguished by empty Portuguese Colonial terraces and wandering tourists puzzled by the hotel's vacant grandeur. Carrie voted for the posh but now undervisited Copacabana Palace. Remarkable, we agreed, how little difference an art director's California fantasy makes once you are here.

"Do not tell anyone you are visiting the Carmen Miranda Museum," we were warned before Esther's party. "Cariocas hate it, hate Carmen Miranda because she was born in Portugal (not Brazil), and hate Hollywood for what it did to all South America." The museum, a concrete doughnut, three times was virtually empty of people. Glass cases hold the star's costumes, photogenic chokers, and marriage certificate (to a film editor). A poster and T-shirt, but no postcards, were offered for sale.

Back in the States, at Theater 80, we see Carmen Miranda's first two U.S. achievements: *Down Argentine Way* and *That Night in Rio*. These are sluggish wartime vehicles for Latin stereotypes and North American condescension. Busby Berkeley at least had the sense to send up this bad Good Neighbor policy in *The Gang's All Here,* where, in the 1943 battle to woo Brazilian products, Manhattan chorines teach nightclubbers how to dance the Uncle Samba.

Flying down to Rio, not the film, begins to correct years of lies. Their real orchids and moonlight, thank goodness, continue.

My New Career

Back home, I dream of walking on the Rio beach, two aluminum kegs strapped over my neck. *Maté, maté e limão,* I yell, which is heard as "MACHee, MACHee ay leeMAU." Sinewy, indefatigable vendors walk back and forth, hawking cold, sweetened maté tea and lemonade, yelling *maté, maté e limão,* over and over again.

(2/22/1983)

Only Connect

The Brooklyn Bridge, now in its centennial year, has stood for a lot. It attracts artists and writers, perhaps because Roebling's beauty stands for opposites conjoined: massiveness as well as delicacy, height as well as length, means as well as end. I don't remember his lines exactly, but Russian socialist poet Vladimir Mayakovsky celebrated the bridge, in spite of its name, as Manhattan's connection to the great U.S. mainland . . . i.e., to New Jersey. Geography never stands up to inspiration.

The Manhattan base of the Brooklyn Bridge can be seen from the side windows of the Bridge Cafe. More importantly, you can't avoid the hum generated by car traffic. (Would it sound, sans cars, like a monstrous aeolian harp?) The song of the bridge so close up could drive you crazy, but the kitchen of the Bridge Cafe, and its popular new chef, Leslie Revsin, must feel the sound's better influence, for they send out specifically inspired food. The Cafe looks to be the same old big bar, small-table, checkered-tablecloth place it has been, and you expect to be served a crusty hamburger and mug of beer, or at most a broiled fillet and potato side. You get, however, food prepared with such exactitude that its contrast with the physical restaurant can be described as poetic: opposites conjoined. This is remarkably instructive. Would such food, a modest number of superficially barlike selections, be unexceptional in a tonier setting? Can all forms of food preparation be called exact if each is the best possible of its kind? Can the cues of surroundings literally affect what you taste?

Using the food, I'll try to explain what I mean. We choose an appetizer of calamari in rosemary-flecked dressing, a usual starter in a bar-restaurant setting. It appears not as a pile, which of course it is, but almost as an arrangement. You can smell a bit of squid before it hits the tongue; and once it does, the chewing turns silken, with no rubber-bandiness at all. Initially this is difficult to understand, for the balance and timing that went into such a dish is expected—and rarely achieved, incidentally—only in hotsy-totsy places like Revsin's last outpost, the long-menued and nouvellish 24 Fifth Avenue.

Perhaps we're in an especially sanguine appetizer mood . . . but no, the slices of white garlic sausage shuffled among a lightly oiled "salad" of mimicking potatoes; slices of rare tenderloin accompanied by an anomalous assortment of endive, red-cabbage slaw, and presently fashionable horseradish cream; a muddy black bean soup, more a puree, that tasted only of bean and just a hint of hambone (no garlic, citrus or vinegar that I could tell)—all proved our feeling. Even the cold tortellini salad, a mistaken conception at the start, tasted rich and fresh, not gummy or dry.

Exactitude, to the tune of the hum, is necessary in order to succeed with the few entrees the chef has chosen. It shows at once in her calf's liver, cooked to order (medium rare here), gently crusted on one side, and napped, as they say, with the softest sauce of balsamic vinegar. Liver like this smells of sweet flesh, with no cloying touch of blood. My companions told me they had never tasted better—and the price, I should add, is $10.50, a fair half-stop between bar and banquette.

We enjoyed equally the less-unusual chickens-of-the-day, and delighted fully in tilefish sauteed with tomato, black olives, onion, and garnished with slivers of ginger and a bit of fennel. The ratio of ingredients makes or breaks this dish, and it was faultless. Half a roasted duck came cloaked in acidic, sable-colored sauce jumping with globules of green peppercorn: crisp skin; pink, luscious, slightly fatty meat; a pungent battle with the sauce. Another evening the sauce was much less acidic and the meat slightly mushy, which is the only variation we could find in our extremely constant happy eating.

The bargain of the menu is a $7.50 mop of on-time linguine, which hid slices of sausage and shreds of woody sun-dried tomato. The unaccountable failure of the kitchen was a fish stew, the solid parts of which held no flavor at all. Accompanying potatoes, spinach, zucchini, and wild rice don't compete with main dishes but do retain their integrities; desserts, except for a gloriously smooth pear and ginger pie, are up to you. The wine list, something I don't usually mention, is well-balanced and reasonably priced (a $7 Zinfandel, really), an opinion verified by an oenophilic friend.

Because the chef, who has succeeded professionally despite the tremendous sexism of the restaurant business, enjoys a devoted following, the Bridge Cafe is jammed for dinner, usually with pushy tweed. It lets up around 9 or 10.

The restaurant is a five-minute walk from City Hall. Since the Brooklyn Bridge itself cannot be viewed or heard without thinking about Walt Whitman, and since on Tuesday of last week I walked to the cafe from City Hall, the site of public hearings on Intro I, the proposed gay rights bill, I will end with this:

The ignorance and narrow self-interest shown by the City Council committee members who voted against passage of the bill is New York's shame. Citizens cannot allow them to take public office again. Their bigotry, which I observed, and simple long-due human rights, are opposites that can never be conjoined.

(3/8/1983)

Caviar and the Masses

The argument went like this:

How can we account for the growth of restaurants in New York serving gussied-up versions of this country's regional food? Texarkana, Santa Fe, Carolina, American Harvest, and the former Cincinnati—now the Maryland Crab House—have defined a restaurant category which I call New American Regional. These places don't attempt historical authenticity, for few of their menus recreate the treasures buried in old Cincinnati or New Orleans cookbooks. Instead, the kitchens use traditional recipes as sources, but they do things with Smithfield ham, for example, that would not go down well in its place of origin. Texarkana serves a duck breast sauteed rare and sprinkled with emeralds of jalapeño pepper. At Simon's, a riskily thin crayfish bisque is offered with a picturesque sample of the main ingredient perched suggestively on the bowl's rim, sign and signifier all at once.

Nouvelle and Japanese cuisines, I had said, the major kitchen-influences of the '70s, embraced and married all kinds of American foods. Why else would some of these restaurants plop kiwi ovals or zucchini fasces next to whatever part of the country was on sale that week? Cooking-school nouvellism, watered down to $10 or $15 entrees, throws its affectionate arms around a great deal.

Don't get the idea that New American Regional is necessarily bad. In fact, the application of novel methods and tenets to out-of-fashion native material sounds powerfully creative; some of the results are terrific. This country has always gleaned pleasure from flirting with foreigners, bringing them over here, and adjusting their "sophistication" to the requirements of our rolling hills and skyscraper canyons.

But why should New American Regional, and its more diffuse cousin, American Nouvelle, appear now? The supposed "new nationalism" has been suggested as a paradigm, resulting in a sort of states' rights of the kitchen, or, at the very least, a cuisinary balance of trade. Yet fits of nationalism recur every few years, like malaria, without bringing Upper East Side "American" gourmet shops along with them.

I suggested two other reasons. Look, for example, at the marketing of native roe. Iranian and Russian caviars are simply too dear even as a treat, so entrepreneurs got the idea to package our very own salmon and sturgeon eggs, first cheaply, as second-best but good caviar-for-the-near-general, and then expensively, as a rarity in itself. Regional is exotic: a predictable paradox in the business of food. In paradisal times sturgeon clogged the upper Hudson: fishing and pollution thinned them out long ago, and this newer greed will finish the job in the rest of the country unless someone takes care.

Conservation, though, is an impulse *behind* New American regional food. When an economy that favors restaurant chains and similarly efficient monotonies equally disfavors restaurants small and various, then local public outposts of regional cooking—Cajun, Creole, Tex-Mex, New England, black Southern, and many others—must fight for their lives. Raw ingredients themselves are threatened, as Ray Sokolov points out in his book *Fading Feast*. Truck farms are replaced by condos, tomatoes are bred hard and square to facilitate mechanical harvest, and centralized food distribution squashes the smaller local tidbit. Have you read about the mild Vidalia onion? You can pick one up and chew it like an apple, for the flavor is more rich and earthy than hot. It grows this way only on certain soil, in a certain Georgia location. But as soon as someone smelled profit, the purposeful and public-minded Georgia state legislature voted to extend the "definition" of Vidalia onion territory into a few dozen surrounding counties. This is called the legal dilution of the real.

Profit-determined economy is the culprit, and I concluded that big-city New American Regional food, for all its bangles, is a last-stand effort to save dying regional cuisines.

I was asked to work this out by an inventive editor at *In These Times,* a socialist weekly paper that comes out of Chicago. It was an excellent suggestion, and I wrote the piece. When it appeared, however, something disturbed me, which I mention not to criticize *In These Times* in particular but because it elucidates a conflict faced by progressive, politically committed readers and eaters when asked to think about something like fashions in food.

The article was printed pretty much as I wrote it, but the headline read, "Down home cooking is a hit uptown." The teaser followed with, "Regional food is threatened as agribusiness weeds out pluralism in our produce," and the caption to a Norman Rockwell Thanksgiving dinner finished, "Unique regional dishes are disappearing from dinner tables and small town diners—but turning up in chic restaurants."

Perhaps I am wrong, but the caption especially seems to imply that "chic" restaurants are somehow responsible for the disappearance of regional food. Since only the solvent and urban can eat chic, chic is bad. A cluster of tired suppositions rises up predictably: that small-town is better than big-city, that old-fashioned is pure, and that pure is correct.

I neither implied nor stated any of this; that the article was moved in that direction is a textbook example of how formatting can alter the meaning of a piece. But I must admit that these thoughts make me defensive. Recently I've been speaking with critics who write about clothes and fashion, and write from their love of the human inclination to decorate-communicate. They have a look in their eye, as if around the corner someone is waiting to accuse them of "enjoying life." Maybe we can defend the creativity we hope finds its way through what we consume, and still fight to allow that everyone is clothed and fed. Maybe we can defend uncensored sex and still fight sexism, as a few brave souls claim. But activism and pleasure are rarely thought about together, and that goes far to ruin any promise of both.

(4/19/1983)

The New York Delicatessen on 57th Street

Deco on Rye

Almost every person I took to eat at the New York Delicatessen had been there before, years ago. "My daddy brought me on Saturdays, and let me drop the nickels in the slot if I wanted a dish I could reach." "That's nothin'. *My* daddy let me have pie before we went to the movies."

These are folks who haven't said "daddy" in years, but their memories reactivate promises behind windows, coins, and Daddy. They are recalling the mechanization and masculinization of public eating. The New York Deli on 57th Street, once a bookstore, even two bookstores, was first a Horn & Hardart's Automat.

Before this party gives his opinion on whether or not the New York Deli makes it into Deliland, let's have a moment or two of reflection on a dying American form: the cafeteria, and its glamorous appendage, the Automat. Wait, how can a working-class outpost be glamorous? I dunno. Perhaps it's the chromium polish on the fixtures; it certainly wasn't the food. Maybe it's because nostalgia per se is glamorous: but as we'll see, the New York Deli's particular success disproves this historical aphasia.

We could hate cafeterias, with their steam tables, linearity, and noise. They evolved as a method of feeding workers rapidly so they needn't lose time or gain pleasure by eating their sandwiches outside the factory, in the sun. We should quote Marx here, or Gramsci, to curse officially the profit-motive that extended the assembly line into a worker's lunch line. So we shed double-edged tears for the walk-through cafeteria: it charted the spread of Taylorism into supposedly private life.

And yet . . . the nickels, the quiet release and pop-out of the door, the empty stage that—when did it happen? I didn't see it—fills itself with another piece of pie . . . this is magic. I'm supposed to say how the Automat is a simulacrum of modern consumerism, where need plus coin in the house of capital awards you a quantum sandwich, all humanics eliminated. But no dice.

The real evil to associate with Automats is pictured in Mitchell Leisen's 1937 film *Easy Living,* screenplay by Preston Sturges. Sturges's hungry unemployed try to sit out the Depression in an Automat, all its tiny windows promising what the closed doors won't allow. But movies too are magic, for Automat employee Ray Milland, in a fight with Mr. Boss, trips the secret mechanism we all know exists: and every door opens up with food, food! Now comes chaos and exhilaration and a pie-in-the-face revolution that Mack Sennett never knew.

The Automat is fun only when, nickel-in-fist, you are just a little hungry.

Is the New York Delicatessen still an Automat? No, of course not, just imagine conflating the two genres, a nickel—click—a shtickel. However, Brad Elias, who redesigned the space, retained, repaired, and recreated the Automat's Art Deco interior and exterior. His result is an equally welcoming, even festive, public space.

There aren't too many open-armed eating spaces on 57th Street; the pancake shops price their wares like bullion, and most of the restaurants large enough to qualify as spaces charge too much to be public. Art-hoppers drawn by the street's galleries never know where to lunch. Now, some may associate Art Deco with pricey onyx chatchkas or even with the tendrilous elegance of Ruhlmann furniture, but American deco from Woolworth's to Radio City was intended for mass enjoyment. What second-hand fakers would have us think Depression Glass was too ritzy for the Depression?

Well, Elias recast the metal railings, split-leveled the eating areas, and asked single-name artist Moser to rim the balcony—opening this fall—with his distinctly undelicatessen murals of night-hawks in evening wear called *Amorous Disconnection*. All together, it's decoeclectic: Chinese wall screens, ghastly hanging lamps, pink-stained wood tables, and sub-Naugahyde seats. This is fun, the customers whisper, a facade brought indoors. And everybody recognizes inexpensive fun: the New York Delicatessen is one of the very few restaurants in this part of town that attracts a racially mixed clientele.

One of the others that does is Wolf's Delicatessen, right across the street, named after founder Dave Wolf. But after Wolf sold his pastrami interests to Mark Packer, he must have missed his schmaltz, so he scouted for a site, found one—and opened the New York Delicatessen. What must he think, when he looks across the street, to see his immediate rival carrying his name?

The 24-karat question is whether or not the newcomer makes it again into the charmed circle. There *are* fake delis, you know (and that's all I will say, for it's not polite to make Nebraska deli jokes about pastramis on white, hold the mayo). So here: yes, it's a deli, though a few bugs have to be ironed out. Wolf's new waiters, for example, just aren't nasty enough. Give 'em time. I had a terrific, just-enough-fat, brisket sandwich ($5.25) one day, another a little more typically dry the next night. Pastrami is thin-sliced, with too much variation sandwich to sandwich; no one likes those dry chips cut from the butt. I won't compare this place to Carnegie's or even the old Wolf's—that's for you to enjoy—but I will say they make a good gefilte fish, sweet and almost fluffy, and we had also a nice chopped liver (it's nice to say "nice" and have it mean something). But the kishke is *eh* (hold the gravy!), the stuffed cabbage *feh* (ditto), and the french fries are from hunger, just like they should be. When we ate the crackling crusts off all the rye bread in the basket, all of us (six at a time) hallucinated our fathers' warning: "Lay off the bread, you won't have room for anything else." It's a real deli.

Someone asks, do Jewish food and Art Deco go together? Well, go down and visit the Deco District in Miami Beach, and admire the cheap '30s Flash Gordon hotels once filled with needle-trade Yiddish unionists on their happy vacations. This is the way the future was, utopian, communal, affordable. You know what New York Deli's naked deco sylph offers in her outstretched hands? A matzoh ball. Welcome back, Mr. Wolf.

(5/3/1983)

Mr. X of Rye, New York writes:

All my life I've preferred sandwiches to anything else, and so I don't go to restaurants, at least the kind you review. Does this make me, to use a term another food writer has coined, "blind of palate"?

Dear Mr. X,

No, not at all. In fact you may be the most postmodern of eaters, for you are among those who can testify to the existence of . . .

An Ideology of the Sandwich

When the interviewer from Swedish Public Radio asked me to talk about the sandwich as an American obsession, I really didn't know what to say. Swedes have their own open sandwiches. How would the Club Sandwich Controversy translate into Swedish?

"Oh, don't you worry," the cheerful interviewer said, "almost everyone in Sweden understands English, as long as you speak slowly and don't use too many three-syllable words."

So I began with John Montague, the Earl of Sandwich, who liked to gamble. Refusing to leave the gambling table during one of his marathon bouts, he slapped some beef between bread and played on. Just think, if another, later, earl had done this, we would now be eating cardigans. Anyway, the sandwich was conceived to provide time for more important things than eating. More important things than eating!

She asked if this gambling stuff really happened, and I replied that all accounts I had read referred to someone else's account. Is that history? she asked.

Of course medieval laborers employed bread as *trenchers*—platters, even laptables. Farmers in Provence have eaten their lunch on bread for centuries. Yet it took the English to name them, tame them, to cut off their crusts, cream their butter and stamp them into tea-canape hearts and diamonds: those old gambling shapes. American workers of the 19th century ate hefty sandwiches with their coffee, but this was not genteel. Boston's Fanny Farmer pushed only the dainty sandwich, with interesting instructions to "spread bread [with creamed butter] before cutting from the loaf." This is "finger food," food that exists to show you are able to eat politely but stand beyond hunger. This paradox enables a healthy young man such as Oscar Wilde's Algernon Moncrieff to make a pig out of himself over quite a small quantity of cucumber sandwiches.

"What about sandwiches with funny names?"

I'd have to research the reuben. Hollywood studio commissaries and Brown Derby-type restaurants named sandwiches after stars, but I don't remember what composed the Greta Garbo (the interviewer smiled), the Judy Garland, the Gloria Grahame. They've stopped doing this, I think. One theory accounts for the demise of the Hollywood star system by observing that there's nobody left you'd want to name a sandwich after. Who, really, would be thrilled to eat the Tom Selleck, the Pia Zadora?

"And what about the submarine, the hoagie, the

grinder, the hero?"

I thought for a moment, and things began to stack up. I remembered the Dagwood. The Dagwood is the largest possible vertical sandwich. Dagwood constructs it on an accrual basis, as a way of claiming his corner of Blondie's kitchen.

He steals her leftovers before she has a chance to mince them into tomorrow's hash. His Dagwood is butch construction, the very antithesis of slow, female cooking. Only he makes it, only he eats it: the Dagwood is neither a communal nor a generous act. The Dagwood is Dagwood's independence from Blondie, Alexander, Cookie, even Mr. Dithers. The Dagwood is compensatory male behavior; it is contemporaneous with the skyscraper. The Dagwood is an act of aggression.

"Then why do women eat sandwiches?"

I said I didn't know, but I did know that the phallic sandwich is only one of the American male's many signatory artifacts. It's quick, portable, almost indefinitely expandable, and in this way parallels the hegemonic spread of U.S. culture. And there's another American connection: the sandwich, structurally, is a small, replicable model of the late Herbert Marcuse's concept of "repressive tolerance."

"Marcuse, from the Frankfurt School?"

Right. You have slices of bread, uniform, infinite, available. The sandwich is defined by filling these blanks with anything, everything. As kids, I remember, we tried to imagine the worst sandwich in the world: sardines and peanut butter, salami and whipped cream. But my father told me that his favorite sandwich, his real favorite, was a chocolate sandwich, two Hershey bars between two slices of white bread! The point is that the sandwich can bracket anything in the world, and whatever the filling was before its recruitment, the entirety becomes the same thing in the end: a Sandwich. It feels like variety, but it's nothing but containment. To spur yourself out of sandwich deadness, you will be forced to scour the world for oddities, strip it of rare fungi and ortolans—in order to make a better sandwich. Yet you will fail. It will look like choice, this American imperial cornucopia of sandwich spreads, but it is only a ghost of choice, an ideology of small change.

"You like sandwiches, don't you."

I didn't know what to say.

"I do too, I am learning to like them, but not as much as you Americans."

(5/31/1983)

Permanently Fresh

A penniless child out of Dickens looks into a tavern window at a steaming roast of beef.

The result is emotion, a product of many contrasts. Between what is seen and what is tasted. Between what is perceived and what is owned. Between what is real, insofar as one can obtain or control the real, and what is a dream.

What if you reverse these miserable contrasts, and by doing so turn them on their head? Make a model of a hunting scene, a battle victory, a coronation, out of spun sugar, jellies, gums and crusts: these medieval set pieces were called "subtleties," when that word was still accruing its meanings, before it settled into its present rhetorical state. Please don't eat the subtleties. And who would eat them, considering the pleasure they give uneaten, contrasting edible material with elevated form? Which viewers of such expensive artfulness would be hungry enough to ruin it?

What about duplicates—or, rather, replicas—of the desired food? Replicas of cooked and uncooked food have been made in Japan since the 1920s, when restaurants began to serve unfamiliar Western dishes to curious clienteles. Replicas were used there in the same way sushi and sashimi replicas are still used here: this is a *steak*, these are *french fries*—and you watch the gleaming promises darken and collect dust over the years. You watch them constantly, like it or not, for these fakes do much more than save the waiter an explanation. For when you ask yourself, in spite of yourself, if the restautant's *real* sushi is so dusty, if the kitchen moves the food as slowly as this, you begin to see the power of these replicas. Must the kitchen continue to imitate, season after season, these authoritative forms? Do the signs determine the cooking they stand for?

The firm of Minoru Iwasaki is the largest fake-food maker in Japan. Soho's new showcase of Japanese design, Gallery 91, pulls dozens of Iwasaki samples out of their utilitarian windows and isolates them as objects of interest all by themselves. Designer Yoshiko Ebihara, who opened the gallery, called the replicas art, superrealist sculpture, and I won't debate this Duchampian proposal: the replicas are certainly displayed as art. Gallery 91 is right next door to a superb dinner gallery, Chanterelle. Remember, we are in Soho, this is the art world.

Here sits a scatter of tangerines, some whole, some peeled or peeling, under Plexiglas. They are objects. Gelatin was poured over the poor original to make a mold, the real food removed, liquid wax mixed with oil paint and brushed underneath, wax and cotton wool added for body, the mold pulled away, and the form painted to mimic the inspiration. One person works on a piece from beginning to end, with pride, maybe rivalry, as the result.

The tangerines "look just like" the real thing. But of course they don't, because the real thing varies. Although these are near-perfect replicas, they are not idealizations because the peculiarities of the original are reproduced. They are "perfect" only in their deceit.

I noticed that the tangerines did not make me hungry—

they emblemize but do not advertise. A spurt of pleasure comes from something else; the "tangerines" are an introduction to the poetry of replication.

We move on, and see that the fake foods fall into two categories: the convincing fakes (though we know they're fakes) and the flops. Of the latter, the most moving to me is a roast beef. I have been moved by roast beef before, but never in such a way. This roast is clearly too solid—no juicy depth, too red, too immobile. It *sits,* bare on the pedestal, and the word "forlorn" comes to mind (and Keats, and joy's grape). A sad lump, it is more steer than roast. The viewer's tendency to project emotion onto an inanimate object, Ruskin's dreaded pathetic fallacy, is in full swing here, begun by the contrast between what a roast should be and what this one is, and continued by free associations on the hoof. This replica is good because it is bad.

The other contrast is the old poetical saw: the stopped motion, the frozen laugh, and in this case, the frozen food. There could be humor here, if it were badly done, but though the show's tour de force, brown beans metamorphosed into a stream of coffee, is tricky and therefore petty, nothing can be taken as only a joke.

A few objects are set apart on a plate to be touched: a scallop shell, a potato chip, an ice cube, a sugar cube, grains of rice, and a peanut. The brittle sea shell collapses into softness and virtually disappears. The opened peanut, a breathtaking replica, is somewhat frightening the way its disposability now demands attention. The sugar cube is getting soiled by smudgy fingers. Each grain of rice has a seam, which denies its riceness.

Why does fake American food "work" better than fake

Japanese food to Western eyes? Perhaps we require a file of food-familiarity to make the replica a screen on which to project our memories. It may take these replicas, these quotes, to pull our feelings into the light: and for this reason fake food is successful. Real food needs representation to become visible.

(7/12/1983)

The New West

Southern California

New Yorkers who have never taken the California plunge are afraid of it. Their fear manifests itself in Disneyland sarcasm and a temporary public alleviation of their annoyance with New York. It's easy to say New York is da centa of da woild if you've never been away. Also, it may be true. Those who have left and come back say, "New York is the center of the world." We don't count the ones who got lost and never returned.

It's been easy for me to assume that New York has more good restaurants than any city in the country. It has more restaurants, period. I live here. This is the center of the world. People in this city are serious about eating out. Chicago, with proper pride, claims the greatest number of Lithuanian restaurants, and each locality in this country possesses its only-here, but there's never been a 20th century challenge to New York.

But maybe you've smelled some hype about the "eating revolution" in San Francisco or, less hyped, the recent increase of restaurant quality and ethnic variety in Los Angeles? Well, hype is hype by definition, but where there's fire there's smoke, and likely it's smoke from the mesquite charcoal of San Francisco's grills. I've spent two weeks (scratched the surface) eating down the California coast, and even though I selected restaurants likely not to

disappoint—if I did the same in New York I would be deliri-
ous with pleasure—still, the eating was extraordinary. I
did not hit California in neutral: I was prepared to be let
down, and in some of the most frantically touted places I
was. Yet the amplitude of innovation in restaurant food on
the West Coast, especially in San Francisco, is so great,
and so unusual, that even a dullard or a New Yorker must
see that something's going on.

Vietnamese, and Central and South Americans, have
settled in southern California during the last 10 years and
made whole communities for themselves. My friend Bill
Stern, restaurant reviewer for the *L.A. Reader,* drove me
to the town—city?—of Westminster, a half-hour (car time)
south of L.A. proper (whatever that is) and technically
part of Orange County. Westminster identifies its streets in
Gothic English script, and these signs, to a novice, are the
only locators on a perfectly flat Cartesian grid. Westminster is like Kansas with buildings. Grids are supposed to
help you locate a point, but this one accomplishes the opposite, and we rode around and around—or more accu-
rately, left and right, back and forth—until one of the many
shopping centers we passed seemed to Bill different, and
familiar, for he had eaten here.
    L.A. Rule One: restaurants, good restaurants, are often
found in shopping centers. Corollaries to this rule: you
must know where you are headed, no walking, no brows-
ing, no "I'll stop in somewhere to get a bite." You drive in.
The whole urban balance between the getting there and the
goal is redefined, for all is anonymous in the driving until
you arrive. This is why New Yorkers wonder, when they

land in L.A., where it "is." Angelenos think this confusion ridiculous, and honk their horns.

The shopping plaza in Westminster was like any other, newish buildings with Swiss chalet roofs—but the signage was Vietnamese. *All* the signage: the camera shop, the Xerox (I assume it was a Xerox), the tailor, the pharmacy, the supermarket (full of unfamiliar leafy vegetables), and the restaurant.

Two small rooms made up this restaurant with a large party-room in the rear guarded by an eight-foot-high knotted dragon. The menu offered almost 200 items–more than any Vietnamese menu in New York—and I walked back into the plaza heady with the flavor of fillet of catfish baked with peppers and herbs in a brown crockery pot. Its sauce was a reduced slick of soy, fish juice, and vinegar, the crackling pungency of which make the sweet catfish even more delicate. About $6. Perhaps that Swiss chalet style was simplified rural Vietnamese.

Another Vietnamese-signed shopping center two streets away, somewhat older and less architecturally uniform, included a Bob's Big Boy-type family restaurant (ugly glassed trapezoid) converted to serve Vietnamese food. It was crazy-cheap, hospitable, apparently flourishing. Disjunction between the sign and the thing signified was uppermost, and I had visions of abandoned drive-ins countrywide serving pirogi and kim chee.

We were the only non-Vietnamese in sight. Bill thought few folks from L.A. came to eat "Westminster Vietnamese" after he wrote about it, though he had no explanation for this except laziness and ethnocentricity. It makes no difference to the restaurants, for they, like all the other

Vietnamese shops, exist to serve their own community. How many Vietnamese have settled in L.A.? Even the Census Bureau doesn't know, but shopping centers of this moderate size handle thousands of people each. There is a small Vietnamese middle class. Bill said that because of the demand Vietnamese have set up a farm to raise catfish.

We passed a generic hamburger stand in Westminster— all white, called "Hamburger Stand"—on the way back.

Next day for lunch we drove to a restaurant in L.A.'s "sweatshop" garment district ("Are there sweatshops here?" asked one L.A. native) called El Salvador Cafe (531 East Pico Boulevard), a modest stucco-fronted single room with bars on the windows and . . . a guard at the door. Except at coffee shops next to police stations, I've never eaten where I could see a full holster as I chewed. But what wonderful food: sugared *platanos* fried in a lozenge with creamed cheese and beans, superb chicharrones and *yuca*, lettuce/cabbage slaw tossed with flecks of fresh oregano, and more. Miniature hammocks swung from the ceiling, Salvadorans chatted in Spanish and ate oblivious to us, the Anglos, looking up only to admire the entrance of a rosy-faced young woman escorted by her young date, his rosy face shadowed by a giant cowboy hat. Tables lingered over coffee after coffee; this was Saturday, and what better place to be? The guard never flinched nor smiled.

In another part of town we visited Managua (932 N. Alvarado Street), a four-year-old Nicaraguan restaurant with serviceable food. We did not ask what brought them here. L.A. has more than half a dozen Central American restaurants—just two or three 10 years ago—because it has a new Central American clientele.

What else is new in L.A.? Bill claimed he "would have never been able to do his job 10 years ago" because there weren't enough reviewable mid-priced restaurants. Angular eateries calling themselves "cafes" are springing up like chanterelles, and one is supposed to know which are good and which "merely" good-looking in a city that buries a tail-finned Cadillac headlong into the two-story facade of the Century Cafe, a facade that can only be seen from your car as you pass? The Cadillac's skewed taillight blinks obscenely as the red ball lowers in the west.

San Diego, California's second most populous city, plods along, restaurant-wise, as it always has, notable mostly for cheap Mexican joints, deep-fried (!) abalone, and a scatter of preliminary European. I should say that the worst Mexican restaurant in San Diego is better than all the trashy new Mexican restaurants in New York City put together. In San Diego they do not brag of knowing nothing about Mexican food.

But now they know something about Vietnamese, for there are probably more Vietnamese restaurants—ethnic-Chinese, Khmer, and Hmong—in San Diego than anywhere else in the country. All during the '70s San Diego provided modest housing in poorer neighborhoods for Vietnamese refugees, arranged for training, and helped find jobs. Now there are Vietnamese cluster-communities and shopping districts interspersed within the city's predominantly black and Chicano areas—with some tensions as a result.

None of the six or so restaurants I tried, from the disappointing egg-rolly Le Lotus Room in gentrified Hillcrest—

the only "chic" looking Vietnamese restaurant I've ever seen—to the popular and oldest ("the food is falling off") A Dong, served anything remarkable. They were just *there,* offering so many versions of Vietnamese cooking— a cuisine full of contrasts and amelioration—that a stranger might actually get to know it.

San Diego has broadened. From one corner, near San Diego State University, we could see: Bloomer's, a Jewish deli; Chicken on Fire, black fast food; a Vietnamese ice cream stand (serving American ice cream to Vietnamese, not the other way around), Vietnamese fast-food stand (barbecued duck for $4.50), Vietnamese movie theater, doctor's office, pharmacy; and a Middle Eastern restaurant. Many Iranian students who came to study in San Diego could not or would not go back, so small Iranian restaurants are opening up, for ethnic restaurants in this country, however welcome, are too often symptoms of national pain and flux.

San Francisco, Eureka!

On arriving at the San Francisco airport, I picked up a copy of the *Chronicle*: S.F.—A City of Taste, 92.6 Restaurants Per Square Mile. This was front-page news in 72-point type. Its lead paragraph was custom-made for my lead paragraph:

If all 705,700 residents of San Francisco decided to dine out tonight, San Francisco's eating establishments would have a seat for everyone. "They may not like the place, but we'll get them a table somewhere," said Mark

Chan, a health department official who. . . .

At the luggage trough, a man and woman argued so insistently over which was better, Chez Panisse or the Santa Fe Bar and Grill, that their luggage passed them twice.

At a cocktail party, acquaintances who didn't know my eating purpose in their city could not wait to exchange the latest restaurant dish. "Did you hear that Alice was going to be on the cover of *Newsweek* but Brezhnev bumped her because he died?" ("Why did he pick *that* week to die?") God help you if you don't nod in recognition of "Alice" (Waters) or "Jeremiah" (Tower). Your cocktail friends will tense their wine-glass grip and walk away. I discovered from eavesdropping that Waters personifies calm, Tower energy; Waters is yin and Tower yang. These two aren't politicians, actors, gurus, or writers. They are more important than that. They are chefs.

The mid-sized stage-set city on the bay has a bubbling political life, cultural life, business life, ethnic life, and gay life, but if you happen to see a pair of hands flapping away in the air, punctuating vital conversation, you may assume the party is discussing food. In the last two years restaurants have become the punchbowl into which San Francisco's middle-class citizens pour all their urban pride. They grin like new parents when they say that chef squads fly from Tokyo and Paris to eat at Chez Panisse and the "grills." ("Grill" is a magic word.) "We" are lively, they are not too shy to admit, we are inventive, we are— deep breath—world-class. New York haute cuisine, for all its meat and splendor, sits in France's wake. We are new.

Who is this "we" they cite? The citizens have *become* their restaurants, which indicates how enormous the need must be for unqualified collective pride in something. Vietnam has lingered a long time, and the '49ers spread only so far. My friends glowed with the mission of pleasing their guest, as if they personally were responsible for this unquestionable source of happiness. In a despotic world, at a particularly chaotic time, any reason for true civic pride is an unexpected blessing. Its wellsprings are utopian, but that will be clear as we approach the food.

In my week my guests and I could visit each restaurant only once, so descriptions and impressions are only that, not evaluative reviews. I made all my reservations weeks in advance, false name as usual.

Located in a renovated wharf on San Francisco Bay, vegetarian Greens (Fort Mason, Building A, 415-771-6222) is run by the Zen Center along with their older bakeries (remember the *Tassajara Bread Book?*). I was going to say "funded by" instead of run, but Greens apparently funds the Buddhists. It is open for dinner on Friday and Saturday only, and though the lunch is popular, the demand for dinner tables is so great that in July the first available reservation, I was told, could be made in November. Luckily there was a cancellation, but I had to identify myself to get it: an unethical first, but since the prix fixe menu ($18) is set, my identity would make little difference in the food. I hate to rush these descriptions. The wharf room had the highest ceiling I've ever seen in a restaurant, and the view of the Golden Gate Bridge and Marin County was such that I made arrangements with Robert, my regular eating companion (thanks for your help, Bob, and Denny, Michael, Pam, Evelyn) to switch seats halfway through the meal. The sun lowered, the fogless sky—rare here—softened into lavender and honey, and the lights on the red lattice twinkled alive. A tension between natural beauty and grand artifice, which was so dramatically articulated through this window, became the presiding spirit over all my San Francisco meals. The bridge melted into our buttery, cloverish, St. Helena Chardonnay (Stony Hill? vintage? mist mars my notes). We looked in the direction the wine was made.

A first course on a small plate: tiny, woody, marinated string beans; golf-ball sized "rose fir" potatoes with a walnut sweetness, the kind you either grow yourself or find at the bottom of a supermarket bin; ordinary beets in a mild, orange-flavored vinaigrette. This was a gestalt appetizer, for at one moment it seemed small and demure, the next a symphony of pure flavors. This second alternative takes over when we are told that most of Greens' ingredients are grown across the bridge on their own land. All vegetables are organically farmed.

A search for purity is the health-food root of new California cooking, a leave-the-system answer to a country where unprocessed, chemical-free food (air, water) is almost impossible to find. Greens proposes a '60ish solution to the underlying threat of ecological disaster: tend your own garden, save the whales, so to speak, not by forbidding slaughter but by growing your own. That the result tastes better is natural, but ancillary.

The spinach and basil soup had a broth too weak to bind the two. Pleasantly bitter, though.

The main dish, in a meal where anything could be minor or main: a corn timbale in tomato sauce, sauteed zuc-

chini, and pattypan squash. A failure, for the timbale
never jumped over into the land of the vegetable idea. We
were amazed at its sullen dullness, yet the squash was
essence-of, superb.

An oiled salad of Green Gulch lettuces. What is Green
Gulch? The flawless—and I mean flawless—leaves must
have been marathoned over the bridge in cool hands.

I was beginning to get the idea, that these were the best,
freshest lettuces that not only could be found, but could be
made. Their origins were on the plate. Months later I can
still taste this salad because its idea-quotient carries it into
memory; without knowledge of its origin it might have
been just a great salad, and I would not have noticed much
of anything about it. This is not a trick, or a joke, for it
only shows that ambitious cooking is based in a web of
thought.

A dessert will prove my thesis. You could choose from
four, but there is one that turns out to be a model for food-
as-thought. The menu called it a lavender honey mousse,
but this is how the chef, Jim Phalen—a lovely man who
suggested, in his modestly outfitted kitchen, where else I
might eat—described it: we get our own cream from Napa
Valley and steep our lavender in it refrigerated, overnight.
The next day we whip in egg yolk and a small bit of clover
honey, mostly for flavor, not sweetness.

The resulting pale cloud spews from a flaky, noncom-
mittal ball of puff pastry. You spoon the cream. It possesses virtually no body, no texture. But as it slides down,
your inner nose is walloped with the scent—the flavor—of
lavender and honey. All that is solid melts into air; it is a

wine of a dessert. The lesson is that spirit can overcome the corporeal; and I remember who runs this restaurant. The sky, I said above, was lavender and honey.

Rumor has it that the Zen Center wants to close Greens down because its fame has run too far.

Just as calling a new restaurant in L.A. "Café" will generate first customers, so calling a place "Grill" in S.F. will draw them too. "Grill" connotes hearty, mahogany, male, but also plain, pure. Grill implies raw fire, and if mesquite charcoal is used, grill attaches itself to the repopularization of Southwestern and native American cookery. Forget that France grills, Italy grills, China grills: Grill is American.

The Santa Fe Bar and Grill in Berkeley (1310 University Avenue, 415-841-5525) could stand for San Francisco's others. Jeremiah Tower, its press-happy chef (and Waters's former co-chef), may have helped the other grills around the city take off. Praise of the Fourth Street Grill, Hayes Street Grill, and even Zuni (1658 Market Street, 415-552-2522), a superb storefront grill with the defining menu but without the name, can be overheard all over the city. Not every steak or onion in grill-land has its provenance checked, but local fish and vegetables are used, supplemented by regional oddities; sautéing gives way to *a point* grilling, supplemented by stewing, smoking, poaching, and steaming. Chiles become the grill's *fines herbes*. This is new, and not new.

The name "Santa Fe" refers not to the tribe directly but to the railroad—the restaurant's richly fitted, festive rooms were once waiting rooms of the Santa Fe Railroad's Berkeley station, a famous gay cruising spot of the '40s and '50s. It's too busy and noisy for cruising now. A baby grand pumps Cole Porter and urbane jollity as Berkeley's obvious down-and-outers hang around on the sidewalk outside.

Almost everything we sampled here was at least well-prepared, and much was novel, but the whole is obviously greater than its entrees, for the same reason that San Francisco's best new restaurants are great: reactive ideas inform them.

Some of the notable offerings: salad of curly endive with shiitake mushrooms, red bell pepper, and ginger. In New York the endive might lose its curl, but not here, and shiitake fashion in this country began in California. Steamed clams with polenta, tomatoes, herbs, and Parmesan cheese. Grilled Pacific snapper with chili butter. Halibut with ginger-lime butter. Santa Fe prepares its own sausages, all quite peppery, dry, and unmysterious. Vinaigretted lentil salad comes with goat cheese from your local goat, garlic, and . . . mint. Sounds good? It is, and even better, Santa Fe treats its own inventions as a matter of course. This is what you *should* be eating.

More: grilled chicken breast with lobster butter and watercress; marinated pork loin; and the menu's big failure, a watery, tough, misconceived pot pie of braised sweetbreads, mushrooms, ham, and herbs.

The restaurant is epitomized by its appetizer of small cornmeal blinis accompanied by tissues of home-smoked fish and American caviar (roe to us). It announces: we are beyond the Russian Tea Room, the action is here, the old world is too old to be good.

To interrupt the new with the discovered, let me alert San Franciscans who don't already know to a word-of-mouth delight of the old-fashioned kind called Nippon (314 Church Street). Be prepared to line up at 5:30 p.m. outside the dozen-table closet in order to partake of the gorgeous sushi, sashimi, nori rolls—the clam-neck sashimi made my heart jump—prepared by athletic dramatists who know their stuff. The prices, New Yorkers, are literally one-third what you'd pay for anything comparable. Nothing in Manhattan is comparable, however, to Nippon's "avocadoness" and lack of chichi that invigorates this sheerly Californian neighborhood restaurant. Mine may be its first review.

If you've not heard of Chez Panisse (1517 Shattuck Avenue, Berkeley, 415-548-5525, or ask most anyone), then you don't read periodical prose. A narrative has grown around its development; chef Waters has stated that the restaurant, opened in 1971, grew out of the Berkeley counterculture and Free Speech Movement. It was at first collectively run. A friend I trust told me that after losing money from bad planning, the collective met to determine how to divide the restaurant into an expensive downstairs and less expensive upstairs cafe, recognizing the profit potential in the class differences of its clientele. This was decided in politically correct Berkeley-consensus fashion.

I ate at Chez Panisse in its third year, and had mediocre rabbit. This summer, its $35 set menu offered me rabbit again. The meal was almost simply perfect in itself, and when you add the restaurant's pork barrel of accrued ideas to the food, it even becomes complex.

Chez Panisse has grown to combine the tropism toward purity exhibited by Greens with the aggressive—though sometimes spurious—rediscovery of American dishes and methods of the grills. But it adds to these an acknowledgement of the need for sophistication. Waters and friends realized that the best way to supersede the hierarchical assumptions behind classic French cuisine—where royal chefs learned to translate their work for a 19th century bourgeois empire—is not to ignore France, but to swallow it up. The restaurant was not called *Chez Panisse* for nothing. In nouvelle cuisine the French have flirted with the demand for novelty and purity of flavor, but they retained or reinvented certain elite signals: conspicuous consumption (through too little rather than too much), chef overlords, and codification. None of this for Alice and her friends, though the media's need for a "star" may threaten the Californians' democratic impulse.

Chez Panisse is a surprisingly small two-story house with only a couple of dozen tables downstairs. Its Missionesque appointments are as elegant as that chunky style will allow, quite beautiful, and also both old (serious) and American at the same time. Tables can look directly into the spotless assembly-line kitchen, which therefore becomes part of the restaurant; Vivaldi that originates for the staff only accidentally makes it out to you. Servers dress in formal (Europe) black and white and glide around as if the eyes of the world are upon them. Berkeley, San Francisco, even California have never boasted restaurants of this caliber, or so their posture says. New York, for all its problems, can pull off importance with more ease.

Grilled leeks with Catalan (Europe) sauce: almonds,

olive oil, satisfying, undistinguished. Young carrot soup with chervil: carrot is a difficult soup, often too sweet or pulpy no matter what the stock. This was so right and balanced that it made me wonder where the carrots grew. A swizzle of cream (Napa Valley, I'm sure) decorated it, just as it decorated soup at Zuni and Greens. This is a small town as well as a city.

Rabbit in red wine and garlic. French? Not on wide egg noodles so finely wrought and cooked that we knew why they name them egg. Equally sized light and dark curls of muscle on top, in a sauce of rabbit redux. Five or six warm huckleberries to punctuate, rusty-colored and sweet. The rabbit, succulent, is properly minky, noodles are rich, wine sauce is unctuous: so the berries, when they break, acidify and "fruit" the whole to an exquisite achievement. It takes confidence to make so much out of rabbit and noodles, and a lot of nerve.

A garden salad followed. All the restaurants I visited take lettuce seriously, so that the concept of "lettuce" is renewed after decades of snipping and gopping down. The emphasis on simple lettuce is French, of course, but it now becomes American: that's the tactic. I am supposed to imagine nimble fingers caressing the heads.

To end, a peach crisp with hickory nuts, hot, brown— the whole dinner was ruddy—and echoing poor people's food. Since the waiter served it right upon the salad without allowing time for us to meditate over our dregs of Cabernet, we asked that she hold off. The shock on her face was profound. Who are you to tell us? Yet she did remove, kept the desserts warm without allowing them to overcrust, and we modestly enjoyed them.

Many of the most adventurous "New Californian" chefs are women, as a fine feature by Ruth Reichl in *California* magazine has pointed out. There are reasons for this, some accidental and some a long result of the French and American cooking establishment's recorded disdain for and fear of women in their club. It must give the new female chefs some pleasure to be creating such a stir.

Benicia, a pastoral suburb an hour north of the Golden Gate, for about a year served as the capital of the new state before Sacramento took over. In contemporary history Benicia may be known as home of artists Judy Chicago and Robert Arneson, and because Judy Rodgers cooks at the Victorian outfitted restaurant of the Union Hotel (410 First Street, 707-746-0100). My last meal in northern California stood as the most enjoyable, assimilating the lessons of Chez Panisse, the liveliness of the grills, and Rodgers's need to refurbish the noble tradition ("everyone who stays here eats here") of American hotel fare. Also, Julia Bycraft, the pastry chef, is a genius.

Can you imagine the colors of thin red garlic soup floating leaves of purple basil? (And the texture of "cream" biscuits that sing?) Can you see the spread between tradition and innovation in the young grilled chicken marinated in red wine and draped with circlets of grilled red onion? Where else do we find these home-cured grilled pork chops spread with fennel butter (though a little too strong, a little too sweet)? These are $25 to $30 meals all told, the crystal gleams, the service melds care with informality, and I would do anything to return.

Over dessert I considered the differences between new restaurants in California and New York. In my nine visit-

ing meals—not enough, but almost—only once was anything over- or underdone. Never was anything less than
superbly fresh. Everything pleased the eye, neither killed
by arrangement nor piled and ignored. Wines were judi-
ciously offered and affordable. There is imitation and
repetition, but of each other, not of a tired imagined
France. No deco sconces attempted to replace the style
that should be in the food.

Could New York restaurants grow their own? A few
could. Need they bow to the Southwest to be inventive?
No. In any case, inventiveness in New York menus, when
it shows up, is rarely followed up by careful and uniform
cooking. Regional ideologies, such as California hippie-
dom, vegetarianism, ecological obsessiveness, may account for the direction California cooking takes, but first-
rate preparation is first-rate anywhere, ahistorical and
forever.

This, over plum ice cream (of Sonoma cream?) that
palatized us so we understood the puckering flavor of
the plums used, the cream used, and then moved us on
to concentrate both perceptions to a final fluid peak.
Marionberries—I hope that's spelled right—are druped
Oregon fruits that look like raspberries, smell like strawberries, and taste like something else: simultaneously
sweet and tart. The pie Bycraft made from them, with a
short crust, I would never have expected to come out of a
restaurant kitchen, and to me.

Last, we broke through Bycraft's hot, crackling caramel top and pushed into a cool, flowing custard of that
same grassy cream. Not unusual, but I lifted the spoon up,
hard noisy beige broken in soft white, and I remember ask-

ing myself as I tasted, how does it feel, to be soothed and excited all at once?

(10/4/1983)

Beautiful Soup

Most of us assume that a desire for money motivates the opening of a restaurant, and anything else, such as joy of cooking or personal obsession, is secondary. There is evidence for this, of course, in the advertised pressure within the restaurant trade to balance salability with profitability, "salable" being the telling synonym for tasting good enough, just good enough, to be bought.

If you look, however, way under the surface and through the history of restaurants, past the obvious spurs of greed, necessity, and entertainment, you may find a transhistorical channel, like the spring under Spring Street, which time and again breaks through, that consists of a motive entirely unexpected. Call it hospitality, succor, even love. Very selfish, this motive, giving yourself pleasure through feeding others. But most who have cooked for others recognize, if only once out of many tired times, that "doing something" to ingredients, overcoming their inertia and transforming them into a soup, a stew, a pie, is an archetypal way to embody labor and spirit. What better definition of idealism than to mobilize spirit to change the physical world?

Idealism is not presently the norm, and probably has never been, but it breaks through when it can. With all my problems with "the church," it sometimes attracts those who wish to prove that idealism is an active force. There are thousands of hungry persons in New York City whom

only these few will feed, or feed with grace, and it took a
group of artists—artists also deal in the battle between
profit and spirit—to spread this word further.

They call themselves the Food for the Soup Kitchens
Committee (call 675-4042 or 505-8369 for more information). They have put together a benefit exhibition and sale
of artworks at the Bronx's Fashion Moda (2803 Third Avenue, near 147th Street). The show spreads on the fame
range from Wegman to . . . , on the price range from
$5000 to $300, and is altogether a mixed "young" show in
the graffiti-expressionist mode. If you forget about food, a
fine bowl-of-soup painting by Huck Snyder will remind
you. Steve Whitesell is preparing a map of Manhattan's
shelters and soup kitchens to give out to those who want to
know where to eat. Money raised by sale of artworks and
assorted benefit performances will be divided among four
kitchens, and since one of them is in my neighborhood, I
visited.

Lorraine Wynne and Andrej Kodjak coordinate various
volunteers from New York University, the neighborhood,
the parish of Nativity Church ("Please thank the church
for us"), and from the 400 they serve, in shifts of 60, every
Sunday. The two are volunteers themselves; do all volunteers work with such good-humored intensity? Relax your
ideas of "soup kitchen" for a moment, for this could be a
restaurant review: as I walked downstairs into a sunlit
room the smell of garlicky meatloaf started me salivating.
Tables were set: fruit salad, mustard, utensils. "We want
to give a sense of being in a restaurant, a restaurant without
a cash register." They have waiters, decorations, "but we
would love to have tablecloths," which would go far to re-

move the stigma of the institutional feed. Lorry and chef Andrej were full of working details: we like to have one menu because people don't realize how important it is, to those who depend on this food, that they know in advance what they're getting; we'd make more than meatloaf but as things stand we can't cook on the top of the stove; musicians are welcome to come and entertain; damp cloths keep the trays of bread from drying out.

They began in May of this year. Why? Lorry couldn't answer; she was understandably halted by the complexity of trying to explain unselfishness. Andrej: "We think hunger is a result of greed and not lack." Who comes? Here is where they explained most carefully. Ten times more men than women, little overlap with those who use the men's shelter across the street ("I didn't see the same faces," said Lorry), all races, all ages. They want to fight the "fearful defensive attitude toward the poor." Of course there are those, Lorry told me, who will never be able to manage for themselves, but the kitchen serves a wide variety: addicts, those down in luck, a man with a baby whose wife was in the hospital, and who simply could not spend the money for a meal. Transients, young people, the out-of-work. "We don't even touch the most destitute." And then Lorry did touch the reason she was here: many, most of the people who come to eat, need this help now, temporarily. They are not fated to their "lot," but if they don't get some kind of careful, compassionate assistance—what a humane society would call their right—then their "fate" is secured.

A New Jersey mayor is trying to keep a church from running a kitchen for the poor "because when they're not there they'll be out in our streets." I like the "our."

It costs $257 per week to feed 400; a $10 donation covers 15. They need a hot water heater and commercial dishwasher so they can move from paper plates to china ("to make our service more dignified and to offer a better meal"). Volunteers are welcome. Of course, this is one of many private soup kitchens, and they all need help; call the Coalition for the Homeless, 460-8110, for the one nearest you.

Anyone is welcome to eat at the University Soup Kitchen on Sunday; Andrej Kodjak's meatloaf is excellent, if a bit spicy. (I forgot to mention Andrej is chair of the Slavic Department at NYU, Lorraine is an administrator for the Graduate Faculty of Arts and Sciences.) Prices are reasonable: free if necessary, $1.00 otherwise.

We end with the recipe, Andrej's:

Meatloaf for 75

15 pounds ground beef
4 1/2 loaves of wheat bread
30 eggs
1 quart tomato juice
5 tablespoon salt
3 tablespoon black pepper
1 tablespoon garlic powder
1 tablespoon oregano
2 pounds chopped onions

Mix. Set in flat pan. Bake one-half hour at 500 degrees, and one hour at 350 degrees. "We make six."

(10/18/1983)

Why There Are No Great Restaurants on the Upper West Side/Part One

It's like criticizing late industrial capitalism or *New York* magazine: how can you argue with, uh, success? Most of Ernie's 350 seats are occupied at dinnertime, even until 10 or 11, which is 2 a.m. in Upper West Side Standard Time. "It's our Soho restaurant," one proud eater told his friend, his eyes sweeping over the painted exposed pipes, brick walls colored to imply graffiti that has outlived its impulse, and the free-standing bar, its space defined by suspended architectural cornices and shards, the Elgin Marbles of '70s upscale. He did not, in his sweep, include the fussy enameled ceiling-fans, the brass handrails, and the suburban brick fireplace way in the back, desolate, a Levittown memory which restaurants like this are supposed to bury and replace.

Our Soho restaurant? No, no, not Soho, Soho has its own problems, conveniently summarized in a restaurant's press release that characterizes the famous shopping district as "achieving the rare sense of a tightly knit community of several diverse groups" ("retirees . . . young businessmen from Wall Street and families, singles, and young marrieds of all sorts"). Artists, factory workers, Italians from the old neighborhood don't knit. But folks sometimes travel to Soho to eat. Who, who among you, will make the trip to eat in the Upper West Side? I risk tautology, perhaps falsely creating a "people," but Upper West Siders (young businessmen from Wall Street and families, etc.) eat in the Upper West Side. Upper West Siders eat at Ernie's.

It's wide open, it's there. It's welcoming. The brittle din takes us back to Ocean Avenue's Lundy's—good-bye, Lundy's, even your Teresa Brewer room couldn't keep you alive. If Ernie's food were rough, like Lundy's, or even good, then we could throw our arms around the whole display. But the food holds the restaurant in balance. If good, then we customers are an attractive lot, chatting intensely about art, lust, love. If not, we are nothing but ill-clad, easily led drudges who wouldn't know a good time if it sat on us. You could delight in community, or you could suffer involuntary fun. Food has that power.

After signaling possibilities to my companions at the table and shouting out decisions to the waiter, after eating at least half the giant menu, hoping that this would be the place that turns the Columbus Avenue spinach-salad jokes inside-out; after dyspeptic night-thoughts, after long silence, we have concluded that there lives a spirit which takes a dish so chic-sounding as a hot salad of mussels, tomatoes, pignolis, and pepper on tepid vermicelli, and turns the result to tasteless anarchy. This is the spirit of 76th Street, the spirit of the Upper West Side. You know how Charivari-type sportswear (Charivari, out-of-towners, sells nice clothing in five Upper West Side stores) looks when thrown on altogether, as if the store's label guarantees any combination would work? That's how Ernie's dishes taste.

I am not a spiritual person, but how else can it be explained? All best intentions of decor . . . and someone chooses those fans, that solipsistic brass, those TV-tray tables for two. A remarkable menu, full of pignolis, pestos, wilted this, grilled that, fresh seaweed, and "exotic tomato," enormous bowlsful, friendly fast servers . . . and what can I recommend? The grilled baby chicken ($9.95), garlicky and juicy if you eat it before it and its oily pile of vegetables fall off the side of the plate; the grilled venison sausages ($9.95), woody and plain, and the thin-crusted dinner-plate pizzas for one, the best possibilities here, providing a base for such combos as duck sausage, leeks, fresh sage ($7.50). Could Ernie's make money serving only these hearty but fine pizzas to 350 times three? Would they have the nerve?

Not on your life. I didn't taste one high-quality pasta; some was so al dente I heard the bite. All sauces, well-conceived or ill-, sat on the bottom or top and tasted as if the ingredients were arranged, not cooked. I'm sure you know what I mean: reasonable raw materials not coaxed into meeting each other and shaking hands. Nicely priced pork chops were grilled tough. Mozzarella in carrozza, lumps of fried cheese in a charmless bright tomato sauce, had cooled just enough to reach the texture of warm bubble gum. The piece de resistance, "fegato di anatra sauteed with capers and mustard," Englished as duck livers served with polenta: I was brought a plate that held as unattractive a load of brown matter as I've seen in recent restaurant years, with only a scrape of polenta on the bottom. And the polenta seemed to be flavored with fruit or a sweet glaze. This is not cooking, if a dish can come out of the kitchen so quickly, looking, tasting, like that.

I truly pray I've missed, by terrible accident, the really good food that everyone is enjoying. I get no pleasure out of this.

I've heard other reasons for the dullness. Ransoms
called rents force out the small place that can experiment;
night life creates an opportunity for adventurous cooking,
but increasing crime keeps the spenders early to bed. All
Manhattan neighborhoods suffer these constraints—and
the Upper West Side sits in a trough lined with dead lettuce. Any restaurant with some style, such as Nishi or
even Ernie's, cannot, will not, need not bring its food into
line. Ernie's, I'm afraid, is an idea that doesn't respect the
palate of the careful, *individual,* eater: for you can be an
individual in a community, even a community of clients.
Ernie's takes no risks except size. It denatures its own style
with comforts, and the menu, to be generous, tries to
please the way designers who mistrust their public try to
please: with averages and guesses about what's "popular,"
what they may want. Invention? Creation? Passivity names
this local spirit, and it's the restaurants, more than the
eaters, who are to blame.

It's an extraordinary situation. In a neighborhood which
is the very definition of gentrification but which retains a
multiracial and multi-income mix that holds on for dear
life, in a neighborhood supporting hundreds of restaurants
feeding tens of thousands, in a neighborhood where a
large proportion of the middle-class population reads restaurant reviews, not only for use but for daily conversation, in such a neighborhood, you find the absolute worst
restaurants in New York. Not every one is bad, of course,
and we are entitled to our friendly favorites, but eating on
Columbus Avenue or Broadway is like being trapped in the
largest renovated Center City mall in the country.

I have tried for years to understand why. Many of these places were designed for profit only, during a time when "disposable income," "the singles revolution," "low cholesterol," and "quiche" (which ain't low cholesterol) spiced blurbs of more and more New City Magazines. White wine befuddled a whole generation on its way to rejecting at once suburban fast food, French high prices, and ethnic discomfort. This is the agreed-upon theory.

Yet I don't think you can blame the eaters for what we are served, for not standing up after a few years of dusty hamburgers or phlegmatic pasta "salads" and simply walking out. I sometimes wish you Upper West Siders would. You've won rent strikes, so why not unfurl your sanguine banner, stash the would-be-spent money and plastic in a safe-deposit box, air your repressed complaints, and eat downtown? Why not good-bye, Columbus?

I have only begun to answer the headline's question, but this is just Part One. I expect, but do not hope, there will be a Part Two.

(12/20/1983)

Order in the Court

Everyone knows that food and restaurants are shit compared to art and literature. The more an object of study is an object, the less important (objective) its criticism can be. Art comprises objects? You need not own art to see it, or so they say. Books are marketable? Ideas are pageless. But anyone, or almost anyone, or some of us anyway, can enter a restaurant and buy food. Eat it, it's gone. Food becomes shit, another pound, maybe a memory. Food writing smells of its source.

Well, if you believe this, you'll understand why Michael Chow, of Mr. Chow's restaurants, branches in London, Beverly Hills, and New York, felt he could sue the 1981 *Guide Gault-Millau* for libeling Mr. Chow's on East 57th Street with a bad review. You'll also understand why Chow won, $20,000 in compensatory damages, $5 punitive.

This was a juried trial, and the prosecution tried to prove . . . what could they prove? The guide says the service was slow, and describes the pancakes served with the Peking duck as "the size of a saucer and the thickness of a finger." I quote from the December 7 *Times:*

"To counter this argument, Mr. Chow sent Stephen Yim, the chef in charge of his noodle-making staff, to roll pancakes before the jury, which apparently found them appropriately paper-thin. Mr. Yim demonstrated how he rolls a 10-foot-long noodle in 60 seconds, a feat for which he was given a place in the Guinness Book of World Records." (A nice *Times* detail.)

"The jury and Judge Thomas F. Griesa also saw videotapes of the cooks at Mr. Chow's preparing traditional Chinese dishes, as a means of rebutting the guide's contention that 'sweet and sour pork contained more dough (badly cooked) than meat,' and that most dishes had 'only the slightest relationship to the essential spirit of Chinese cuisine.'"

I walked around the *Voice* office, dazed, waving the *Times* clipping in front of Nat Hentoff, Vladimir Estragon, anyone who would pay attention. Nat knew the judge, "a nice man," and said it didn't surprise him. "Theater will be next." Later Vladimir: "Next thing, it'll be theater." Three others, independently: "Watch out, they'll go for theater."

Theater critic John Simon refers to actress X, in a musical version of Euripides's The Trojan Woman, *as "looking more like the Horse than Helen."*

"Your honor, ladies and gentlemen of the jury, may I direct your attention to Exhibit A, a model of what experts at the British Museum agree was almost without question the true Trojan Horse. Would the jury like to leave their seats and walk around it? Of course this is only a scale model, for the original was 40 to 50 feet high. Yes, you'd be looking up into its mouth. Those are wheels—they did have wheels—or rollers at the very least.

"Exhibit B, you see here, is a computer-assisted composite of Helen of Troy prepared by the police department's own Detective Charles Pooter. It's based on

descriptions of Helen of Troy by Vergil, Kit Marlowe—a man, he's British—and Cole Porter, all specialists in their fields. Move that around, George, so they can see.

"And finally, Exhibit C [applause] who will now perform for us, just as she did on opening night and just as she continues to do six nights and two matinees a week, her Second Act number 'Ladies Who Launch.'" (More applause.)

As the curtain drops, a court officer strikes the set and the twelve peers are instructed by Judge Ziegfeld to determine if Exhibit C more closely resembles Exhibit A or Exhibit B. We needn't leave the courtroom, says the foreman, it's as plain as the nose on her face. Damages are computed by multiplying The Trojan Women's *mezzanine ticket price by the audited circulation of* New York *magazine.*

A chastened Simon says that in future he'll review only dead performers, which, he reminds the reporter from WNBC-TV, *is what he's been doing all along.*

I wake up, slumped over my typewriter, in a cold sweat.

We assume, we hope, that the authors and publisher of *Guide Gault-Millau* will appeal. I appeal to you. The *Gault-Millau* pan was a combination, like it or not, of momentary descriptions, hyperbole, and, hold your breath, metaphor. You know, "love made my heart sing," the building blocks of simple creative thought. What videotape do you drag in to discredit a metaphor, an idea? The problem is not whether a review is "correct" or wrong; whether a critic is "good" or a jerk. Who says criticism is the Word? If criticism was supposed to be "true," all reviews of the same restaurant or book would be, should be, the same.

What a garbagy, mechanical, commercial view of the world this concept of truth implies. By the way, if New York restaurants love the truth so much they wouldn't lobby so fiercely against the long-needed truth-in-menu law; I should sue *them* for every "Fresh Trout Fried in Real Creamery Butter" I've had to read. The truth Mr. Chow's wants from restaurant critics is the kind one finds in ads. Advertising, at least, sells it like it is.

(12/27/1983)

Eating Backward

Long ago, in the utopian early '70s, a group of teaching assistants and younger professors tried to alter the "Humanities" courses that all our students were obliged to take. One obvious adjustment involved the inclusion of women, not as teachers, for their lack needed no demonstration, but in the syllabus, as what the Dean of Humanities liked to call "voices from the past." We proposed the idea to the suave and likable Head of History.

"Women haven't written anything," he said.

I have been reading a wonderful book by Dolores Hayden, 10 years later, called *The Grand Domestic Revolution*. It charts the history of 19th century "material feminists," those who thought that men's exploitation of housework, domestic labor, is the greatest cause of women's inequality. "Women's inequality" sounds old-fashioned, doesn't it? But what a vision they had, Catharine Beecher, "angry housewife" Melusina Fay Peirce, free-lover Marie Howland, and dozens more—men too.

They proposed to change the way people lived. Apartment-hotels, kitchenless cottages, spacious row houses would be connected by common areas, gardens, promenades, restaurants. Cleaning of houses, sewing and laundering of clothes, cooking of meals would be accomplished by working in large groups or by outside "specialists," financed through cooperative business ventures, husband-paid wages, or the coffers of the state. Some of these proposals were begun, and a few seemed to succeed, for according to Hayden the mid-19th century was a time when democratic hope for enormous change was not derailed by capitalist false promise, when "visionary" and "failure" were not yet synonyms in the political dictionary.

The material feminists' needs sound not so different from ours, and their implements of change were recognizably practical. Charlotte Perkins Gilman defended a door-to-door cooked food service in her novel *What Diantha Did,* employing language laughingly similar to that of a hack restaurant review:

> *"Why—why—it's like Paris," she said in an awed tone.*
> *. . . The meat was roast beef, thinly sliced, hot and juicy . . . Mrs. Ree enjoyed every mouthful of her meal. The soup was hot. The salad was crisp and the ice cream hard. There was a sponge cake, thick, light, with sugar freckles on the dark crust. The coffee was perfect and almost burned the tongue.*
> *"I don't understand about the heat and cold," she said; and they showed her the asbestos lined compartments and perfectly fitting places for each dish and plate. . . .*
> *Mrs. Ree experienced peculiarly mixed feelings. As far as food went, she had never eaten a better dinner. But her sense of Domestic Aesthetics was jarred.*

Eating in halls or eating subscription dinners delivered to your own lovely home, eating together or alone, eating meals of great affordable variety and better than you could cook yourself, with time to talk, get up, and do your own important work: these are the ideals that hang on, even in a debased way, to our remnant of pleasant eating in a social space—the restaurant. Don't let mercantile ideals (an oxymoron if I ever heard one) convince you that it's only the food that drives us out to eat. Sure we want fine food, "the best I ever tasted," but we require more. Families of lovers and friends who don't eat out tell me they prefer home not just because they can cook better—sometimes they can't—but because at their own table they feel "connected" to each other through the food. That connection, but without unpaid or involuntary stove-slavery, without the narrowness of the same everyday company or recipe, might have been possible if some of the Grand Domestic Revolution had prevailed. We'll never know the pleasures of those cross-class, flower-laden eating halls or private dinners-to-go, which collective decision and action would have helped to create. Our privately enterprising restaurants will have to do; sometimes they do very well.

In the middle of my read, I received a press release from San Francisco's Local 2 of the Hotel & Restaurant Employees and Bartenders Union, announcing that the local has reached an agreement with Luisa's Restaurant on Castro Street. It's a typical story but with an unusually good outcome in these times. This summer 12 employees were fired for wanting a union. They picketed, protesting their dismissal as well as their lack of a health plan; lack of paid sick leave, vacation, holidays; no breaks in long shifts, no overtime; and flyspeck wages. Luisa's business, mostly gay male business, dropped 80 percent in sympathy. The owner began to negotiate, and the workers won much of what they didn't have, including Gay Freedom Day as one of their five paid holidays.

Gay Freedom Day in a union contract!

Gaining some control over one's life, a reasonable 19th century ideal, almost always entails working with others. I am moved to see this ideal renewed in 1984, when to be called visionary, in any arena, marks you either a fool, or a survivor.

(1/10/1984)

Cooking Backward

You have every right to think New York is so large and mysterious that once a city flavor gets established, it won't disappear. I felt that way when I read about—or did I imagine?—the pneumatic-tube subway constructed sometime in the last half of the 19th century. It didn't work, or its financier lost his capital to some Astorish machinations, I don't remember, but just before or after its completion the plush, chandeliered station was sealed up. Was it truly airtight, this Victorian Tut's Tomb? Has it been marauded by bands of antique dealers, or does it, undefiled, still hold damask secrets, dusty but otherwise intact? Had they stored food down there?

These fantasies, the night-dreams of those who hoard old menus or paper dolls, defend against the fear of permanent loss. Even restored landmarks sometimes turn contemporary, through their shopping mall context if not their intention. Better to clean, polish, maintain, and if the edifice retains a use as well as its shell, we can claim some continuity.

It goes without saying that anxiety over losing the past is mostly about unhappiness with the present.

Paddy's Clam House, "Seafood Specialist Since 1898." What, you exclaim, that old thing? Why I ate there with my father, my grandmother, her grandmother; they could serve 80-year-old oyster crackers from the bottom of the bin. My mother, who sold cosmetics at Macy's before and after the war and froze in her bathing suit on the floats of pre-TV Thanksgiving Day parades ("They'd have fired us if we'd refused"), says she lunched at Paddy's every third day, alternating with a Jewish deli around the corner and a Chock Full O'Nuts nearby.

Was Paddy's always old? Thirty-fourth Street, as you walk west from Herald Square, 80 or 90 years ago changes from the bumptious Tenderloin to the southern border of treacherous Hell's Kitchen. It's no coincidence these neighborhood labels were eatin' words, for food's metaphors ranged through all other brands of pleasure. Police captain Alexander C. Williams knew he would be understood when, newly transferred to the district in its heyday, he said, "I've had nothing but chuck steak for a long time, and now I'm going to get a little of the tenderloin." Reformers called the area "Satan's Circus," but Captain Williams's meat-name stuck.

You can't turn a freshly shucked oyster to fast food; even on Paddy's chipped, matchless china it will carry some particle of Diamond Jim Brady in it. A stew buoying half-a-dozen of these milk-swollen oysters slicked with drops of butter red-edged by flavorless paprika, will warm your shopping lunches even on Paddy's scuzzy, torn green-and-white oilcloth. Fashion can't dim their ruddy Manhattan clam chowder, a recipe at least as old as this city's first IRT, even though we know it's "not supposed to" have onion and potatoes cooked to falling apart, or a broth thickened with flour and fragrant with so many clams. Our fantasy of a continuing past anchors on Paddy's chowderpot that must, like a sourdough sponge which can trace directly its physical ancestry to a Gold Rush bucket in a now-dead town, pass some scrap of soup from one batch to the next. This can't be true except in a fanciful way, but if a soup can be an edifice whose structure is old but function and pleasure intact, then such a soup deserves protection and a plaque.

Paddy's cooks and waiters will be embarrassed by praise, for they just keep going, resigned to no change. You can order a simple broiled fish or sea-scallop sauté dated by signature paprika and be pleased; the $5.45 lunch special (chowder, fish, potato, sweet but crunchy cabbage slaw, lemon meringue, apple, or Boston cream pie included) must be the new Tenderloin's cheapest trip down seafood's memory lane. I wouldn't bother with anything else on the menu. You may look in the door, shrug your shoulders, and walk by, but I take comfort that New York still holds Paddy's Clam House up, that innovation has some constancy to stand against.

(2/14/1984)

Eggs for Lunch

There must be American men and women, I don't know how many hundreds of thousands, who have eaten two eggs every morning almost every day of their lives. Mother blended yolk into baby's first mash, then she mashed soft-cooked egg whole and tried to spoon it more in than around. Baby spit up, egg on our face, but baby knew. As soon as morning became "breakfast," as soon as the little member hit the negotiated world, Two Over Easy became a daily four-bit birthright.

Three hundred and sixty-five times 75 times two. That's not a lot, if eggs is how you measure a life.

The February 16 *New York Review of Books* carried an article called "The Lost Mariner" by neuropsychologist Oliver Sacks, in which he describes a 49-year-old man he calls Jimmie R. A healthy, quick, and friendly patient, Jimmie R. not only can't remember anything past age 19, but can't retain what happens to him longer than a minute or two from one moment to the next. (The brain can fault so specifically; in an earlier article, Sacks tells of a man who lost all concept of "face." Sacks titled his history "The Man Who Mistook His Wife for a Hat.") Jimmie R. can play checkers but not chess, can keep a journal but can't believe *he* wrote what he did the day before. Every few minutes he cheerfully renews his acquaintance with the doctor; Jimmie recognizes only one living person from the past, his brother, although he can't understand how

200   Jeff Weinstein

brother grew old so fast. Jimmie's own white-haired image in the mirror short-circuits his ever-present mind to panic.

The sympathy with which Jimmie R.'s story is told makes it the strongest periodical writing I can remember in a long time. Sacks makes a case—beautifully but not convincingly—for a personhood that lives without or beyond memory: what some call spirit or soul. I shivered throughout the piece, not in fear, but wondering where I or anyone stood in all of it. Try this: " . . . As a savory smell drifted up from the dining room, he smacked his lips, said 'Lunch!' smiled, and took his leave." Or Jimmie's journal: "His entries remained unconnected and unconnecting and had no power to provide any sense of time or continuity. Moreover, they were trivial—'Eggs for breakfast,' 'Watched ballgame on TV'—and never touched the depths."

When Jimmie smelled food, the particular aromas of the meal made him hungry. How much of the anticipation of food depends on memory? Had he a watch he'd know it was lunch, but he also possesses a 19-year-long "dictionary" that gives him the tools to create teenaged anticipation. Animals salivate at apt or conditioned stimuli, and so do we, but who says animals can't remember a smell? They can, we know they can. A dog anticipates its satisfaction? Its master would believe so when master is the stimulus for a wagging tail.

Eggs for lunch. Runny yellow bags barely cooked enough to warm them; tough "scrambled" shards peeled off the pan and reeking of margarine and metal; your first restaurant omelette, French spelled, mucoid, and a big mistake. Elizabeth David taught me to cook eggs *en cocotte*—rather, her *Summer Cooking* taught me—and they didn't smell at all until whatever parsley or basil I snipped in was freed from the white's hold: these eggs released their creamy air only in my mouth.

Can you anticipate a *new* smell? This is how novelty is sold; more eaters are convinced they know the best Peking Duck than have ever tasted Peking Duck. Duck eggs for lunch? But they're "foul," my friend likes to pun, by which he means gamy. Decades ago his mother, blessed with a surfeit of duck eggs and little else, whipped dozens of duck whites into gargantuan plain cakes. And what did she do with the nauseating yolks? Does he remember? He says he doesn't know, doesn't want to know.

Jimmie smells something he has never smelled before. It doesn't chart up with anything cooked for him at home, or in the navy. Pungent, that would be the word, sweet, burnt, foreign.

Does he become hungry, assuming he wasn't already? In five minutes, with the smell still there, does its intensity diminish, or must his put-upon olfactory troops constantly blaze new ground? If aroma can bridge the gaps between forgotten bites, in a calculus of eating, then the eater's memory may be extended beyond the innocence of eternal first impressions. Sacks argued that simple narrative art, because each part refers to the whole, is comprehensible even to Jimmie R. I make my bid for the leitmotif of smell.

And I remind myself that, in the case of food, "eggs for breakfast" needs to be replaced in order to be remembered. Without new breakfasts, the same fried eggs will trail you every waking day. Without novel tastes, the old ones lose their life.

(3/6/1984)

Ask Not What Your Restaurant Can Do for You . . .

New York's New American Food: I

I'd hoped to take back all the knowledge and advancement that mankind has made, but instead I find . . . vegetables.

Not so bad, some would say, if they were really *good* vegetables. Rod Taylor is the whining time-traveler in George Pal's 1960 film of H. G. Wells's *The Time Machine,* and the veggies he meets are the race of bubble-heads called *eloi,* typified by Yvette Mimieux in one of her best roles. The *eloi* eat fruit, only fruit. They are all fair-skinned blonds. They swim and sun themselves by day, stay in at night. The word *eloi,* some believe, sounds suspiciously like L.A., but it's not clear if Wells had vacationed in California. George Pal didn't have to.

You can make fun all you want, but California now proposes that vegetables, properly prepared, are this decade's meat; if you can prepare a vegetable with skill and respect, you can cook anything else. The French have understood (though not always practiced) this for years, and the Italians too, but reinvention in cooking takes such different forms that it might as well be innovation. So-called California cooking isn't a single, codified style, but its Californian manifestations so far draw on the same—sometimes conflicting—"ideologies": Buddhist vegetarianism, "natural" vegetarianism, counterculture antiestablishmentarianism, save-the-whales ecology, me-generation pleasuring, and jogging-generation personal health. Mix these with the culinary influence of Japanese aesthetic freshness, Southwestern chiles and grilling, and the validating familiarity and homey rite of provincial French; dredge in young talent, much of it female; roll in money; and, as Californian M. F. K. Fisher would say, serve it forth.

California cooking isn't a simple concept, obviously. It grows the way such cultural artifacts grow, not through the practical application of discussed ideas, but by being taught and passed around, piecemeal, from chef to chef, by being talked about, by being enjoyed, by being profitable. Ideas enter the air like odors, are perceived, and effect change, but in this culture at this time analytic ideas per se don't engage the chef. If they did, perhaps New York's attempts to import Californian and other national cooking wouldn't be, in most cases, so passive, so dim.

The two most ambitious "new cooking" restaurants to open in the city within the year are Jams and An American Place. Before we start I should warn you: they are each so costly that I can't review them in a usual way. Some of you will afford them, and others fascinated with the development of cooking styles may wish to save up. But most readers, I expect, cannot or will not spend $50 per person before wine. My individual bills, ordering randomly with a bottle from the bottom of the list, came to $120 to $140 for two. Why so much? Whatever their merit, these are some of the classiest, au courantest meals in the city, and you pay for fashion as well as food. Similarly stylish meals in California pick your pocket but not with so deep a hand. Of course, running a tony restaurant in Manhattan costs plenty, and few do it for toque-fame alone. But you can't ignore money as you parse the significance of the food; free-ranging chicken takes on new twists when it comes so dear.

The two places differ. Jams lifts itself from the California laboratory by its own two hands: owner Melvin Master directed the presently "sexy"—wine talk—Jordan Winery (at least it sports a sexy Cabernet), and co-owner chef Jonathan Waxman developed a California nouvelle menu as executive chef of Michael's in Santa Monica—kiwi cum avocado (metaphorically), fruit vinegars, glazey sauces, teeny portions, sorbet-to-pastry desserts, eat-in garden, $140 for three and no chiles when I ate there a few years ago. An American Place, on the other hand, attempts to slide in on more widespread American resurgence, making a California, as it were, of the whole nation. The chef here is Lawrence Forgione, formerly of Brooklyn's disappointing River Cafe.

After a series of meals, it seems that one sinks, the other doesn't. Oddly enough, the cooking and service in both restaurants are adept. My companions and I enjoyed our dinners at Jams more than at An American Place; that sort of preference is, on the surface, not so unusual. Both restaurants have trouble with their physical plant: a smashingly low ceiling and beigey decor that already looks smudged at An American Place; occasionally poor ventilation (from the open mesquite grill) exacerbating the booming noise on the ground floor at Jams. When small things, such as tap-water ice cubes in Jams's gold-priced Evian water, got on our nerves, we were really being pissy about money: after all, for $140 we're entitled to blah blah

blah; one of the worst things expensive eating can do is appear to justify, even breed, a kind of royal snottiness. But pleasure in Jams and disappointment in An American Place arises from an unusual culinary situation, one in which the meanings of a menu and restaurant transform the food, in one case improving it, in the other letting it down. Ideas, for good and bad, can be tasted. I'll elaborate next week.

(4/17/1984)

Local Imperial

New York's New American Food: II

My friend the waitress at my favorite coffee shop looked sincerely puzzled. She knows that raw materials aren't free and that restaurant staff should be properly paid. She could understand spending so much money on exotic French food. "But American food?" What did An American Place and Jams serve that could be American and still cost so much?

Part of this column will try to answer her. However, one of my eating partners at Jams said he was surprised that eating out costs so *little;* he was counting the men and women giving and taking at table, the aprons flying in the open kitchen, the art, real contemporary art, on the walls. Art dealers must miss the work they sell, for at every Jams dinner we could recognize a gallery parent keeping tabs on his or her former chicks.

Since I was not able to sample more than half the dishes in both restaurants in the usual way—"budgetary considerations"—I am limited to more selective impressions. I trust these impressions, though, for no great variety in duplicated selections or any variety in style over a number of visits spurred me and fellow eaters to question each restaurant's feel and accomplishment. If I have missed the apex at An American Place, or the "turkeys" at Jams . . . well, in your randomness, you might too.

An American Place, on the site of Le Plaisir and Claude's before it, is friendlier than it looks—the staff, I mean, not the rigorous clientele. Usually we don't care too much about table setting, but the glass candle and paper doily put us in mind of nothing so much as the guaranteed Republican inoffensiveness of a Horchow's catalogue. Food must stand out against such a background; it has no choice.

The menu, of not more than eight or nine appetizers and the same of entrees, changes frequently in increments that mark both the chef's invention and, just as important, the far-flung ingredients he can obtain. For my coffee-shop friend, this is some of what we ate for starters: sweet breaded frog's legs, bits of lobster, and lengths of lettuce were arranged as radii around a hub of dressed white beans into a pattern usually found on a quilt. A thin but sturdy plate-sized crepe embedding snippets of herbs was spread with goat cheese (from where? what goat?) and trimmed with brown butter sauce: so melting, arid, almost cloying, one could have been chewing crushed velvet. Colors of these are brown, predominant textures smooth. A plate of similarly rotary game sausage, asparagus, tomatoes could not balance the intensive labor of its production with the dry, assorted, somewhat salty result; Albemarle Sound pine-bark "fish" soup, a tawny broth covering pieces of tomato and smoked ham, sent up steam laden with fresh marjoram and a soupcon of "wood," an exotic, disembodied signal in a surprisingly hefty taste.

Not even off the appetizers, I see that I risk listing and yea-naying all our food without flopping over to what's really going on. There's no great disagreement among critics about the cooking at An American Place; "adventurous" in intent though sometimes "bland" or "tasteless" in result. I don't demur, but I wonder about the restaurant's vague "adventurous" concept. The chef has set up a distribution network to provide wild American mushrooms, buffalo steaks, wild mallard, Michigan beef, and other native delicacies (and not-so-delicacies). This has a good effect on renewable supplies because it solidifies a demand, but it could deplete foods that require more careful nurturance and protection. Okay, let's say we're not hurting for lamb's quarters and Willipa Bay oysters; what's the outcome? Freshness does not seem the point here; I've had fresher shrimp elsewhere, no matter that these were lifted from Key West. Invention isn't the thing either; An American Place's desserts are best when they make minor adjustments of resurrected unpopular tropes, such as the slices of bread pudding in a syrupy bourbon sauce. Is it American culinary history we're after?

I see geography, not history. The difficulty in obtaining certain American ingredients holds An American Place's otherwise unconnected recipes together. Instead of scouring the world, as an imperial Rome did for its pleasure, in this restaurant (or country) we scour our own provinces just for the sake of showing the lengths to which we can go. You might expect a more generous menu-profile, a straightforward, pluralist homage to American regional cooking, or even—something of a challenge—a seasonal Eastern seaboard selection that dips into culinary history. But the chef chooses to ignore or (and this is interesting) overshadow and neutralize pointedly regional styles to such an extent that you wonder why, with so much obvious skill and effort, you leave An American Place, carrying few flavors in your I-won't-forget pocket. This tour de force of national imperialism, and not dull ingredients or bad cooking, is the reason for the blandness others have perceived.

You can't avoid, shouldn't avoid, the activating tension in so-called New American cuisine. In dietary dialectical war, rural struggles with urban, plenitude with rarity, tradition with invention. Local goat cheeses, roes, shellfish, even meats, are sought not only by backward-looking, forward-thinking chefs in L.A. and New York, but by their counterparts and scions in Eugene and St. Louis. In this process, local recipes are preserved and spread around, but also ramified and perhaps diluted past merit; I've eaten some terrible "blackened redfish" in New York this year, Paul Prudhomme's excellent new Louisiana cookbook notwithstanding. The pluralism of local products and cooking has given chefs a push and a palette, but the sources may change beyond recognition with too much, or the wrong kind of, attention.

Next column: California visits New York—via France.

(4/25/1984)

Apples et Oranges

New York's New American Food: III

The wine list at Jams, selected by co-owner Melvin Master, former director of Sonoma County's Jordan Winery, lists a majority of French wines. When I asked the steward—a pleasant, unpretentious, efficient guy who almost single-handedly pulls the mood of the restaurant free of conformist snoot—why this was so, he said it was not so odd, that many of Jonathan's (Waxman, the chef) dishes and methods were French.

Like protozoa near a grain of rice, young cooks and servers rush toward, from, and around the centerpiece of Jam's theatrically open kitchen: a waist-high mesquite grill.

Early in the evening, at first seating, men wear ties and women pearls as if they never take them off. Postures indicate ritual, not enjoyment. Later on, voices carry (and carry on), races mingle ever so slightly, and possible business mixes with likely pleasure. Slouching begins. Little hats appear.

As is increasingly the case in New York's expensive restaurants, the greeters and seaters in leather skirts and truly hospitable smiles look more stylish, better dressed, than their clientele.

Some of the food carries fresh air with it, the way it feels to eat in California: as if the door were open. Other food, excellent food, like grilled mallard breasts atop a puddle of

210

pinot noir sauce, looking like rare liver and tasting like rare beef, reminds you which ocean is closest by averaging California (mesquite, pinot noir) with France (duck, sauce method, unctuous concentration of result, as in "old money").

Lucky the wine license came through, or so said a customer familiar to Mr. Master. Yes, they solemnly agreed, it was embarrassing for Princess Margaret to be bagging it, and with the bring-your-own law so unclear.

Wasn't swordfish a mercury collector? They should know about that in California. The logic is, if you must eat it, eat it here, once a year, mesquite-seared with prison bars just to the point where soggy water leaves, moist essence stays, and dryness never shows up. Portions, a citrus-zested puddle (California) and shallots (France) right beside, are not skimpy; grilled swordfish, similarly planned, at An American Place was so thick and spacious it showed slight strata of doneness and sank under its own fresh weight. There we were full before done. Few comparisons are close enough to illustrate so exactly the importance of portion to taste.

So, why then do we receive more grilled, free-ranging chicken than we can shake a stick at? Even though the melding of uncommon (birdy flesh) and common (chicken, chicken, chicken) drove us to finish? And the bootstring french fries? If the American in you must repedestal chicken 'n' fries (*French* fries), make certain the vegetable doesn't wilt, even ever so slightly, in the fat, or begin to cool as you begin to eat. No variation allowed here.

You won't find this silverplate pattern in your bridal register. The handles mimic wood-grain. This is not only fun—and fun don't come easy in joints like this—it also urges you to consider, as you finger a spoon, the relationship of: poor to rich, medium to message, expectation to surprise. This "fun" floats over to the food. Not bad for bad taste.

We move toward our flavors. First, though, some overdone scallops in fresh tomato ragout, so we don't exaggerate.

Mary twirled, fork-into-spoon, thin homemade (not my home) egg noodles into a scallop, through "thin" cream sauce, and onto the tablespoon of golden American roe in the center of the mound. More autumnal colors, and in spring, too. There's no explaining how it works, for soft to soft to soft shouldn't possess the resistance, sweetness, and tang her spoon carried. We passed it back and forth, sometimes the spoon, sometimes the plate. It's an appetizer, but the price, $13, corresponds to the recipe's central importance to the meal.

For vegetarians who like meat: warmed shiitake (Cal-Japan) and "oyster" mushrooms on mache, Belgian endive, and radicchio. Three-oil dressing (count them, three, walnut, hazelnut, olive, baby) and the chef's choice of whatever confettied vinegar. But watch out, Virginia, for the bit of (America) Smithfield ham.

The goat cheese salad, at its bright-hued origins.

Most entrees come with a tour de force, baby-vegetable bouquet. Most of the baby vegetables come with some meat or fish.

Sugary grapefruit "mousse" in a crust, and ginger (Cal-Japan) crème brûlée in pâté sucrée—now, anyone who thinks France is dead, just count the accents—that everyone's drooled so much about. I'll take two, to go. As they say in renaissance England, I die.

The folks at the next table were actually writing down "ideas" they found in the food. "Freshness," he said, "the main point." "Mixed metaphors, modernism, collage," she replied, "without breaking from tradition." She lifted her Margaux. "De-meating meat," he rejoined. "Revegging veg," she jotted.

"And yet, dear, was everything . . . perfect?"

"Of course not, but I tasted each bite so clearly, as if through crystal."

When will mesquite mean New York?

(5/1/1984)

Why They Eat: Deborah

How does she choose? She chooses, she says, what she's used to.

"Did you ever see that '20s ad for, I think it was, the *Book of Etiquette?* A photo of a miserable victim at the table with her new boyfriend, the one she wants so desperately to impress—as if there could be a situation where she wouldn't care what she looked like or said. So here she is, fingering her fake pearls, but underneath she's crying to herself that John thinks she's a dummy because she ordered chicken salad the last three times they lunched at Chez Je Ne Sais Quoi, but what can she do when . . . she can't pronounce the French! Needless to say, she doesn't know one knife from another either, and hasn't even heard of class mobility, the pitiful advertising creature.

"Well, maybe she *liked* chicken salad. I like chicken salad, and I can't even tell when they put ritzy stuff in it.

"A menu isn't a choice, it's a test. What if you order something you've never eaten before and it's garbage? I never think about ordering as a skill; it just seems like something I have to do to get the waiter to go away. But if a waiter came over and asked me, if you could have anything in the world what would you like to eat, I would still have the same trouble. I can handle ordering in pieces, like when someone's going out for sandwiches and wants to bring me something back. "What bread?" Rye, that's easy. "Meat or cheese?" Anything, no make it cheese. When I'm tired I just say I'll have whatever you're having—they're so fed up with my saying that.

"Most people think I'm stupid in this way or have no sense of pleasure. That's just not true. Liking to eat out isn't a biological imperative. I'm not even sure liking to eat is."

Part of this may be a function of being "taken out."

"When my parents took me to Chinese or Italian they'd ask me what I wanted and then steer me to what they thought I'd like. I remember this process, but, now that I think about it, I don't recall the food. No, they were great people, and wanted me to be as independent as they thought I could manage. I would have hamburgers with my girlfriends because we did everything together and I didn't care, I always got what they got, but eating out on dates was a chore and eating out alone was worse, because when they asked me how I wanted my burger I didn't really know. I wanted it with no trouble, that's how I wanted it.

"I don't cook well, but at least no one but me is waiting on me. I don't think I'm a bad cook, but really, how could I tell? It doesn't make a damned bit of difference. I'm not against restaurants, in fact I eat out three or four times a week when I'm too busy to shop for food. I like lentil soup, and, even though they're bad for my skin, I like grilled cheese sandwiches, if the cheese isn't so hot and gluey it burns the roof of my mouth. I like raw vegetables."

Some of this must be connected to her weight problem.

"When I went on a diet, I had to start worrying about eating too much. I wasn't a glutton, ever, but most people expect that if you're fat you ate to get that way, either as compensation or from neurotic bullshit or because you loved the feeling of stuffing yourself. I hated people thinking that about me. But I began to look at what I ate: eat less crap, and eat for my health. Restaurants, by the way, aren't keyed up for careful eating. Even the ones that pretend to health food make greasy tempura or oily salad dressings or carrot cake with more honey in one brick of them than any sane person would want in a year. So in a way, when I look at a menu, it isn't that I ignore the flavors entirely, it's just that, healthwise, most menus look alike.

"I dream about food, not about eating it, just about the packages. That means most of the dreams are in supermarkets, the kind that my mother shopped in before we moved to New York. Light from plate glass windows flooded the aisles and bags of cookies impressed me with their glossy reds and blues and made me happy. I wasn't a cookie kid, I liked ice cream, but the stacks, their fullness, must have satisfied something. New York markets are vile. I'd love to teleport one of those blue-haired cart-jockeys, the kind who'll run you over if she doesn't like your brand of soap, to a giant Ralph's in L.A. just to see the look of confusion on her face, with no one to bump into.

"I've never been a waitress, though I probably could be. It's a trade like any other.

"I never dream about flavors. Who does? How do you recollect a dream about something so devoid of objects as a taste? And yet I know I have sensual dreams."

Can someone like this alter her opinion about eating out? It may be more valuable to ask why she would want to change.

"When someone proves to me that eating out is inextricably bound to kindness, ethics, art, or health, then I'll feel guilty about not knowing how to use a menu. Pleasure, a definitively relative quantity, is all I can see I'm missing. What if I get it elsewhere? Why should I lose my good humor if my fillet was not everything I expected it to be?"

(5/15/1984)

Postmodern Meat

You trust that a driver in an oncoming lane doesn't switch into yours. You trust that your neighbor won't knife you in the laundromat because you know her and why should she, you wouldn't knife her. You trust that your next meal won't destroy you. Every time I unconsciously open my mouth to eat something someone else has prepared, I give the lie to the terrible Hobbesian assumption that I must defend myself against my fellow. Hospitality, which some cultures consider only a lack of war, almost always uses food to define itself. I give you this stew, it won't contain your children; I drink this wine and place myself completely in your hands. The trust implicit in eating is similar to that in sex, opening your inside to the outside, your self to the other. None of this should surprise anyone, but sometimes I am amazed that we enter a restaurant, or even someone else's home, and assume that no bond of trust is being formed, or is even necessary. Of course it is necessary. But, you can also ask, how can we "trust" even a can of beans when signs indicate this is a hostile and stupid world?

Some food analysts have accused Upton Sinclair of exaggerating when he wrote his 1906 attack on the meat industry called *The Jungle*. Not all sausages were made from spoiled raw materials chemically seasoned to cosmetically "preserve" them, not all sausage makers were tubercular, and not all cattle, fed on brewery wastes, developed boils that spurted during slaughter. Nonetheless, the gullible American public believed the man and cut their consumption of meat by half; the first Pure Food and Drug Act was passed just after *The Jungle* was published (according to Waverly Root and Richard de Rochemont's *Eating in America,* a similar bill was lobbied out of existence by meat packers when proposed in 1889). In terms of trust, the lesson becomes industrial: when profit is host, bring your taster with you. It's nothing new to cheat the public ("the public" is itself language that carries the potential of manipulation and gulling on its back); milk has been watered since it came off the farm. What's novel is the extent of the danger, its possible spread, and its beguiling delay, according to Orville Schell in his new book *Modern Meat.* I haven't eaten liver easily for years because I know it corrals the toxins that modern flesh is heir to, but now, I'm sorry to say, I don't think I can eat it at all. And I feel about beef and pork the way I did about liver.

Schell, who worked for a while as a California rancher, spent years running around the country to interview folks who owned, worked in, supplied, publicized, inspected, and criticized the American meat industry. Just to get it out of the way: interviews rarely make good writing. The book drones with I arriveds, I askeds, and he saids. Schell uses description to make gentle but unnecessary fun at his beehive-coiffed or potbellied subjects when one might wish to make fun of their ideas; he does this for "color," which the book sorely needs, though I wouldn't seek it through whispered conversations with the sweet wife of the "King of Exotic Feeds." He does succeed in explaining, dullness be damned, the primary science of his two big subjects: the use of subtherapeutic doses of antibiotics to promote animal growth, and the use of hormones, especially the now-banned diethylstilbestrol or DES, to do the same. "Feed technologies," like the nutritional potentials of good and bad garbage, industrial wastes, plastic pellets shaped like derbies, and shredded newsprint (restaurant reviews!), provide some bitter, some comic, relief.

Schell seems shocked about the commercialization and bottom-linings of agriculture; he knows he shouldn't be. He admits that plastic hay, which so amuses him, sounds like a great idea. What he should be upset about, and is, are the attitudes the meat capitalists—who term themselves the last of the free-enterprisers—show toward their customers. It's pretty clear that the tons of antibiotics mixed with feed have already resulted in bacteria, bovine *and* human pathogens, which are immune to most or all antibiotic treatment. People have become ill, some have died, but chemical and meat industries cite every lack of "conclusive" proof to retain their extra pounds of growth per head. No one has shown, they say with the same logic, that tiny residues of DES in meat-muscle cause hormonal imbalance or cancer, even though Schell finds evidence that uncontrolled use of DES on poultry in Puerto Rico has resulted in five-year-old girls with adult sized breasts and ovarian cysts. We eat our meat, and we're fine.

The facts are bad enough; according to the FDA, DES is still being used after being banned in 1979, and sales of other legal hormones are increasing. But belligerence and an odd passive hypocrisy make the facts almost incomprehensible in themselves. Many meaters hate the government for trying to "strangle" their American know-how and take away their ever-shrinking margin of profit: drugs keep them in business. "All I know," said one, "is if one of those sons-of-bitches from the FDA comes snooping around our lot, he's going to get his teeth knocked so far down his throat, he's going to have to stick a toothbrush up his asshole to clean them." They know where the beef is, they eat it, they see no connection. The government waffles and says it can't prove X causes Y. Says one FDAer, "If you want to have enough inexpensive meat for everyone, you're going to have to use some of these drugs. But personally, I'd rather eat meat that was raised without them."

My editor just asked me what he should do, what he should eat. First, read Schell's book. Personally, I'm bewildered that even though I knew a little about hormones and antibiotics for years, I never let this knowledge stop me from ordering a steak; I was immune. The answer for some may be to stop eating meat, but this is an individual decision, not a collective one. Asking a whole culture to stop eating meat—without any immediate perceptible danger—is like asking men to stop wearing pants. May I fling some suggestions out? If you're given a choice in the market, buy meat raised hormone-free—which is not as drastic as meat completely "organic." Proof of this claim, of course, is hard to come by. If you don't have the choice in your market, ask for it. This is one way to support the farmer who raises healthy and unadulterated animals; disdain for the precorporate farmer helped get us into this mess in the first place. I don't know what to advise about restaurants. Know who supplies our schoolchild's lunchroom burger; bigger is rarely better. Stay away from reconstructed hams, glued-together roasts, all the creations my mail from the National Pork Producers Council ("The New Pork") tells me "we" will love. Ask or demand that elected officials enforce the food and drug laws already on the books and stop decreasing on-site slaughterhouse inspection. Elect a government that can support business without attacking the customer: or find a new way to proceed. One slice of glorious roast pork from last week's Havana-Chelsea is floating in front of me, a goad, a promise, and I seriously don't want to lose it.

(6/5/1984)

To Av or Av Not

"Am I joining the enemy by praising a chic new eatery in the East Village?"

I wrote this sentence exactly four years ago as the lead to a piece about the opening of 103 Second Avenue, a restaurant whose address is as much its meaning as its name. One-oh-three was feared as a harbinger and aggressively avoided by many of the East Village's tenured residents, who saw its clean, angular, designed presence as an invasion over which they had no control. Why not walk in, I asked, and make it part of *your* neighborhood? After all, the hamburgers are no more expensive, and taste much better, than burgers in acceptable neighborhood venues like Leshko's or Phebe's. No, they said. Look who's going in. And they pointed to youngsters who were getting their hair clipped at Astor Place (before the lines) and suited adults who ordered martinis and chili before La MaMa. No, I won't wait to be shown to a table of the proper size. And they strode back to the Orchidia, the world's only Italian-Ukrainian restaurant, to mutter and predict.

Leshko's still bounces its pirogi and Phebe's its burgers and fries, but the Orchidia is gone forever, killed, some of them say, by 103. But when they say 103 they mean more than the restaurant, which hasn't doubled its prices and provided parking places for limousines. They mean the new neighborhood, the artist groundbreakers, the yuppie singles, and most of all the owners, the Owners, the ones who force us out.

Well, a few weeks ago in *New York* magazine we see another 103, a Japanese restaurant, this time next door to the Pyramid Club on Avenue A. It calls itself Avenue A (103 Avenue A) because that's its meaning too: where it is. For those of you who live up- or out of town, Avenue A is two street-strata east of Second, and until recently, any fashion it possessed never made the magazines.

Now, we all know that if magazines were buildings, *New York* would be the first co-op on the block. Even when one of its tenants tries to make a good point, about the gentrification of the East Village for example, the "owners" won't allow anyone to devalue the "property": hence the article's absolutely glamorous photo of restaurant Avenue A. The glamour in this photo is an odd kind of glamour, an idea from an archetypal outsider's point of view of what glamour in the big city is supposed to be. "Look as if it's happening here," the photographer demands of the subject. Glamour, a media creation, has always entailed the anticipation of being looked at, but the innocence of the delusion in this case can appeal only to those who have never opened their eyes to New York City: what gentrification and that aspect of *New York* magazine is all about.

The poor little restaurant. It's a pleasant month-old situation, about as inexpensive as 103 Second was when it opened. The cooked food is largely inferior to the excellent a la carte sushi and odd "specialties" such as Dynamite (scallops, mushrooms, smelt roe with sesame seeds baked in a small tin-foil boat), Tiger's Eye (layers of salmon, nori, and spinach encased in squid, heated and sliced to form six or seven overlapping namesakes), and the refreshing Bonsai Tree (crab and roe wrapped in cucumber). Walls, ceiling, and floors are black, and someone got the bright idea to use purple spots on the black columns, which presages the style of the soon-to-be-chic '60s. It should be, would be, a welcome neighborhood restaurant. Why not?

"Gentrification" has always impressed me as too simple a term to encompass all the changes economically passive neighborhoods must bear. Here's a restaurant both comfortable and affordable, and the list of folks who are "excluded" (exclude themselves) is as long as the wait for tekka-maki on a Saturday night. You will not see families, extended or otherwise, pass through the 103 door. You won't see neighborhood blacks or Latins, neighborhood Ukrainians or Poles, neighborhood poets or neohippies, unless—and here's the trick—they are dressed in the cheap, inventive, sometimes-educated style of the New Artist Class.

I love this contemporary East Village look (and I like the sushi at Avenue A, woe is me) but one of the less attractive social imperatives of a style so delicately urban and easy to rip off is that its practitioners will choose surroundings that show them off exclusively to each other and to those who, like glamour-hounds and art scouts, need them. They can't risk dilution by their pluralist, class-bound surroundings because the New Artist Class, as a style, denies class. Blending with the neighbors socially would be like turning the lights up before the night is over. And the neighbors, technically allies in the fight to keep the East Village affordable, obviously feel the same way. Don't most families want to eat at home?

(6/19/1984)

Czardas Memories

Eating and. . . . It has never made any restaurant sense. Eating and music, eating and art, eating and theater (that's dinner theater), eating and sex. Acceptable as preludes or postludes—which is why the words preprandial and post-prandial were invented—but not at the same time. Music, art, and theater require attention that should attach to the food; sex requires attention and coordination: your hands are full, your eyes too big for your mouth. And terpsichore isn't even in the running. Have you ever seen someone at a bar mitzvah get up from the table between chopped liver and roast beef and try a hora? Don't stand in the centrifugal path; the stomach can't take such exertions, or only under very special circumstances.

Consider the Bohemian Hall in Astoria. Its cornerstone dates 1910, which sets the "b" firmly in uppercase. The afternoon of June 9 hit the mid-90s, but as the sun lowered and the light stayed, the air in the spacious tree-ceilinged garden adjoining the Bohemian Hall cooled to a graciously tolerable degree. If, because of the temperature, you hadn't been hungry for days on end, now you could be. You could even imagine moving your body for pleasure and not just for work. Yes! That's it, the space next to the Bohemian Hall was a pleasure garden.

The Ethnic Folk Arts Festival, formerly the Balkan Arts Center, chose the site of its ninth annual Queens Ethnic Music Festival well. Concerts and workshops in the day's heat included performers of Albanian, Armenian, Bulgarian, Epirot and Pontic Greek, Hungarian, and Calabrian music, but the more lively evening drew on most of them and dozens upon dozens of paying guests to dance in a general party. I came because of the food, a traditional outdoor lamb roast (put together by Takis Petrakos and Leslie English) including Greek and related *meze* appetizers, spiced meatballs, spanakopita (spinach-cheese pie), salads, and large plastic cups, pitchers almost, of draft. I didn't know I'd be tricked into listening while I ate, into watching people dance while I ate, while *they* ate. If I had known, I might have stayed away; so I am extremely grateful I didn't know, for even though my stomach moved in sympathetic response to the music, and my muscles moved in similarly haptic twitches to the dancing, I didn't expect that my eyes would water up during an hour or so of complete synesthetic happiness. This isn't allowed.

The food wasn't the reason—and it shocks me to say, for the food, as mass meals go, was quite good. Minted and garlicked lambs don't look "little lamb who made thee" as they blacken on a spit. Lambs are large. Wise old men run up with their plates just as the cooks, with hammer, plier, and axe (!) in hand, begin to hack and strip off the best parts. Pignoli and currants don't usually spill out in the rice of cylindrical grape leaves. And when have you tasted *volvoi,* red-marinated wild onions grown into golf balls: summery and delicate?

Eat, taste, and drink the beer which runs directly into channels that spill out sweat. As you lift the last cut of lamb and you see your plate's almost empty, your ears switch on and you hear music. (Bulgarian, with bagpipe, fiddle, flute, and double-headed drum.) The flavor's gone, for now you can't avoid the dancing.

I own a tinted photographic postcard from 1912, two years after the Hall, that shows 70 women dressed in white (I counted with a pin) dancing in a circle on a hill outside Cleveland. Hundreds look on. It was May Day, a celebration, and the photo speaks entirely of its age. Someone has said that Morris dancing and all these other ethnic circles are degenerate forms of Sufi ritual. Sufi ritual dance gathers tremendous momentum as people join, chant, and lose quotidian selfhood. Those hundred dancing their not-too-difficult steps in the Queens pleasure garden left their selves in a different way.

A Hungarian Folk ensemble took over and began a dance in which a violin threaded in and out. The deadpan expressionism of the female singer sounded like that of Nico from the old Velvet Underground. Two pacific, dignified young teachers, identified by green handkerchiefs, cued the steps, and variations rippled out of their movement. Circles broke from the big circle and little chains formed.

A memory of food, the unfamiliar-familiar music, and an obvious delight of dance, where younger to older in all shades of race and dress were as numerous as those watching them, well, this is when it added up, when I realized that the pleasure of a pleasure-garden comes from activity in which more than couples or individuals have a part. My lord, have we gone so far that any summer's expression of cooperative fun should seem so rare?

We, my friends and I, unprepared, almost danced.

(6/26/1984)

Bar Salad

Just the other night, in a restaurant whose prices promised a great deal, I received a plate of salmon so barely broiled it looked like a raw chop. When I asked the fussy young waiter to take it in for a little heating, saying it was badly underdone, the poor thing's nose twitched and turned up to where the air was better: "But theez feesh iz done in ze French manner." French manner my ass—but I didn't say that. I remembered my assertiveness training, mentioned it looked more like feesh in the Japanese manner, and told him it simply would not do. The bill (which more and more means the punchline) for two, for mushrooms on toast, spinach and truffle pate with no spinach, veal fillet in salt sauce sided by a crunchy but technically turned carrot, my bloody fish, and an $18 bottle of domestic champagne, no salad, no dessert, no coffee, came to $110. We literally ran out the door.

And walking home, because you have to walk just to prove your body still exists after such mortification, we passed maybe half a dozen fruit and vegetable stands. Most of them had three or four people—this was 10 o'clock—picking their late dinner, or maybe tomorrow's lunch, with metal tongs from a salad bar. For a moment I envied them: they were smart. Get a plastic container. You like artichoke hearts? Take all you want. Mushrooms? Plop, plop, plop, dot with baco bits, unravel some bean sprouts, count out summer squash slices, cherry tomatoes, canned baby corn, romaine, broccoli—no, that would be too much—chunky blue cheese dressing, weigh in at $2.79 a pound, add a bottle of Saratoga and a container of fruit salad, $4.85. Add, like the book editor, a can of tuna. Add, like my neighbor, a hunk of cheddar. Add, like both of them, a glass of white California wine.

These salad bars are somebody's dream come true. When I first met writer Ellen Willis, in Southern California in the early '70s, she said she had a wonderful idea for opening a restaurant that would incorporate the cafeteria style with all the quirky appetites she could imagine and still be affordable. You fill bins behind glass, in a line, with strawberries, crackers and caviar, artichoke hearts, chicken livers, any precious little item at all. The customer takes a tray and points: two of these, five of those, and he or she is charged per piece in pluralist heaven. Ellen would not be made fun of, you see, for wanting strawberries and liver on the same plate (she could have waited a few years to have her wish and fashion too). Convenience vanquishes the kitchen.

We've come far in our embrace of salads. They're not new; medieval Italians had 'em, and most early English cookbooks included Salletts with greens we now step on. But until recently Americans have mistrusted salads as foreign food or arranged them with peaches as "girl food." You already know what's changed: the price of meat, the diminishment of gustatory xenophobia, the search for youth, lithe, and jogging. When salad bars stormed hamburger's last stand, the war was won. Or was it?

I don't use salad bars. And when I admitted this quietly to friends, some agreed. But why? All I had was a feeling that I couldn't taste the vegetable I was eating. I saw the vegetable forms, saw them so clearly under the banks of fluorescent lights that I blinked and wondered if they were real. I know the pros and cannot argue. Convenience, convenience, convenience. But I did a mini taste-test, had someone cut up vegetables from a stand in the shape of their vegetables from the bins, and compared them: I could always tell which was which. I know some stands have such high volume that freshness is uppermost, but even so, eating a cut onion or green pepper from most salad bars is like tasting them through a scrim. How does the lettuce stay so fresh-looking (the emphasis on "looking")? Could they possibly be washing it with a solution of antioxidizing hydrogen sulfite, the way so many restaurants do? I'm not a reporter, I just use my mouth.

The other reasons for our negative tropism are more fanciful, so take them as you will. Andrea demands to know why she sees no flies around this food. You can't win with this logic, won't eat salad with flies, won't eat it without. Guy tells me he saw a doorman on lunch break test the open jars of dressing by sticking his nose into them (Guy thinks it's silly anyway to pay for liquid weight). The sneeze-screens in restaurant salad bars are touchy subjects, but they are the law; how many produce salad bars do without them?

My final objection is merely aesthetic. I don't think I can successfully choose articles that compose a pleasing dish. This has nothing to do with skill. The unifying principle of a salad is the tension between absolute freshness of vegetables and fruits—dependent upon season, month, or even week of availability—and their combination. Salads mean location, and "now." The art they contain goes further, playing casual against arranged, tart against bland, acid against oil. The more I consider this—and I know I risk offending good people and palates—the more I think salad bars denature the very idea of salad. This is the way junk food is born.

(7/10/1984)

A Country Full of Italian Restaurants

Communist-governed Bologna is exquisite, entirely walkable, provincial and urbane at the same time in a way no city in the U.S. can ever be. By long-time law, buildings may be painted only a few shades of ochre and tan, so Bologna looks now as it has looked for hundreds of years. Graceful, sometimes florid colonnades cover the sidewalks and punctuate the view to the street; the joke, with some accuracy, has it they were built so the Bolognese could shop in the rain. (Middle-class Bolognese seem obsessed with shopping; I have never seen so many shoe stores in so small a space. Can this be called "consumer communism"?) Our superb host Manuela, who grew up here and received her degree from the hoary University of Bologna, sometimes finds the covered city physically and historically claustrophobic and is excited by what she terms the sweep and modernity of America. We understand, but remain entranced.

Bologna is also considered to be, even by other regionally chauvinistic Italian citizens, the eating capital of Italy. In a country where pleasure at the table takes at least one third of the waking day, this sounds like significant praise.

I think it will be impossible in newspaper length to give any but the roundest view of what eating in a different culture—in Bologna, Rome, Spoleto, Florence, Faenza, and Venice—is like. Information per se is necessary, and tedious: Italian breakfast is coffee and a brioche or *cor-*

233

When is an auto grill a cafeteria? When it's a restaurant
over an autostrade.

netto, lunch lasts sometimes until 3 p.m. because business breaks from 1 to about 4, and dinner is not as late as the guidebooks say but begins at 8 to 10, after the twilight cafe or *birra* is put down.

Generalizations are necessary too, and dangerous. Why, for example, has no one mentioned that Italian food is rife with salt? Not one of the food and travel articles, or my swooningly enthusiastic summaries, have warned me that the meats, fish, and salads especially, will pucker the palate and crack the lips. And can we say this is over-salting? Perhaps, freakishly, I ate only in salinophilic restaurants and homes? No. Most likely, the Italian culture is hooked on salt the way American culture is hooked on sugar, and on top of that, American "good cooking" over the past 30 years has diminished its salt so much—for heart's sake and to allow the pallid flavors of our overbred produce to squeak through—that though a '50s tourist may not have noticed Italian saltiness, we certainly do now.

Impressions first? Any impression is forecast by whatever we think Italian food in Italy will be. A country full of Italian restaurants! That's not as silly as it sounds, for it's what we may imagine, as we imagine the ideal forms of pastas, meats, gelati, cafe. You can't have a bad meal in Italy. I heard this over and over and tried to believe it. But of course it's not true—and not only because some meals are not simply good or simply bad. From more than 40 breakfasts, lunches, and dinners in widely various restaurants, trattorias (supposedly simpler), pizzerias, birrerias (beer joints), and homes, wonderful homes, I can say that if you make a graph measuring the "goodness" of a large number of meals, the curve would be the same bell (pepper) shape as the curve of meals in the great U.S., except the peak of the Italian curve would be farther along, would be better.

Impressions. Rome's Pantheon exists to provide a stage for the bars and indoor-outdoor restaurants that surround its piazza. No sidewalk to divorce you from the traffic, just the ancient street stones, the looming past, and waiters. What else do Romans do, on a hot, dark July night, than order porcini mushrooms chopped into fettucine and oil, stirred into the nuggety risotto you've only read about, or broiled alone, quivering in the hot olive oil like some forbidden jellied meat? I followed, on the superhighway (*autostrade*) from Venice to Florence, a large white truck devoted only to porcini. You can have too much porcini, I thought for the first time, and then laughed at the foolishness of that.

Other seasonalities: *fragole di bosco* or pinkie-nail sized wild strawberries, giant raspberries and blackberries. The sweetest, muskiest apricots ever tasted. It goes without saying that a culture which believes the world is plentiful enough to allow you to wait for what's in season will take pleasure in the moment of ripeness. To be fair, I also sampled one tasteless peach and an underripe watermelon—which is a popular fruit.

Another fruit: in almost every bar you can ask for *una spremúta lo pompèlmo,* a glass of freshly squeezed juice of the Israeli grapefruit, or fresh lemon juice, or fresh orange juice. This particular variety of orange results in a liquid much more tart than the candylike Californian, a liquid the color of mangoes and blood. A glass of it proves that this orange's only purpose on earth is to make humans happy.

The bars, which are everywhere, serve coffees, hard and soft drinks in profusion, little sandwiches, sometimes gelati, and if you ask politely, a graceful cooled glass of dry Asti Spumanti. In Florence, amid the best velvet, local elegant folk eat and chat standing up; only Americans and the very tired sit down.

We drove from Rome past a poster of a florid, toqued chef holding a surrealistic platter twice his size filled with roast beef and ringed with vegetables. It advertised the Pavesi "Autogrill," a pun on automobiles and self-service, for this is one of the three or four *autostrade* restaurants, the Howard Johnson's of the modern age. They bridge the road, so they get you coming and going. Each has quite a good bar, a grocery store and "Tourist Shop" (spelled in English), and a cafeteria with salads, pastas, decent cheese, reasonable broiled haunches, and the same sugared summer berries all the trattorias can offer. A three course meal comes to 5000 to 8000 lire, which isn't much for Italians, and for Americans, at 1700 lire to a dollar, is a guilty gift.

(8/7/1984)

Memories of Things Pasta

Invention is half of great cooking; the other half is the unwritten, homey, almost invisible invention over slow time we freeze and call tradition. So what do you do, in a country whose culinary genius is divided into regions, whose culinary secret is the obvious belief—yes, belief— in the "rectitude" of seasonal food, when you wish to invent a new dish and join the international world of contemporary cuisine?

You lighten up, with smaller portions. You use traditional ingredients in new combinations: a warm pigeon "salad" with white beans (the kind you can eat fresh, in season, dressed with oil, in a Florentine trattoria), carrots, lettuce, and herbs in a puckering liver sauce; or tagliatele itself colored pink with tomato, at Florence's cozy and up-to-the-minute restaurant Da Noi. You raid France: sauteed duck breast sitting in a nouvelle puddle of . . . black-olive sauce, sable and delicate, this at Imola's much praised Ristorante San Dominico. Mussolini, by the way, was born in Imola, a town a half-hour's drive from Bologna that looks agricultural but has grown industrial since the end of the war. Ristorante San Dominico is so expensive, we are told, that it is out of the reach of a typical university professor; only foreigners and lieutenants of industry can think nothing of walking in.

One is able to parse the culinary struggle in San Dominico's duck course alone, the breast boned the French way but cooked—we would say overcooked—past the fashionable rose to beige the Italian way, the Italian olives reduced to a superb color but the evanescent taste only a rural memory, the accompanying tablespoon of "potato pie," really scalloped potatoes, hearty in flavor but a modern tease in size. Italy fights France, country fights city, the chef fights the tyranny of the basic flavors he or she must temper in order to transform.

Even in description you can read how "continental" collides with regional Italian in a selection of dishes listed on San Dominico's Italian/English July 12 menu. First courses: back of rabbit in wine jelly, anglerfish mosaic with a fresh tomato sauce, egg-filled raviolo with hazel butter and white truffle. Second courses: composition of Adriatic fishes served in a delicately scented sauce with saffron and carrot, sauteed golden fillet of beef with toasted pine nuts, milk-fed veal kidney with fresh mustard seeds. Desserts: jelly of peach with an almond ice cream, bittersweet chocolate fondant in a vanilla sauce, and, our own popular selection, the cassata (a cake, popular in Emilia-Romagna) with various nuts and candied fruits from the countryside in a fresh raspberry sauce, accompanied by (these are my words) a brilliant mint gelato in which you could taste the moment the leaf was shredded.

One meal isn't enough for criticism, but it is plenty to ruminate. Only rarely in the dozen dishes we sampled that night did the impulse to infuse a primary flavor with secondary ones result in a memorable invention. There was a feeling of spectacular average, though the execution was faultless. Everything looked beautiful on the plate. "A selection of Italy's finest cheeses" included an underripe brie; we did much better with cheeses at the market. The culturally relative raised its head, for my American partner thought the salmon and duck overcooked. We both were surprised at the constant salt; our Italian partner noticed no salt at all.

Ambitious restaurants have other methods to slip off the bonds of traditional or powerful flavor. Bologna's Ristorante Taverna alle Tre Frecce, with three arrows still stuck in its medieval wooden facade (the oldest in the city), took trad recipes and twisted them slightly. A minestrone was coarsely pureed and cooled. A green tagliatele, unusual for Bologna, was sauced with a "ragout" of minced red and green pepper, butter, and herbs. A meatless ragout in Bologna! This was daring, and expressed some wit. It underlined too how difficult it is to reinvent a medium already minimized, protean, and able to incorporate almost all culinary fashion except that which would entail its own elimination. It's no secret, millions know, but I'll add my word anyway: pasta is the apex of Italian eating.

A change of scene: Antella, in the Tuscan kitchen of artists George Woodman and Betty Woodman. We described to them the extraordinary restaurant pasta we'd already sampled: giant tortellini, like deep-sea creatures, serene in a heart-stopping walnut sauce (at Taverna Giulia, a Genovese restaurant in Rome, because Rome "collects" the rest of the country); sweet, downy gnocchi with Gorgonzola, or pesto, or those porcini and oil; pork-filled ravioli brushed with a haunting and unexpectedly lambent sauce of pork drippings and tomato, eaten al fresco in Spoleto (the rest of the meal disappointing). Pasta al dente doesn't mean gritty resistance on the tooth; it means what it should, not overdone. And not once, literally not once, did we receive either fresh or commercial pasta less than perfectly boiled.

Betty reminded me about the gluten in Italian flour, and even though she doesn't obtain the wheat from Antella anymore, she suggested we make pasta right now. You've read how to do it elsewhere; I can add that our egg yolks (from the chickens next door) were the color of the glowing orange jackets roadworkers wear in the rain. Never in my life have I tasted . . . well, I'm stuck, just like the great chefs of Italy, with the task of modifying flavors like that melting basic pasta. It wants saucing, and it taunts the saucer: make me better, I can't be any better than I am.

With that pasta (and a pepper-sauce imitation of Da Noi's, because yellow peppers were so fine in July), we had rabbit prepared the day before by Betty and George's neighbor Margharita Calvelli. This rabbit was raised here, killed here, rubbed with oil from trees outside the window, stuffed with rosemary and sage that are grown here (and salt, Margharita's uninhibited handful of salt). The view from the window? Florence to the right, and everywhere else ideal cypress cones, grown to imitate Renaissance landscape painting, clustered in blossoming olive groves.

Margharita—whom I am now thanking—bakes the bread for the few houses around; my life is better for having tasted her *schiacciata,* a flat loaf fragrant with her olive oil and sparkling with salt. We arose early one morning to watch her assemble a *minestra de pane,* a soup, to be poured on stale bread, made of local onion, cabbage, chard, zucchini, potatoes, basil, parsley, celery, and carrots, cloves optional, brought to a boil in layers, then combined with sieved white beans and boiled three more hours. The television blared in her large, bare kitchen, modern in every way except for the stone fireplace and wooden chair on a platform right beside. If this soup isn't authentic, I could only say, I simply don't know what is.

And I must end with a recipe, given to Margharita Calvelli by a friend. Get out your pencil and your ax, for this is a:

Ricetta del Cinghiale
or, a Recipe for Wild Boar

"Cut it up, and put it in a pan, without any oil to make it lose its water. Skim away the water little by little until the meat is well dried. Put onion in a pan (a lot) chopped very fine and oil and cook until the onion's softened and not brown. Add Cinghiale and brown. When it's almost brown add salt, pepper, rosemary and sage chopped up finely. When it's all well browned, add two or three walnuts, skinned, and crushed with a bottom of a glass (or in a mortar). Crush them, don't chop them. Also two fingers of white wine in the pan and let it evaporate. Then add the tomatoes, cook it with the addition of water or broth. Make it boil very slowly [*piano, piano*] for about two hours."

The walnuts, grown in sight, make the difference.

(8/14/1984)

Artburn?

If I were a museum that served food—I've said this before—I'd offer light but unusual dishes: first, an Oldenburger, a Rauschenburger, a Rothenburger (different meat), and for those who must scrape ketchup off the plate, a Greenburger. Then sandwiches: a Rubens (corned beef, swiss cheese, sauerkraut, grilled), a Francis Bacon (lettuce and tomato), a Frederic Remington (Western sandwich), an Abstract Expressionist ("club" sandwich), a Duchamp (rroast beef on rrye), a Salvador Dali (just ham), a Warhol (soup 'n' sandwich), and a Magritte ("this is not a sandwich"). Appetizers and complete meals would include Keith Herring, Sole Le Witt (or Marisole, or Fischl sticks, or Janet Fish of the day), Veal Parmigianino, Chicken in a Basquiat, and a Caraveggio special with Applebroog Brown Betty and Penck lemonade. In keeping with art world custom, women are half-price.

Why do museums open restaurants while most concert halls do not? Obviously, time is scheduled differently, but still, looking at art shouldn't make us any more hungry than listening to a Shubert quintet (like the "Trout"). Perhaps it's the walking a museum entails, or a synesthetic response to color and form that inclines one toward pate. Maybe—and I'm not kidding here—art creates a need to *buy* something which museumed art can't satisfy, hence the gift shops and restaurants. Maybe art should be as

243

much a part of peripatetic life as eating. Maybe there's money in restaurants.

Everything about the refurbished and expanded Museum of Modern Art makes it more comfortable for the consume . . . for the lover of art. Escalators glide you in style to the style you prefer (now where on 34th Street have I seen escalators like this?), guards tell you which way to enter a room and which way to leave, and lines for movie, I mean film, tickets move smoothly, even at the most popular shows. Best of all, the members-only Restaurant and the everybody-else Garden Café have been granted large, almost gorgeous situations in which to do their stuff. The results are in: sculpture makes food taste better. Even bad sculpture has this effect, on even bad food.

Finally, however, the class worm has turned, for the hoi polloi's vittles at the Café taste livelier and cost less, much less, than the members' victuals upstairs. The new cafe is set up cafeteria style, like the old one, but it doesn't offer its predecessor's hot entrees, which I remember as often burnt, greasy, soggy, steam-table stuff which postwar (WWII) baby boomers associate with the free-form '50s. It's now the '80s, and MOMA's almost caught up. These cafeteria trays are surfaced in black rubber, with cut corners so four trays puzzle together at one table. You may place on them romainish salads, a soup, a few good sandwiches, pastries, elegant bottlettes of iced white and unadjusted red French *vin de table*. Sometimes the staff, always friendly, seems new or puzzled, as when, after a ham and cheese sandwich, not on the menu but visibly possible, was requested, the sandwich chef placed the cheese on top of the top piece of bread.

For the most part, MOMA's Café has copied the "boutique" fingerfood aspect of center-city museums that gained ground during the '70s and holds sway even now: nothing can offend, nothing will excite, and its contempo chrome or (now) black rubber will guarantee that new clothes won't suffer by comparison. And yet, some minor genius made a wonderful decision: the hot dog. You can buy hot dogs, hamburgers, and cheeseburgers, nicely cooked and with satisfying garnish, at a grill in the corner. All the rest of the place reads Cincinnati or L.A., Artland, U.S.A., but the grill reads New York, New York.

Too bad they got no hot dogs upstairs. Now here's a restaurant, and frankly, it's one of the best spaces for a restaurant, with one of the best views, in all of street-level midtown. And that's the secret word: looks. The food looks great, lucky members, yellow blending to red in a chilled corn and red pepper soup, predominant pastels of the curried chicken salad playing over the cubes of fowl and spheres of grape, cold poached salmon sauced in biomorphic green. Everything, appetizers, cold entrees, baked fish, grilled veal chop, poached pear with sabayon and raspberry sauce, creme caramel, goodness gracious, it's all gorgeous.

It tastes like Valium feels.

Except for some perfect Mission figs, not one dish got beyond see level. The chef will be angry with me, I am sure, for not saying exactly how the fish was denuded of flavor or why the grilled chop flopped. Nothing went bad, and no recipe except the aforementioned corn and pepper soup—imagine trying to spoon down cold pink succotash—was entirely ill-conceived, although I hope to never see or taste that green sauce again.

Before the Restaurant opened, MOMA staff was asked to guinea-pig the new menu—at half-price. Generous. The result? Unanimous agreement on its inedibility; that chef, for whatever reason, quit, and things are better: museum members are the permanent subjects now.

(9/11/1984)

Why They Eat: James

Anytime a new restaurant opens you seem to be in it.

Sure. Wouldn't you be? Wouldn't anybody?

No, of course not. Not everyone is so interested in food.

Well I don't really believe that, but okay, it just so happens that I don't feel alive unless I know what's going on in the food world.

Can you tell me how you got this way?

You think I'm obsessed, but most people don't take anything seriously enough, anything at all. Food and cooking are the most basic, most important . . . no, I'm not gonna convince you, I shouldn't have to. You wanna know how I got "this way"? Can't you tell?

Your parents?

I was adopted. My mother was a frankly mediocre cook but we always had dinner on the table on time, and on weekends my father made something he considered special, steamers, lobster, tuna salad, nothing fancy but perfectly good. They wanted me to go to college, but other than that they figured I would choose my own direction.

My brothers knew what they wanted as soon as they realized it wasn't hard to make money as long as you had a little to start with and nothing much else on your mind. I read all the college pamphlets and liked the idea of doing something with my hands. I tried Pratt for a year, for graphic design, but switched to the Cuisinary Institute after a girlfriend of mine mentioned that her brother, who had graduated two years before, just received a review in the New Jersey edition of *The New York Times*. It all came clear to me at the institute, how terrifically important cooking is, and how difficult it can be to prepare food for other people. Now when I think of my mother, I imagine her running a restaurant for five, three times a day, almost every day of the week—and for no money. I never would have let Dad mess up my kitchen, either.

What happened at the institute?

The only stuff I wasn't interested in was the mechanics of opening my own place; I'll leave that to my brothers. But everything else! Did you know how important marketing is to cooking? Where you have to go for herbs, for decent shrimp? Can you taste the differences among unpasteurized creams? I can, now. I became a chef. I can't really call myself a chef, I should be a cook, but I know that with the right work and in the right kitchen I can manage with the best of them. I would make it the right kitchen because that's what I do better than anyone. I'd make it hum, I'd harmonize it.

So where have you worked?

Hmm. First at the Restaurant X in Soho. It was terrible, the chef cut his butter with margarine and his cream with half 'n' half, so I quit.

You quit your first job?

If you don't quit your first job, you'll never get your second, which was in a much better place. I was sous chef. I was fired, though, for being too even-tempered for a chef, even an underchef. I was too nice to everybody, especially the waiters.

Have you tried waitering?

I'll never be a waiter. I couldn't stand being so close to the food. Now I'm driving a cab. A fare once offered me a job on stage, in the chorus, but that's not for me.

So instead you're what, an eater?

I'm just keeping up with my profession the way any serious professional would. Let me tell you how I do it. I drive almost 14 hours a day, but I take my breaks and sleep-time before dinner. On my off-day I make a list of the week's restaurants I have to check out and call in my reservations that same afternoon—that way I'll know enough in advance if a place is booked up. I don't ever want to be without a restaurant. I use my real name. After I'm done, an hour before I start work, I go back to my room and take notes.

Can you really do this on a cabbie's income?

You think I'm kidding? Look how I'm dressed; I have one good outfit, and only because I need it. It's lasted nine years. I live in a goddam fleabag in order to pay for this. Actually, I get a kick out of taking cabs from the hotsy-totsy places and watching their faces as they realize where I'm getting out. I don't spend my money on anything but restaurants. If you liked them as much as I did, neither would you.

Do you ever take anyone else?

[He acts as if he doesn't hear.]

Does anyone go with you to dinner?

No, I, uh, wouldn't have time. They wouldn't get *why* I'm doing it. It's not necessary to have anyone else, not necessary at all.

This is one of an occasional series.

(9/18/1984)

Meals on Wheels

Ever since I started to write about food I knew the following memory would make itself appropriate. I don't
know why we were out there, the desolate eastern border
of Nassau County, but once or twice a year Mom drove my
brother and me to a sunny shopping-center lot. We walked
into the one place we knew, sat ourselves on stools lined
around a big rectangle, stools usually filled with "little
kids" (we were seven and nine), and waited until, all of a
sudden, it came out of the back, loaded with hamburgers
and cheeseburgers: a Lionel train! It puffed smoke from
smoke pellets, and occasionally delighted the unwary with
a wheezy electric whistle. "Don't get excited," my mother
said. Can you imagine, don't get excited. What I didn't understand, and still don't, is how the conductor knew where
to stop. I wanted more than anything in the world to *grab
the burger as it passed,* I didn't care whose it was, but I
was a good boy and would have been mortified to eat
"someone else's food."

Does anyone out there remember this bubble of the
'50s? It may have been named something sensible, like
"Hamburger Express," but a little-boy voice assures me it
was really called "Hamburger Choo-Choo."

Dine-O-Mat, a seemingly adult bubble from the '80s,
has opened on Madison Avenue to serve the lower Manhattan department store crowd. Before I get excited, let me
explain what it attempts. Someone, maybe a graduate of

one of New York's tandem culinary-business schools, figured that profit could be made with reasonably priced,
small portions of chic New American food—if turnover
was high (I mean customer turnover, not apple). So this
virgin entrepreneur thought: fast food with class, where in
history do I turn? The cafeteria, the automat, dim sum? I
need something novel, I need a gimmick . . .

Walk through the postmodern deco door, take a look
and stare drop-jawed as saucer after saucer of fashionable
but (therefore) not immediately recognizable food passes
by, quivering on its slightly tremulous conveyor belt. (At
this point, my editor is excited. Where do you sit, he wants
to know, where's the belt in relation to the counter, does the
food get cold in transit, do you—and this is more to the
point—take a dish you want, eat it, and grab another when
you're done, or do you fill your tray with everything and
eat all at once, or one by one, or . . .)

Stop. When you walk into Dine-O-Mat and sit down, no
one tells you, nothing tells you, how to organize your appetite. The belt resembles that in a Japanese restaurant
nearby and many others in Japan, moving food at arm's
reach, below eye level, slowly enough to allow temptation
but quickly enough to withdraw it if you don't make up
your mind. Some plates are evenly spaced, some bunched,
but at lunch-time they march, march, march like colorful
soldiers out of the kitchen window, and inexorably back
again. Only selections to be eaten lukewarm make the
rounds; at closing time, salads look footsore and marinated eggplant accrues sepia tones.

All Dine-O-Mat's customers, a sophisticated, restaurant-
wise lot, are left hanging for just a moment, not knowing

how to play. Watch them—yourself—in this free time. Can I touch the food? Does that make it "mine," and will I have to pay? Could I steal a piece? What if I grab every single dish I like? A fantasy of infant power wipes across cool, middle-aged faces: for as soon as you choose and remove your little pile, another appears. Cornucopia is always full: only gods can do this.

But children, there are some rules (for it's a game). Menus on the wall divide selections into soups, salads, cold food, hot specials, desserts, and drinks. Prices are coded by the hue of the plate; almond a dollar, rose $1.50, gray $2.50, and black $3.50. Color, therefore, equals cost; this consumer equation, which provides almost everyone with a burst of confused pleasure, begins the process that makes Dine-O-Mat more interesting than its food. Because you must assemble a meal without immediate guidance, Dine-O-Mat forces you to question the assumptions upon which "meals" are made.

Although the middle-class, three-course Western restaurant meal didn't shape up in the form we know it until the 20th century, its elements were seeded hundreds of years earlier. Look what we assume now: that dinner will proceed in linear fashion with small course, big course, then small course, savory, bland, sweet; hot or cool, hot, cool; no mix of fish and meat in the entree—it's easy to go on. Of course variations to these rules are common, are invented as we eat, but a variation is defined by the invisible, assumed structure that generates it. The structure itself changes over time, thank goodness.

In the first weeks, Dine-O-Mat arranged its list of two dozen offerings not as soups, salads, entrees, desserts, the usual cues to how you should eat, but according to the color-code; all the rose items in one column, all the black in another. It didn't work; no one knew what to eat first. But we had three meals . . . not meals, I mean eating times, before they switched over, and can tell you that the freedom to have sweets first (as some Renaissance Italians did), to follow with green salad with crunchies and garlic dip, to combine fried strips of Mississippi catfish and wasabi mayonnaise with lamb ribs and honey mustard on the same tray, or most shocking, to begin and end with the same item, the same apple-onion hush puppy or mocha fudge cake, as a delicate reprise, well, this exhilarated us the way only basic rule breaking can.

From these exploratory maneuvers I learned how deeply engraved course habits really are. We couldn't compute calories, or even recount with any ease what we ate, or in what order. Sometimes we jammed three or four selections on a tray at once; another time, with equal appetite, we spaced them out in such a way that it took hours to finish (not endearing customer behavior at this, or any, restaurant). I realized for the first time that it isn't the particular type of course pattern that helps us measure our meals, but its regularity, its dailiness.

Portion size didn't help. The amount of crayfish jambalaya salad on a Dine-O-Mat plate fits no preconceived idea of fancy food: slightly too much for an appetizer and too little of a main dish for either lunch or dinner. Two of 'em? It's "wrong" to double: taking two of the same "main dishes" cues piggishness, and there's an odd nausea that comes from backing up, as it were, and starting again. The only portions we recognize as typical '80s are desserts and apple-cabbage-onion slaw; even sandwiches, such as the excellent lukewarm chicken barbecue salad on cornmeal bread, have been copied in Dine-O-Mat xerox at 80 percent. It's not so important to me whether or not this is a business "mistake": the portion anomaly throws the conventions of portioning into welcome relief.

Dine-O-Mat the restaurant, as opposed to Dine-O-Mat the idea, has chickened out of any relationship to pure form. They "menued" the menu. "Hot specials" must be ordered specially, as must desserts with whipped cream. Snooty booths far from the conveyor belt supplement stools, those solipsizing/democratizing symbols of Edward Hopper's America. If you sit at a booth, the whole edible kinetoscope disappears. Recipes vary in execution—this is high-food talk—but since you can look at many offerings before you taste, it may be novel to let your eyes be your critic. I especially enjoyed the blueberry shortcake, prosciutto and sausage strudel, and the soft-shell crab, in that order, and one after another.

Dine-O-Mat would, I think, offend the French to their very bones, if it didn't also fascinate them as a predictably American monster—half speed, half pretension. I can easily imagine, looking through the window, all the stools occupied with Levi-Strausses and Derridas, the former methodically stacking up roses and blacks, the latter shutting their eyes and swiping the first plate that comes by. Their essays on Dine-O-Mat would appear a year later, first assembling, then deconstructing, the structure of the urban American meal.

(10/23/1984)

Tearoom Trad

Recipes die. They are mourned tersely in cookbooks, feelingfully in memories, falsely in nostalgia. Nostalgia kills memory because it replaces what's true; when you *want* to believe something, you'll eat anything and think it Mother's Best. Her real mashed potatoes never stand a chance.

I would take advantage of the opportunity to meet recipes that are on their last legs, at least before someone attempts a regional resurrection of dated food that isn't yet cold. You can still find spoonbread and fried weakfish at the Chalfonte Hotel in Cape May, but otherwise the news isn't good. The soda fountain in Bigelow's on Sixth Avenue has gone the way of marble slabs eroded by dishrags and elbows. Lunch counters in our beloved Woolworth's, linear paeans to grilled cheese sandwiches and malted milk, have only a few months left. When Madison Avenue's New York Exchange for Woman's Work shut down a few winters ago, that was it for the particular kind of middle-class ethnic cooking called "women's"—except nearby, at Mary Elizabeth's.

We have no way of knowing if Mary Elizabeth's is the last of the restaurants in which food has gender. Though female, its behavior is bisexual, attracting both men and women, young and old, to lunch at table, to order soup and sandwich downstairs, or to dip nutmegged plain or sugar-cinnamoned crullers into coffee at the Cruller Bar. The potential for destructive nostalgia is so great here that I want to face it head on and get it out of the way: doilies, pinkies, creamed butter, aprons, mint, relishes, embroidery, coconut, gloves.

Even the facts waver. The menu says Mary Elizabeth's was founded in 1910, a newspaper says 1903, a former owner says 1908. Art director Barbara Richer had once wanted to do a book about Mary Elizabeth's, and over lunch (East Indian Shrimp Curry for her, Shrimp Salad on Our Freshly Baked White Bread for me) she told me the restaurant was named after one of Fanny Riegal Evans's three daughters—and not the one named Fanny. The father of this genteel family, a Welsh musician, apparently left them to fend for themselves somewhere near Syracuse, New York. And so they did, making candy. At one point they opened a teashop in Newport, Rhode Island, with a floor so damaged that when customers appeared the women hired the son of an undertaker to come in and stand over the hole. (If this story doesn't illustrate all the parameters of the apocryphal, I don't know what does.) Their tearoom in New York has moved a few times, once to the ground floor of Alfred Stieglitz's Fifth Avenue gallery "291," and, perhaps finally, to the present 37th Street address in 1938. The head cook, Virginia Drummer, started in 1917 washing pots; she had to stand on a soapbox to reach the sink. Although she threatens to quit, she's still there.

How's your curry? It looked like a camel-colored white sauce that had immobilized five innocent shrimp. Barbara didn't answer, but said that the original recipe was a gift, a secret, from Rabindranath Tagore, the poet. A large, flat tray of condiments was offered, holding salted peanuts, coconut, the dried fishy preparation known as Bombay Duck, and a portion of Major Grey's Chutney, which the restaurant used all through the Depression in spite of cost because it was "the best." I don't know how my shrimp salad could be better, so I commiserated. Its many shrimp in chunks were very likely fresh, not frozen, lightly mayonnaised, bedded in a slightly sweet white bread with a moist crumb. You're wrong: the crust was on.

The problem with evaluating most of Mary Elizabeth's food—aside from the obvious knockouts such as shrimp salad, crullers and cruller holes, cloying but zesty lemon and orange layer cake, and the toasted cheddar sandwich with a bacon bow—is that when something impresses us as bland or lifeless (like the meats in sauces) we don't know if the new owner is cutting corners or the recipe itself is breathing its last. Take the baked spaghetti in tomato sauce with cheese and bacon. You'd have to invent children, if they didn't already exist, to eat food like this: sweet and savory, warm, wriggly, comforting. Kids, by the way, adore this place, and not because they're catered to or seated in plastic cars. So the baked spaghetti tastes like Chef Boy-Ar-Dee? This is what Chef BRD is the pale imitation of! For you adults, they serve "tomato rarebit on toast with fresh herbs," but without the herbs. This rarebit poses the relativity problem and, as you lean back after sucking up every drop, answers it too. As food it's nothing, bad for you, too sugary, no cellulose, and on a cold afternoon you thank God it exists.

You won't be alone here. Much has been made of the career waitresses and their multidecade tenures, but they're also active, obliging, and patient. It's perverse fun to think about "blue-haired old ladies," B. Altman shopping bags permanently at their feet, chewing spoon-dropped codfish balls with dignity these 40 years. However, the lesson is not that some older men and women eat here, but that they are excluded or invisible almost everywhere else. I like to think some one of them would read this, and go to Mary Elizabeth's for tea, for the very first time.

(11/27/1984)

Bring Home the BLT

Oh the new year. Some battles know no anniversary. I recently read, for example, about a West Coast attempt to make a perfect BLT.

Some would say, riding the subway from the office, the Mobil station, the high school auditorium musty with decades of overheated paint, that any BLT is perfect, as long as it's in my hands, still warm, at home. In this reverie, the tension of sandwich preparation begs to be imagined: immediate gratification from eating each strip as it comes sweating from the pan versus the laudibly adult repression involved in timing the toast, slicing the fruit, spreading the white, constructing the edifice, and falling to. If any idea can stand up to a hot strip of bacon, it's the BLT. A BLT "tastes" before it's ever eaten. So, you can understand why I was confused by the news from California, when any BLT is perfect.

Then I thought about it, and slept on it, and thought again. Something fishy is going on, something very like a theft. The perfect BLT, we are told, starts with the perfect pig, raised on the perfect slop (I imagine someone means here free-ranging pigs, tumbling over and munching wild anise and fighting Alice Waters for the best of the basil).

I proposed this to a carful of eating friends, who proposed in turn a pig tank in the window of the Perfect BLT Cafe. Point to the one you want, gloved hands lift it out, and, three months later . . .

Only the innermost leaves of lettuces will be used; if a leaf ever shows its outer side to the air, it will be discarded.

The bread will be made with wheat grown in sight, on land naturally mulched, vivified by water containing all the right minerals and none of the wrong everything else. It will be baked "the same day." It will be sniffed by a white-haired old lady, smiling.

The mayo will always be spelled in full. It must be homemade, never before thunderstorms, with oil pressed from—wait? A conference will be called in 1985 to determine which oil makes the perfect BLT mayonnaise. Then such a source will be grown on land naturally mulched. The oil must be cold pressed. (You *can* taste the dif between cold- and hot-pressed oil. My tailor agrees, just as he can feel the difference between cold- and hot-pressed trousers.) The eggs will come from chickens who ate herbs similar to, but different from, what the pigs ate. They (the eggs) will be both white and brown. They will be equally nonfertilized and fertilized, if the Supreme Court will allow the latter option not to hatch. Eggs already have a perfect shape (Raymond Loewy), so that's taken care of.

Any perfect cook can anticipate what follows, but I should add that the thickness of the bread and the mesquite over which it's toasted will make or break the result. Menu charge should be computed the way all other entrées are priced, factoring in per-hour labor. This BLT is a labor-intensive sandwich, which should make it popular.

The absurdity doesn't bother me, because great art rises from the absurd. However, someone is having his or her sandwich plucked from his or her hands with only an oily smear left. Once, everyone could claim a BLT. New Yorkers thought their coffee shops invented it, Floridians loved the way it complements juice, Ohioans could imagine they were east or south, and Iowans could claim the pig. Only Californians were lost: the best tomatoes (the most, at any rate), a glut of bacon, fastest toasters in the west, and it didn't taste right. Too New York. There was once a lunch-eonette on Melrose where the BLT was second nature, but it's gone the way of all fresh.

Any class (and most religions) could claim the generic BLT. And this is California's revenge: they are stealing the sandwich from those who have always owned it—most of us. When you make the perfect BLT, all others become versions. You can argue the versions, complain about the fancy-pants organic one here or the whole wheat mutation there, but the true nature of the sandwich has been threat-ened, its ability, whatever the realization, to stand for unqualified satisfaction. The BLT is a perfectly vital meta-phor for the egalitarian potential of this country, and it's under attack.

An elite appetite has done this; it's a skirmish in a famil-iar war. This little one we can win, though, win it so thor-oughly we can even go to this silly restaurant, order their abysmal geegaw, down it in 30-second pleasure, and ask for another. "One BLT never fills me up." Aren't we enti-tled, in BLT terms, to as much as we want? Why not this year?

(1/8/1985)

Rich Food

A couple is shown to a table at one of the art-parasitic restaurants in the new East Village. Her preworn fur, retrogressing into skins, is back-door Fendi, and her Gladstone bag could have been handled by its eponym, but, no matter, she looks up-to-date, whatever the date. The bag goes on the floor.

Another couple comes in, rejects the table they're shown, and looks around the room (two can "look" as if they were one) for a spot that would suit. They decide, throw their coats over the extra chair between tables, and after an odd five minutes of no menu reading and no talk, sweep up their things and leave. Has the restaurant offended? Is it beyond their means?

As the first two get ready to divvy up, she sees that her bag is unclasped. Her wallet is gone.

In the last month this has happened twice to people at my table, and the *Voice* has received calls from others who, it is likely, were robbed in this way. I've wanted to tack a warning on the end of my column, but it might shout louder as a lead. Also, I realized that this modus operandi, if increasing, is not unrelated to something that's been on my eating mind for some time.

The clientele of New York restaurants is changing drastically. I have no data-laden proof of this, but since I've been eating around New York City almost every evening since 1977, and eating professionally around the country

263

since 1971, I trust my impressions. The feeling began about five years ago, when I started to receive letters about the cost of eating out. I had blamed inflation: 10 years before (1970) we found $5 to $10 dinners in mid-range restaurants, and in 1980 the price had risen to $15 to $20. I had predicted the median would hit $25 to $30 in another five years. Well, it has, and surpassed that: those who still care for more than one course—in other words, those who wish to eat without thinking about money—must be prepared to peel off two Jacksons, or his plastic equivalent, at the very least.

But Carter wasn't reelected; hasn't inflation let up? Perhaps we shouldn't have assumed milk-and-butter inflation was the culprit; uncontrolled rents, for example, affect cost of operation severely. And high menu prices reflect something else. A few years ago, market logic dictated that fewer and fewer of us would be able to eat out. Cafes would shut their doors all over town, and I'd be forced to give up my column and take a real job. Logic doesn't work, however, in a city whose "us" became potentially more and more a "them."

We have no hard information about the number of people who are implicated in the urban restaurant boom. As usual, booze and business lunches float restaurants into the black, but entrée prices have risen to the highest level the city's glossiest stratum, the mayor's walking tax bases, can comfortably afford. It could be that even if more tables are occupied more frequently, fewer *different* people are able to taste tomorrow's green chili mousse. That is my impression: fewer young families, fewer singles from the boroughs (except at purveyors of the frozen margarita), fewer under-30-thou professionals, fewer blacks, fewer Latins, fewer single women. The superficial corollaries: more ties and jackets, more dresses, more dirty looks from maitre d's than I have seen in many a year.

Some of this could be cultural swing, certainly, a long, dead reaction to the denim and turtleneck '60s. But culture, as we should know by now, always uses the mirror of money to put its makeup on. Ultimately the restaurant boom incorporates simple economics: prices eliminate pluralism, the apple of New York's eye. So, in spite of hysteria to the contrary, we're not seeing an expansion of interest in restaurants; we're seeing a consolidation of interests, and a possible decline.

This is why I've been reviewing so many "expensive" restaurants: even the cheap ones are expensive. Truly inexpensive places, the ones that haven't closed, have been reviewed to death if they're any good or are forced to relinquish ideas—the creative cooking that makes food worth reading—to the dim exigencies of bottom line. I relish exceptions to this, and search for them constantly, but I shouldn't have to tell you that pickins are slim.

I had wanted, as well, to mention the effect that this progressively homogeneous clientele has on eating out, but I don't know how. You can't criticize a crowd, exactly, just because that crowd excludes others, or you. They may be nice people—*you* may be nice people. There never was a golden age of eating out, but the excitement I remember of placing a reservation, falling into a new menu, looking around at a random shuffle from the human deck all gabbing and waving our latest fork-finds in the air, has attenuated and changed. With so many restaurants from which to choose, with active experimentation in so many kitchens, I feel surrounded, paradoxically, by a herd. When people look alike (and money helps people look alike), it's easy to believe they eat alike, think alike, even if they don't. Terrible thoughts.

So it's no surprise that even those with just a fiver and subway fare in their wallets get ripped off. Only the rich eat in restaurants, everybody knows that.

(2/19/1985)

Home Sweet Home

The late O.O. McIntyre, Columnist, says: the Best Fried Chicken Dinner I Ever Ate was at KING'S TROPICAL INN . . . Have just had an Elegant Meal at the famous Home Dairy Restaurant, the largest and best appointed restaurant in the United States . . . State Cafe, the Most Sanitary Restaurant in the City . . . The Best Ventilated Restaurant in Chicago . . . When in Winchester don't fail to see this mirror in the METROPOLITAN RESTAURANT, it is the only one of its kind in the United States. Value $7000 . . . the Most Unique Dining Room in California . . . Southern Arizona's Most Attractive Rendezvous . . . Your order of OYSTERS A LA ROCKEFELLER since 1889 when this dish was concocted by Jules Alciatore at The Restaurant Antoine is number *1277165* . . . The Longest Lunch Counter in the World . . . 200 Waitresses, All with 200 Smiles . . . World's Largest Seafood Restaurant, Seating Capacity Three Thousand Two Hundred . . . Serves 5000 meals daily in a tropical Spanish atmosphere . . . Fine food served amidst living tropical plants . . . The food is world famous, as MILLIONS of patrons can testify . . . The charm of the old world in a new world setting, and where HOLLYWOOD begins!

I could go on. If this were America before or between the Wars, I would go on, and on. We may be understandably ashamed of the baldness of it now, but America once had something, or stood for something, that no one else had, or stood for. You ask what? No one knows exactly what, but whatever it was, it was more than anyone else, and first. It was clean. It was in italics, in capitals, in bold-face, all at the same time. It was worth going to, then worth staying at, and finally worth dying for, again and again.

Five men own America, which seats only 500. Whether they intended to or not, perhaps even against their better instincts, they have created the most American restaurant I've seen in years. Please don't assume it's the food. Concentration on the quality of cooking, the so-called aesthetic criterion, is not American but bastardized French. Our defensive deference to the gourmet, the reluctant bow to Europe from our regional waist, is American too, but this isn't the America we particularly love, the America of the whale's spout, the gusher, the cheer.

America, on 18th Street, is gross. Its ambition, its size, even its mediocrity, is gross. It tosses every regional and pop-'50s resurrection it could profitably think of into its prairie-pink menu: the fashionable grilling, the giggly alligator oddity, the ridiculous pasta primavera, the phony-nostalgic iceberg lettuce, the sushi, the Hangtown fry, the Yoo Hoo. Taken seriously, the menu is an insult to the quiet meal; taken seriously another way, the menu is a symptom of culinary history, of the meaning of history to an aggressive restaurateur: an open field free to plunder. Hungry customers, not used to pastiche at dinner, scan the menu, put it down, pick it up again. Shall we start with ham scrapple or duck pate? Sourdough pancakes, egg foo yung, or four-cheese pizza? Sopaipillas, grilled pineapple with "raw wildflower honey," or Death by Chocolate?

(My review? I ate too much, or too many. As in life,

stick to the basics, like hamburger, grilled fish, or steak, otherwise you'll probably be sorry. This is the only place I know that serves black beans—alongside almost everything—al dente. Get drunk if you like, have fun. Think how interesting that the orders come out accurate and reasonably hot.)

America makes you fight to get your table; this breeds strength. Many folks come to cruise at the split-level bar, so on weekends management plants a bouncer on the steps outside to field the diners from the trash. This young man is a prick. Oh, pardon me, I mean he doesn't seem to know that a few innocents approaching the entrance actually wish to be greeted and fed. Can you eat in a disco? Isn't this a disco?

But once you show proper servility and push open the tall doors, you're met by a space, a volume, from the past. A Red Sea of oaken tables, white linen, slatwood chairs is cleaved by an aisle to the bar and Olympic skylight above. Statue of Liberty and fighter plane: American history in dumb pastel. Overall, an elysian hum. Never mind what we look like, as if a tube funneled underground from 59th Street and Lex to here. We sound busy, democratic. Gargantuan restaurants at the turn of the century, feeding a new middle class infatuated with department stores, electric lights, and their own gaudy figures, sounded this way. Low-ceilinged shore restaurants of the '20s, kitchens like metallic hell, sounded this way. Frenchman and Frenchwomen are aghast; Japanese, no strangers to number, are repelled by the scale. We don't care, it's another storybook image of the city's promise. Those with $200,000 condo studios for homes, mousehole work stations for offices, and VCR living rooms for Roxys or Radio Cities, stretch your eyes.

Food needn't die here. They could cut the menu viciously with a red pen and provide items that correspond spiritually to the din: oysters, clams, lobsters, shrimp (from one place, not three), chicken, steaks, roasts, burgers, mashed pot, corn, soft beans, tamales, pies, puddings, fruit, wines, beers, ice cream, perhaps reflecting in recipe some of the demographic spread this age requires. These needn't be gourmet "great": they shouldn't be. They should only be the best the kitchen can simply do, the largest portions, the lowest price. Will the result, a more uniform national memory, cost out? That's the risk, but if a restaurant called America can't take risks, it might as well fold its tent and go home.

(4/9/1985)

Why They Eat

I have been asked to do a "sociological analysis" that would explain why yuppies of all ages eat what they do. This, however, is dangerous. If I dare to write that the typical yuppie—a redundancy if I ever heard one—eats this or that, the typical yuppie in real life, being what he or she is, will hear what I have written from a friend who reads, and then go out and demand to be fed what I said. This contemporary phenomenon, media analysis as promotion of product, is usually associated with another of the Murdoch magazines, not the *The Village Voice*. We must be extremely cautious.

There have been yuppies in the past, but they were older, a sparkling middle class that flocked to the festive public spaces—department stores, amusement parks, and restaurants—erected just for them. They lived in the city or across the rivers, in the first suburbs. The postcard reproduced here, of Churchill's restaurant on Broadway and 49th Street in 1913, pictures this ruddy crowd, most of whom weighed more than typical yuppies today, although they were much shorter. At the arrow, left, you will see a younger and thinner version of the animated folk around him. He doesn't look happy, exactly, but he knows he's dressed properly and has no question he's in the right place. This is the first yuppie.

New York yuppies today have moved back from suburbs as far away as Dallas, although most rejuvenated city cen-

The first yuppie.

ters train their own. There's no need to describe their appearance or behavior, the way they stop in the middle of the sidewalk oblivious to whom they block, for example, unless it applies to their feeding habits in restaurants. We may be acquainted with some very nice and well-mannered individual yuppies, but the only time you see them verifiably alone is when they are trying to decide between spinach and watercress, "that big green one or the little green one," at a Korean salad bar on an evening they must eat at home, for work reasons, by themselves.

It's no secret that yuppies choose restaurants that are already broken in by relatively small—fewer than 10 at a time—expeditionary yuppie bands (can we read the menu, will we be outnumbered?), but the food at these favored restaurants falls into only two categories: pepper and nostalgia. I should say right off that just because yuppies like a restaurant, it doesn't mean the cooking is bad. Gulf Coast, for example, still serves excellent grilled swordfish and rich shrimp gumbo to all comers, and the Great Jones Cafe continues to blacken its doorstep with some of the sweetest redfish in town. But I'm getting ahead of myself.

The pepper theory falls into two subcategories. (1) Yuppies like anything with chiles or cayenne—hence Mexican and faux Cajun—because yuppies are so bland themselves that they need the heat, the burning sensation on the lips and in the sinuses, to "break through" and signal where they are at the moment or remind them where they were the night before. Of course, the "bland" metaphor makes this thesis attractive, but it falls apart as soon as you ask why yuppies avoid Szechuan, Thai, and Indian food like the subway. The answer lies in the next possibility . . .

(2) Native New York yuppies were served Szechuan takeout by their parents, so these parents could attend rent strike meetings or lengthy foreign films. Their neo-baby boomers therefore became hooked on pepper and black beans but associated the paper-carton cuisine itself with political and ethnic liberalism. To be desirable to them now, anything hot must be geographically American, or potentially so. Mexican food, if you call it Southwestern, fits the bill perfectly. Wasn't Mexico once Texas? Mexican food, by the way, is the only food that's native and "native"—American and foreign—at the same time, which opens up whole worlds of bad behavior and racial condescension to the yuppie eater. And since we all know the general state of Mexican cooking in New York, where lava and sand (beans and rice) overwhelm variously named and protein-filled rubber bags, jalapeno-aroused yuppies needn't worry about what's right and what's wrong to order. They need not worry about anything at all.

Some analysts, even some restaurateurs, explain the yuppie attraction to restaurants like Memphis and America and dishes such as mashed potatoes, pot roast, and rice pudding by attributing to these lost souls a genuine, if herdlike, anomie, one that can be assuaged only with generous dollops of E.T.'s (remember?) plaintive cry: home. Restaurant menu-makers, caught between the Scylla of trend-spotting and the Charybdis of costing-out, have more and more taken to anticipating their clientele's memories. A menu of memories would seem to preclude inventiveness in the kitchen, but no one has had the nerve to ask, actually ask, a yuppie what food he or she is nostalgic for: no one, that is, but me. They're supposed to remember cherry Coke? "Cherry coke, isn't that virgin snow?" It's simple, really: the only "foods" yuppies feel nostalgia for are still around, like Tab. Yet the yuppie, in the insecurity that's the flip side of dull arrogance, will darkly conjure up someone else, someone better, someone born of a real mom who baked real strawberry-rhubarb pie, and wonder why he himself or she herself was cheated. Self-knowledge lies in this direction, so they segue to their usual business mode, that of the pecking order. Our bosses are nostalgic for this stuff, they imagine, so I guess we are too. Conformity is the goad to false nostalgia.

The nostalgia/conformity paradox confounds ambitious chefs, because even though yuppies are known never willingly to place in their mouths anything they've never placed in their mouths before, and would starve in certain international situations, they are also aware that they shouldn't drop in on a restaurant unless it's the culinary "place to be." Our presently vivacious American Regional Pudding Cuisine, from the soggy fried chicken at Memphis to America's gritty Tupelo catfish fillet, can claim its own valid raisons d'etre, some of them unconnected to Reaganitic xenophobia, but it's no accident that the food-timid yuppie is paving and paying American Regional's way. Dream-whipped mashed potatoes are the yuppie's Everest: because, for the time being, they're there.

With all these theories, something a server told me may be all that remains to be said: "Yuppies order food, pay for it (sometimes), but they don't eat it." The women pick at their Cajun Popcorn or grilled alligator sausage but the boy-men don't even raise a fork. Last week, at the restaurant reviewed elsewhere in these pages, 18 yuppies em-

JAMES HAMILTON

Yuppie food

ployed by national network television arranged five tables and proceeded to terrorize the small staff and most of the artiste-manque customers, themselves no strangers to self-centered noise. The males began to bellow and roll their chairs into ours—the chairs have wheels—bumping, Coney Island-style, whoever was sitting in their way. They never ordered, not that I could see; one hour, two hours, three hours passed.

But they ate. They held their food by the neck, held tight, until one or another of them slumped to the floor. That, the prone end of the meal, is how you know what a yuppie eats and when a yuppie is well fed.

(4/16/1985)

In Ulster, Among Sconces
and Scones

I said, "I'm going to write about what's considered the best bed and breakfast, and best restaurant, in Ulster County."

"Can you give me some idea of what's identified with, uh, Ulster County?" our editor-in-chief asked.

"Nothing."

I meant to be funny, playing the Manhattan chauvinist as is expected, but my own editor turned beet red. He, I should have remembered, weekends in Ulster County. He could not, however, successfully answer the question on the floor.

"We can call it 'The Best Restaurant in the Catskills'"—editor-in-chief.

"It isn't the Catskills, that's Sullivan County"—almost everyone.

"It's better my way."

There are those who were born to visit country inns. Were I one (a visitor, not an inn), I would probably be as thrilled to stay at Capt. Schoonmaker's 1760 Stone House, on Route 213 in High Falls (914-687-7946), as the readers of the many articles and guidebooks that have included it on their "gracious and intimate" lists no doubt are, or will be. High Falls has a high waterfall and a little gurgling one, the latter providing great natural beauty and white noise behind the big stone house and little stone house that make up this hospitable bed and breakfast. These houses are very old, smelling of scented soap, and comfortable as age allows. You do share a bath. The cost is $55 a night for a couple; travelers are not expected to travel alone.

Your hosts are real people named Sam and Julia Krieg, whose vocation it is to be friendly. Julia remembered my first name the moment she heard it, and repeated it many times to let me know; I found out later that Julia and Sam don't forget anyone's name, at least until a party leaves and the next comes in. I think there must be an innkeeper's school for this, or a mnemonic device. It's disconcerting, John said afterward, to hear your name a half a dozen times at nine o'clock in the morning.

This is when breakfast is served, and no later. "If people came when they wanted, I'd be cooking all day," a laughing Julia explained. The dining room was filled with pewter, maple, overshot, samplers, and about 18 upper-middle-class citizens, each with a different first name.

Julia confided the night before that we'd be having "something quichelike with broccoli," and indeed we did, topped with strips of bacon. Julia's fragrant bread was so hot that Julia couldn't get the knife through it: the loaf squooshed like a pillow. Tongues warmed with excellent coffee and with Julia's prodding, which was how we found out (from Carlos) that the nearby shores were lined with injured folks who had bumped their backsides tubing down the falls; from Alice that they couldn't see the Capt. Schoonmaker sign from the road at night and drove back and forth for an hour; and from Julia herself that many foolish midnight visitors bother the 90-year-old cottager down the lane who had no lights on, asking if there was room at the inn.

Julia bakes. Julia brought out a blueberry danish, delicious. Next Julia presented a fruit strudel with coconut, which only a few of the sated survivors also tried. And then, Julia hefted around a large, iced cake the color of beaver pelt. I thought this was a joke (it was Sunday, 9:35 a.m.) and I offered my opinion that the cake was really plaster of Paris, because no one would have room to find out. Although this was meant as a compliment, you do not call a chocolate, peanut butter, and marshmallow cake "plaster of Paris" in front of its creator.

Julia rebounded immediately and took the opportunity to tell a cake story of her own, about the time, on Sam's birthday, she had the town baker prepare a sponge cake with a real sponge in it. Julia and family then got Sam drunk on three martinis. First Sam tried to blow out the candles, but they had bought those candles that you can't blow out ("you should have seen him huff and puff!"). And when he tried to cut the cake! Julia finished with a coda about another cake with a dishrag inside, at which point it was time to leave.

The couple across from us, a doctor and lawyer from Manhattan, had asked Julia the night before where to eat, and she had recommended the comparatively newish 1797 Depuy Canal House in High Falls (914-687-7700), which was famous, I was told, because it had received four stars from the *Times*. Tom and Kim loved their seven-course meal, which had taken three and a half hours.

"They even had popcorn in the salad," said Kim, the lawyer, a lovely person who kept up on her food. So, that evening, after a look at the menu handily provided by Sam, we went.

The Canal House sits, surrounded by mournful willows, next to a dramatic defunct canal. I think the canal's walls are made of cement; natural cement was first found or invented in this country in nearby Rosendale circa 1820. (It is claimed that hamburgers were found or invented last century in upstate New York as well.) Boats were weighed and tariffs levied in canal houses; this stately building has become a restaurant full of things to look at. In fact, we were urged to tour and watch diners at their wooden tables on planked floors. We were urged also to visit the kitchen, which was more up-to-date (a blackboard read "Cause Without a Rebel"), although it wasn't clear, from the stares of the staff, that we were entirely welcome.

The menu is not Early American. It offers courses a la carte (appetizers at $10, entrees at $25), a limited three courses at $30, and seven courses at $42. These are, we thought, Late American prices. Have you ever eaten Cockles Empal with coconut under sconces? Chef and owner John Novi, who recited the menu, explained that this was an Indonesian dish, though he didn't know, after being asked, where his fresh cockles came from. We were offered, among many other dishes on a menu that changes, "Peach Belini [sic] Harry's Bar," a champagne cocktail converted by the chef to a soup; pheasant rillette with toast points; "Zakuska of Haddock Timbal w/American Sturgeon Caviar on Red Pepper Hull Sauce and Served w/Russian Peppered Caviar" (a post-Revolutionary attempt at dentente); tuna in puff pastry with grilled radicchio and balsamic seaweed sauce; rare mallard duck breast and pate of New York foie gras with either a "Vincent Price Cognac Sauce or Linganberry [sic] Port Glace" for $5 extra.

Bread was served on individual wooden boards.

If you go, may I suggest that you read Craig Claiborne's review on the wall of the bar before you are seated. He loved the place, called it the best of what roast beef country cooking should be. Why, they even browned the edges of the review for authentic effect . . . or is it brown because these four, often-quoted stars are dated 1970? Of course, when you're among history, 15 years is like yesterday, and popcorn in the salad doesn't mean a thing.

(8/13/1985)

Restaurant Row

Again consider how often you see young men in knots of perhaps half a dozen, in lounging attitudes, rudely obstructing the sidewalks, chiefly led in their little conversations by the suggestions given to their minds by what or whom they may see passing in the street, men, women, and children whom they do not know and for whom they have no respect or sympathy. There is nothing among them or about them which is adapted to bring into play a spark of admiration, of delicacy, manliness, or tenderness. You see them presently descend in search of physical comfort to a brilliantly lighted basement, where they find others of their sort, see, hear, smell, drink, and eat all manner of vile things.

Some things never change, for I have made these descents myself. Frederick Law Olmsted's prescription (the above from an 1870 paper called "Public Parks and the Enlargement of Towns") for the disease of urban existence was a park. His parks would be of easy access to all classes, well integrated with the cities they salved. They would purify the air and filter the anxiety created by a world of unmitigated commerce; if commerce is necessary—and who doubts the necessity of "the devouring eagerness and intellectual strife of town life"—then an Olmsted and Vaux park must follow.

Olmsted follows his unmarried parkless example with one of familial grace, where a man can ask his helpmate to put some bread, butter, and salad in a basket, gather the children, and join him "under the chestnut tree where we found the Johnsons last week." They'll stroll to the dairyman's cottage for tea and milk, and take their supper by the brookside. In his Brooklyn Park, Olmsted observed "tears of gratitude in the eyes of poor women as they watched their children thus enjoying themselves."

Obviously, if you can't change the corrosive effect of urban working life, then you must find a way to counter its effect before the damage destroys—or revolutionizes—those who are building the city. Policing of the working classes was inherent in the generous plans for their betterment. Olmsted was convinced that the urban park would act as rustic Thorazine, and he loved to tell how even the most delicate gardening in his Manhattan and Brooklyn creations was left undamaged by millions of once-hooligan hands and feet.

But Olmsted also had a classless vision—rather, an omniclass vision—of parks as democratic arenas for what he called "congregated human life." His Victorian fancies embraced "flocks of black-faced sheep, while men, women, and children are seen sitting here and there, forming groups in the shade. . . ." However, this picturesque imagination also forsaw a unique urban space where the antagonism of rich and poor would be diffused in the general pleasure that orderly nature provides. Promenade behavior does not engender active confrontation, it is true, but the strength of equality felt during a utopian Sunday afternoon could wash over into the working week. Or so a part of Olmsted hoped, fighting greed and government to implement his green zones.

We still have mutually suspicious classes, and we still may enjoy Central Park if we believe that congregated human life is safe enough to risk. A walk through November mulch is just as rectifying as Olmsted promised, much more aromatic than the intellectual strife this newspaper, for one, is heir to. I have been lunching at the Loeb Boathouse, and only the threat of no paycheck can scare me back to subway and office.

Olmsted saw the park as a place to eat ice cream and drink beer, the latter accomplished in the company of ladies (he usually addressed men) so that self-censorship and tipsily tipped hats would win the day. Many park restaurants were proposed and some built, the logic being that if you must feed between four walls in so decadent a venue as a restaurant, let the first thing you see as you leave the door be a tree. Warner LeRoy's Tavern on the Green would have you see the tree as you eat, a tree with a nest of light bulbs in her hair.

The 72nd Street Boathouse was built in 1954 and fitted up with a grill and sodas; in summer, long lines curl from the serving window. The building has just been "refurbished" and now includes a small restaurant cum cafe, with windows facing the small body of water on which the rented boats are to be tested. This month, in lieu of boats, a duck will paddle as you eat.

A concession called TAM (Time and Money), based in Staten Island, is in the process of working out a menu for the middle-class part, which has real linen and waiter service as accomplished as that on lower Third Avenue. The fast-food area smells of frying, as all worthy fast-food areas should; lumps of catfish are placed on a cold, doughy roll, and the dollar cup of french fries washes down the popcorn-cups of beer. Once-trendy pastaed and pasta-free salads are lost among the frying, although the pasta-magnetic effort to draw a wider clientele—read nervous middle-classes—through the gates speaks to Olmsted's pluralistic intention. The middle-classes also eat hamburgers, I am told, but vegetables are good for you, if there are no black-faced sheep around.

The obliging staff will help you forget the grotesquely ugly plastic chairs in which you sit. To the left of these (facing the duck) you will find the door to a tiny restaurant, tiny in relative terms because it is so public, partaking of a public park. All restaurants are public in that anyone can enter, and anyone with money can leave, but privacy is heightened and made Romantic by nature so close under glass. If you try to ignore the park, the restaurant resembles those found in this country's better museums: chicken salad et alia, two excellent omelettes, a $10 roast beef sandwich, a wine list one notch above the solids.

But you can't ignore the park; it's too obtrusive. Your omelette cools as you stare at stacked boats. The Olmsted park is not so much an antidote to the city as continuous with it, sometimes a backdrop, other times a reminder of what we constantly miss or avoid by living here. Of course, you don't find parks without cities, parks you can carry home in your pocket. Nature, unparked, is wilderness and hell to manage, and cities without parks are no better, full of opportunities to pay your bills and leave. Neither alone will do.

(11/19/1985)

The Semiotics of Zwieback

"Do you really like sushi?" My former assistant usually began stories about herself with questions about you, and she continued with her very own sushi experience, as if it had never before happened to anyone: "I took one bite and spit it out, I couldn't get it down, I was so embarrassed, the sushi chef laughed and made me vegetables instead." That was nice of him, I thought. I waited for the inevitable focus of the story, its *cliché d' être:* "I know that people like sushi, but isn't it an acquired taste?"

Every taste is an acquired taste. That's what I answered, and it sounded true. But how do you verify the concept of taste acquired, or even of taste itself? The problem, put as a problem, generates scientific thought, which in turn invents experiment: determine what species or individual animal—Tabby or Rex—will starve rather than eat this or that. Get out the cages and the cats.

Phylogeny tippytoes to ontogeny: when did little Jeff spit out his first _____ (fill in the blank), and why? Knowing little Jeff as I do, he may have disliked the way blank clashed with the hue of Somebody's apron; before, he could take blank or leave it, but after the rejection little Jeff wasn't offered blank again, which is why big Jeff orders purée of blank whenever possible, even in fancy restaurants. I should warn readers who believe this fiction that big Jeff isn't convinced that wordless little Jeff could recognize the continuity of blank from one day to the next, much less dislike the taste of it.

Taste and language are inseparable, so there. Refusing a nipple or throwing down a spoon reinvents "No." Consider, however, the paradox that spoken language tends to repel connection to flavor—in fact, to any primarily sensual thrill. Words that speak of tasting, hearing, touching, and sexing do not come easily and, as any copywriter will tell you, those that do are the stupidest words imaginable. "Good" and "bad," as in "feels good" or "tastes bad," take first and second place, if we ignore "ummm" or "ugh," which don't quite count. "Nice," "awful," "marvelous" work wonders, until we divide the general into the sensorially particular in order to include such warhorses as "delicious." I am not making fun of food critics here, nor of those who need to indicate orally how welcome a meal or lover was. Experts such as oenophiles have invented sublanguages to account for—or to create, makes no difference—sensual quanta, allowing the gentlemen to keep diaries of their tastings for the purpose of quantifying and selling the results. But conversational vocabulary, in every dialect and class, backs away from direct engagement with flavor. Only similes and metaphors are left.

There's nothing wrong with these poetries, of course. John, eating sea urchin roe for the first time, said they taste "like low tide." Wonderful. I knew what he meant—at least I thought I did—because I was eating them simultaneously. Like and dislike are left hanging in his tidewrack's brackish smell.

But perhaps John's low tide was clean, brightening the mica-flecked sand? If I hadn't eaten those saffron eggs at the same moment, I wouldn't have known which low tide he meant. I'd have gotten his gist if I tasted sea urchin roe later, because adults conveniently imagine we perceive flavors the same. Forget that there's good and bad roe, eaten on good or bad days. Ignore memory. Whether we like roe or not is something else entirely.

Shared eating lassos the language we use to describe it. I am certain this is one of the many reasons even irritable humans enjoy eating together: to reinforce the illusion that we can be easily understood. Take a couple who've been together 20 years, place them at the table with a steak and brussels sprouts, but set them talking to dialogue by Harold Pinter. Their sentences fly like arrows misdirected, they speak alone, and their perception of the food in their mouths must be equally hermetic and unsure. Even you, the discomfited observer, can taste the difference.

The chaos this kind of isolation implies is fearsome, and some of us require assurance that our self, our own cartilaginous language, remains both steady and open to the public—when someone says, for instance, that he loves you and would you please pass the salt. For me, it's Zwieback. I speak a Zwieback language, and it's certainly my own, but because I've understood it for almost 40 years it provides my haven in a heartless world. I am not alone: others apprehend Zwieback too. Its reputation as palliative, thought to be based on purity of ingredients and mothers' approval, actually obtains from its continuity.

One may adore home-baked or off-brand zwieback, but when I say Zwieback I mean Nabisco, for I am an American and if the trademark speaks I listen. I have no memories of any kind from infancy, but the coffin proportions of the yellow box have attracted me long as I can remember. I ran my fingernail to break the seam, lifted the top with a rip, and the first, fruity smell never varied. I can rewrite the previous sentence in permanent present tense.

"Never varied." These are shapes only a baby or artist would make, prelinguistic units of texture, comfort, value. First they scrape, then they crunch, and finally they give way to fluid, going in. But they're not anti-intellectual, because they allow counting. For dietary reasons I was allowed just two at a time as a child; oddly, I still don't know how many each box contains.

The baby was changed. This fact applied to the box and, I hope, to me. We are faced with a permanent contemporary baby as we eat. He (I'm a he, it's a he) is white. He is supposed to signify, packagewise, the customer recipient to the real recipient, the parent. But what happens as you grow up, gazing at that baby as you fondle and mouth your flesh-colored food?

You, if I may say so, become continuously baby, forever hopeful and satisfied. This is why no one—except perhaps a genuine baby—eats Zwieback with the carton out of sight. If you are white, if you are American, each Zwieback *becomes* you, reflexive and without history, as the blandness unfolds. Zwieback will be your mirror, and mirrors are the first, the most necessary, acquired taste.

(11/26/1985)

Our Town

This I remember, or think I remember, that my fourth grade teacher, Miss Costello, asked us to write an essay called "My Hometown." Now, Miss Costello was a smart cookie, and she had planned not the usual kiddie lesson in fulfilling expectations—lying—but an exercise in problem-solving.

"My Hometown, by Jeffrey I. Weinstein. We don't have a Main Street, but we have two big supermarkets. They actually do milk cows over in Queens, but I didn't see grass near the buildings they are in, which are dirty. I never met a farmer in Brooklyn, Queens, Manhattan, or Collins Avenue in Miami Beach, the only places I have been to. We are friendly with some neighbors, but just on our block. It feels like a hometown in Seal's Luncheonette on Coney Island Avenue, because Seal and Max say hello and know that I like roast beef on a roll for lunch, rare, with chocolate milk. There are many types of home-towns."

Miss Costello also advised us not to ignore the dropped penny in the street because you'll never know when you'll need just one more cent. She had a way with homely advice; *she* was hometown. She taught me about ethics and social relativity, good training for my present work. To wit, let's look at Denny's American Kitchen Favorite Hometown Dinners.

New Jersey's Route 22 resembles a tape loop of commercials on midnight television, being, as it is, dozens and dozens of miles of uninterrupted shopping. The road's linearity is inexorable, for almost any turn you make—in desperation—leads to a parking lot adjoining . . . BIG DADDY'S TEXAS WIENERS, UNIVERSAL DINETTES, VAN HEUSEN FACTORY STORE, POTAMKIN CHEVROLET, COMPUTER WORLD, HOUSE OF TILES, HOUSE OF SNAKES, HOUSE OF PAIN . . . sorry, I accept the semantics of neon and the philosophy of Las Vegas but after a while, at dusk in the rain, it gets heavy. Route 22 is a tunnel of love through commercial culture. It provides self-defined necessities of life to those who live nearby: it's somebody's—always potentially my—hometown.

In Southern California, once actually my hometown, we met at Denny's for midnight eggs, or, even better, patty melts, although they might have been spelled with an IE. Denny's was a hangout, the necessary factor without which hometowns can't exist. Business, gossip, public boredom, politics, intellectual life, courtship, and fighting could be viewed or practiced on leatherette seats. Persons of all colors bathed in the yellow light of the same sign. You paid for the right to this intercourse, but anyone who could afford a car—those who lived "in" this town—could manage the coffee cover.

Denny's has made a big mistake with its new, additional menu, although it was as inevitable as expansion and consolidation in late capitalism. If Red Lobster can serve blackened fish, the logic goes, then any restaurant can ride on the lobstertails of urban eating fashion as long as it doesn't drop its basic draw. The ideo-geneology of Ameri-

can Cuisine, you may remember, is 19th century rural paradisal, going to '20s and '30s road culture, to West Coast
postpluralism (French added), to center-city sloshing and
grazing. Memory is denatured in all these phenomena, but
only the last two have played creative havoc with history
proper, serving time in a blender.

Now comes the tricking, I mean trickling, down, simultaneously to please the regular car clients and to attract
sophisticated urbanites whose city happens to be the suburbs. The single starter is one wedge of iceberg lettuce
("the way they used to serve it in the Fabulous '50s" and, I
might add, the way they serve it now in Manhattan's Betty
Brown's and America, the restaurant). Denny's has practice with this one and acquits itself nicely. The menu elab-
orates underneath, in eight-point type, the origin of the
term "iceberg" as it applies to lettuce. This urges reading
eaters to historicize our appetites.

Entrees are listed as Maryland Fried Chicken, Jambalaya, Apple-Stuffed Rainbow Trout, Open-Faced Hawaiian Grill, Old Fashioned Chicken Stew, and Grilled Ham
Steak, all about $5 apiece. Menu copy pastoralizes and ele-
vates each ingredient and the whole; only the Hawaiian
Grill, layers of chicken breast, ham, and pineapple on an
English muffin topped with chartreuse mustard hollan-
daise, bespeaks any native ingenuity. Denny's Jambalaya,
really a sick Spanish rice, insults even the cunning, appro-
priating functionary who planned it.

Sliced ripe olives and pineapple rings are tossed everywhere, which fact is explained, if not excused, on the
menu's back page, a grid of trademarks that comprises
Denny's crackerbarrel general store: Clear Springs Trout

Company, Dole, Lawry's, Sara Lee, Sweet 'n Low, Tyson (chicken), California Iceberg Lettuce Commission, Quality California Black Olives, and, the last star on Betsy Ross's flag, Grey Poupon Dijon Mustard, Made with White Wine. This commercial obeisance is not the mistake I referred to above; in fact, such acknowledgment is entirely familiar and expected, congruent with Denny's traditional function as an interchangeable highway home. But you cannot plant a false oak in a real parking lot: both must suffer the doubt that relativity inspires. "Is there really such a thing as hometown?" Decent customers will be inclined to wonder. After that, it's downhill all the way.

(2/4/1986)

The Last Cornflake Show

Kellogg's net sales last year were almost $3 billion. "The company has achieved 41 consecutive years of increased sales . . . " according to its annual report. Of course, not all these dollars reflect ingestion of the cornflake, a quantum of commercial information that the Kellogg Company has successfully rewrought as one word, the greatest word in cereal. In fact, Kellogg's—along with Post and its Grape-nut—has processed and reformed even that original word, cereal, which, after Ceres, once applied to primitive materials unpressed and unboxed. No, Kellogg's sells Eggo, LeGout, Whitney's, Shirriff, and dozens of other words you may or may not comprehend as food, but Kellogg's is a cornflake, is "cornflake," before and after everything else.

I have a single cornflake in hand, straight from the box. This one is about a half-inch across, a rectangle curled at one edge, although the flakes vary in size from breakage. The color is a yellow-beige, just going to brown on the pocks—much lighter in tone than the flake photo on the carton. *Cornflake color.* In my mouth, my teeth go right to it, and it falls into powder. All the essence is available at once in a burst of what early ads called "nutty" sweetness, unhampered by fiber. *Cornflake taste.* But all of a sudden there's a dramatic emptiness, a hole where the flavor was; I grab a handful immediately, without thinking, and throw it in.

In a bowl, flakes race with milk to the finish, beyond which the food turns and collapses to paper, to the cardboard, soaked, from which it had been poured. A bowl of cornflakes ignited by milk is a meal automatically clocked, constructed to speed you up and out. Your bowl of cornflakes is breakfast Taylored to the 20th century. By now this Kellogg's breakfast has accrued as much American nostalgia as a still aggressively going concern possibly can. Therefore, any particular cornflake manifestation tenders an involuntary album of meanings, individual and social, in which the cornflake and its ostensible foodish purpose, its reality, is buried—to the tune of countless, collective, commercial good mornings.

But where do the cornflake's continuity and origins lie? And why did Kellogg's of Battle Creek halt its tour of the cornflake factory, its only tour worldwide, after selflessly hosting six and a half million visitors over 80 American years? On Friday, April 11, I visited Michigan to find out: at the Kellogg's factory, I took the last cornflake tour.

The factory hadn't expected much press attention when I phoned months ago to ask about the final day. But the word did get out, so a press event and public statement were planned to take place on the lawn, in front of the statue of Tony the Tiger. Tony the Tiger has never struck me as, shall we say, a significant iconographic figure. I understand—though do not agree with—Kellogg's apparent objection to a statue of a cornflake, but I would at least have preferred the more historically comfortable Snap! Crackle! Pop! These three, however, were brought out in real life, along with a fuzzy Tony and cubs, to cut capers and pose for the kids and the press. The kids also posed for the press, snap, and the press for the kids, crackle, and for each other, pop.

Joseph M. Stewart, a Kellogg Company vice president, tried his darndest to wrest attention from the animals and imps. He said that "industrial spies" from rival and foreign manufacturers are forcing them to close the tour because Kellogg's is embarking on a half-billion-dollar program to modernize the Battle Creek plant. We wouldn't even be allowed to take pictures inside today! Yes, the cornflakes will remain exactly the same. According to Kellogg spokesperson Richard Lovell, the old factory, which Kellogg's claims is the largest ready-to-eat cereal plant in the world (they own 38 in 18 countries), employs about 2400, "but we don't anticipate much change of personnel" anent the retooling.

A reporter said he had heard that Kellogg's tried to close the tour in 1981, but the town and Chamber of Commerce raised a hue and cry, afraid to lose ancillary tourist income, and the company backed down. Yes, this is true, Stewart admitted, but "now we are investing $500 million in the community." No one asked why the company had wanted to stop the tour in 1981, before modernization and spying were even mentioned.

I had time to kill before the tours, so I drove a few blocks to Joe's Working Man's Cafe, located on a short commercial strip between the Kellogg and the Post plants, for lunch: fried cod, fried bread, macaroni and cheese. At Eagle's Rexall drugstore, the two rows of Kellogg's cereal souvenirs had been picked clean—except for a few Raisin Bran potholders—and they looked as if they'd stay that way. "It's a shame," a woman said to the pharmacist behind the counter, "it's just a shame." I did not have to ask her what was a shame.

Willie Keith Kellogg, born in 1860, had a brother, John Harvey Kellogg, eight years older. John Harvey, a Seventh-Day Adventist, became a doctor and ran the Battle Creek Sanitarium, which, through a combination of luxury, vegetarianism, and the effulgent confidence of its extremely short chief, became a magnet for the rich and ill. John Harvey employed his brother to help run the place and invent the processed grains that were supposed to aid digestion, improve sleep, and revitalize the worn human husk. They sold their "Sanitas" granolas and wheat flakes to proselytize souls as much as to add to the institution's income—John Harvey could never conceive of any difference between the two vocations—until, between 1902 and 1904, 42 other companies in the area began to manufacture "Battle Creek" type cereal foods. But only one besides Kellogg's Sanitas produced a "corn flake"—the brothers had invented a flaking process somewhat by accident (moldy wheat, a surprise flake pried from the rollers, the usual American accident myth) and patented it in 1894.

Will Keith and John Harvey hated each other; W.K. finally took control of the food part of the business. It seemed he had a genius for advertising—a form of proselytizing—and for selling, which he saw as one and the same. He knew how to create a national appetite, and a ritual to support it. He also managed the most difficult thing: to split the label of "medicine" from the promise of health; to, in effect, transform fear of illness into the invisible motor of a superficially happy eating obsession. The Victorian ghosts of masturbation and madness haunt the cereal bowl but, in order to ignore them—and ignore them we must—we will eat quickly, conveniently, and automatically, trusting the original and its signature, assured that W.K.'s food has never been polluted by a human hand.

The staging area, as they call it, was crowded on this last day, as it had been all week; we were divided into color-coded groups seated around white tables. We each had been handed a small envelope as we entered, and one by one we opened them: to find a white squiggle, which, when pulled from the sides, turned into a hairnet. Mamas hairnetted babies, crew-cutted men slipped theirs on with surprising familiarity, so that after a few minutes the whole room looked, well, related. Some took free postcards from the last of the piles.

A woman at my table looked me in the eye: "I've been working here for 26 years." The press had been requested not to talk to workers on line, but no one said anything about this. She was stationed in the "gluing-the-bottom-of-the-box part"; her husband (chatting at another table) was retired from his post at Post. She waved to two fellow workers, and as I watched and spoke with her, I realized that a large portion of this last day's tours was made up of plant employees.

Feelings were high. Some folks seemed upset by management's attempt, they said, to hire young part-timers and break the union. The plant had recently reinstituted eight-hour shifts, moving back from W.K. Kellogg's much-appreciated six-hour day, conceived during the Great Depression to "give work and paychecks to the heads of three hundred more families in Battle Creek" (or so W.K. was supposed to have told the town's mayor at the time). I asked the Kellogg-Post couple if they were upset that the tours were ending. They smiled. "Eighty years, that's a long time." (This is the husband.) "I know what the man said, but it costs them money to run these, and look at the space it uses up. That's the reason they're stopping them."

"And you know," (this is the wife) "it gave us something enjoyable at work. To see people coming through—it's strenuous work, hard work, and this made it easier." They themselves took the tour almost every year, and whenever family or friends visited from out of town.

Arniece, our guide, was hoarse after a grueling day but nonetheless perky on her feet. She gave a snap history, including the fact that the company is using more semis because the "railroads are collapsing," told us to stay in line during the 20-minute walk, and said she'd answer any questions. Two in the audience wanted to know what happened to a cereal I never heard of, a joke about All-Bran was offered, and in we went.

The tour followed the order of the floor, which is not necessarily the order in which the flakes are made. Isolated machines folded boxes. The noise was stupendous; many workers wore earplugs, and we heard Arniece through the stationary bullhorns only if we stopped our ears. My general impression was that anyone who would want to steal these ancient, very semiautomated secrets had to be crazy. It was astounding to see flat, stacked cartons of familiar cultural volumes: as if art, or the Washington Monument, could be deflated. A cardboard sign was scrawled "THANKS, TOUR-GUIDES, FOR A JOB WELL DONE, WE'LL MISS YOU" and signed with a crying, smiling face. My table partner rushed across the yellow line to embrace a machine-tending friend on the other side; it was a barrier that felt good to see broken, and probably felt good to break.

We saw food only once (although we followed its changing aroma all through the factory): at the flaker, where swollen brown grits, already cooked with malt, sugar, and salt, then dried and partially caramelized, cascade through rollers and are flattened. The moist flakes are then conveyed to rotary ovens, something like clothes dryers, and tumbled until toasted and curled. They're sprayed with vitamins later. A clear window had been inserted in a chute near the rollers so we could see what was going on.

A digression: the sweet person who ran the antique store at which I stopped on the road from Detroit to Battle Creek told me, out of nowhere, that her father, John G. Donovan, was a machinist and road engineer who, in the 1950s, set up most of the cereal companies' rolling mills—an extremely specialized job. For a moment I had the idea that anyone in Central Michigan I spoke with would be connected, somehow, to breakfast food.

We were each ("one to a person, even infants") asked to take a box of cornflakes from a mountain at the end of the line, plus a phonograph record, clearly an old three-box-top job, of the Snap!Crackle!Pop! song sung in rock, punk, and country-western styles, and we walked out into the late afternoon sun. A four-piece all-purpose band, having played all afternoon and many afternoons before, was ending its workday on the empty lawn behind the statue of Tony the Tiger: to the tune of "Hello Dolly" they sang, in sarcastic sotto voice, "Tony will never play for you again." I caught them just as they folded up and left.

(5/20/1986)

Forget the Alamo

The recent made-for movie called "My Two Loves," starring Mariette Hartley as a widow who falls for lesbian Lynn Redgrave, was shot in San Antonio because San Antonio provides all the backdrops an urban middle-class soap opera requires. A neon-lit restaurant for trysting: Rosario's, bench-and-table Mexican refinished in funky pink deco. A promenade near water for the denouement: the sunken "river walk," shored-up and lushly planted by the WPA, snaking 15 feet below the dusty, quietly restoring downtown. Truly delightful, the puddly river's cafe-laden shores attract vacationing Texans the way Venice draws Italians from the south.

San Antonio is said to be the nation's tenth largest city, with a mayor—Henry Cisneros—so visible that some local firm named a men's cologne—"Henry"—after him. Since the city's economy is diversified, which in Texas means anything but oil, the joint is jumpin', not the least reason being the area's large, long established, and relatively prosperous Mexican-American population. (In fact, it would be more accurate to say that San Antonio boasts a sizable non-Hispanic community.) After years of self-exposure to idiotic gardener/maid racial assumptions, who know only Southern California are amazed at the confident habits of a Mexican-American bourgeoisie.

The Alamo sits in the center of town. It is much smaller than anything Fess Parker defended.

You eat Mexican-American food in San Antonio restaurants if you want the particular flavors that this area has acquired and bred. I found a living metaphor for all my disgust with run-of-the-mill New York Mexican food in what might be the most happy small eatery I could dig up (with the help of *Texas Monthly*'s Alison Cook, and a number of other guides), a courthouse lunch place called the Little House Cafe (107 South Flores): their tortillas. They were almost a quarter-inch thick, and they tasted, well, coarse, pulling, slightly salty, aromatic, precisely how I now know tortillas should. I must forswear all experience of New York tortillas, which should be used to fill holes in crumbling plaster. Also, this explains why chilaquiles—a casserole employing fried pieces of stale tortillas—are a San An specialty, and at Little House they were served *en salsa verde,* in a green chili sauce of embarrassing vegetable freshness.

Mario's, open 24 hours, a cross between any Denny's and Marlene Deitrich's hideout in *Rancho Notorious* (325 South Pecos), served chilaquiles in green sauce more pungent and roasty, less gardened, than the Little House version; I began to see how differences in a regional Ameri-Mex food could be measured, something impossible to do with the combination plates of our urban area because you can't measure a difference between zeros. I also compared Mario's chilaquiles to their offering of three calf-brain tacos, sprinkled with cilantro. All were victorious.

The blackboard outside Rosario's roadhouse (1014 South Alamo) listed lobster burritos and fresh crab; the sleek graphics translated to price-and-a-half, but even upscale veneer in San Antonio retains some lard and noise. (Prices never exceeded $20 per person for a Mexican meal.) Yuppies and preppies of all races eat at Rosario's, as well as silent neighbors, an obvious gay and lesbian faction, and at least two transvestites, who were notable not only for their nerve but for their superior punkish fashion (dowdy Mariette and Lynn held hands here). Most food is cooked "Tampico" style, which is taken to mean seared in chunks on cast-iron platters, the simplicity ameliorated by typical jumping salsas. The whole ate beautifully, in the pluralist atmosphere.

Alison said I'd be crazy not to take the short trip north into rural Texas in order to eat "the best barbecue in the state, which of course means the universe." Fewer than 10,000 souls live in Lockhart, within an area that grows corn and watermelon, but I'd be surprised if twice the number didn't drive through each week heading for Kreuz's Market, which is a butcher shop, meat smoker, and sitdown barbecue.

You know what barbecue is? Can you be sure, if your food memories consist entirely of what you read a decade ago in *American Fried?* Barbecue is vinegar sauce in North Carolina, pulled pork drenched in hot Georgian tomatoes, you name it. Kreuz's will not be generalized either. It serves barbecue from Mars.

Since I forgot my camera, most of my memories are photo-mimetic. One either knows the spatial routine or is befuddled; for example, you must enter through the back door, directly into the smoking room, if you wish to eat. The walls of the room, and all the regulars behind the counter, are coated sable from dozens of years of live oak smoke. In an hour, you will smell like the meat you eat. We did not know how to begin, until a young cowboy (in chaps!) politely, via a butler's drawl, advised that we ask for our beef or pork by the slice, and could get our pork/beef sausages dry—the fat burned off—or not; he preferred the former. Today they had their usual pork tenderloin and beef, not brisket as would be expected elsewhere in Texas, but shoulder clod; sometimes they offer prime rib. The meat is tallowed in rendered fat, salted and peppered, then sat on a low grate over a sucking fire. Six hours later, the dark lumps are lifted and sliced for you and me, the slices weighed and handed over on butcher paper. You pay the slicer. Texans argue about butcher paper and the concept of authenticity.

The cowboy points you to a door into a bright, high-ceilinged, bench-filled room. Two ladies in stained white outfits dole out piles of ButterKrest bread—Texas Wonder. You can buy red onion, ripe avocado, underripe tomatoes, dill and sour pickles, yellow cheese, and jalapeno peppers by the piece (peppers were 11 cents each), plus beer or soda. Paper towels are dispensed from a holder; Texans argue about that too. You sit down, next to one of a roomful of families, the young and old.

Cowboys are black, Hispanic, and anglo. Some eat the meat fastidiously, cutting with a plastic knife, proceeding in series with bread, onion, and Coke. Others make sandwiches, or make do with their hands. Did you think I forgot about sauce? There is no sauce. Sauce's not right. The flavor would be marred. What is the flavor like? Imagine what it could be like, assuming that the penetrant fumes of live oak are sweeter, less acidic, than those of mesquite. *You cannot find meat like this anywhere else.* I had the bad luck not to be hungry; but it was in fact good luck, because my extreme, potent pleasure must have been generated purely by the object of pleasure itself. I brought nothing toward it: it came to me.

Outside, the fenced backyard was filled neck-high with cords of oak. This is the photograph I would have taken. An ice cream parlor had just opened around the corner, and we tried the chocolate, not the sorbets.

(6/3/1986)

The Corn Is Blue

And Other Savory Hues of Northern New Mexico

On Tuesday two weeks ago I saw the "sodomy" map in *The New York Times;* New Mexico was not on it, or, I should say, was shown to be a state in which homosexual or heterosexual oral or anal sex could be attended to in the privacy of one's affection without threat of outside arrest. Now this does not make New Mexico Shangri-La, because even on the few and liberated streets of Taos my spousal equivalent and I were shouted at by drunken anglos leaning out of their pickup, looking for something to alleviate their angst. I have also read that New Mexico's state legislature has introduced a bill to reinstate its immoral "sodomy" law ("sodomy" is one of those proscriptive, not descriptive, words that demands quotes). But until that time I will sing the state's praises, foodwise and in whatever other way the place allows.

Santa Fe and Taos are special because those who live there are special: Pueblo Indians were displaced by the colonial Spanish, and the Spanish and Indians together were cheated and bumped by anglo settlers from the east. (Anglos are defined as anyone not in the first two groups, which means that a black or Japanese Santa Fe resident falls in the anglo category.) These groups have fought, and there is historical enmity to share, but the tourist sees cultural truce in the phenomena a tourist looks for, or at. I am a tourist here (pretend we're there) in the way that most reporters or professionals are consumers of sensual and factual tchotchkes. However, the homogeneous flow of novelty was broken for me again and again by the intensity, the unpredictable and happily unavoidable power, of three things: the landscape, the "proximity" of history (the way the past constantly breaks through the short crust of the present), and, believe it or not, the restaurant food. Home cooking, from these adobe homes, lies somewhere beyond the sunset.

Northern New Mexico has generated foods and recipes that now influence the fashion and evolution of mainline American cooking. This is our place to eat all things made of blue corn, the place to chart the differences between types of local green—fresh—chiles, the place to dip sopiapillas, twisted serpents of fried dough, into sage blossom honey to dispel the heat of whatever carne adovada (pork marinated in red chiles and spices, then cooked and served in more of the same) we find as specialty of the house. But the present also breaks into the past: the few so-called better restaurants, which once proved their superiority by importing French or "continental" cuisine to the gilded locals, now import "regional" Southwest dishes from Los Angeles, San Francisco, and even New York. Regional food is the trendiest in the country; that it seems to be imported to its region of origin should be no impediment to success. Newcomers help to preserve the old forms, although in a changed, often attenuated, manner. The concept of preservation is, of course, a dialectic whose opposing principles, tradition and invention, won't let each other alone; habit on one hand, and commerce, on the other, effectively control what and who survives.

New words:

Vigas, the exposed pine ceiling-beams of true adobe architecture. Hotels and real estate agents make a big deal of these dramatic supports, with fairly good reason. Building in Santa Fe must conform to either adobe style or a plain frontier-Victorian model with prim cornice, but my friend and architect admits that as long as the facade does not offend, contractors can drywall all they want.

Micacious, referring to the unusual, mica-flecked, buff-colored clay used by ceramists of the Taos and Picuris pueblos to fashion their utilitarian cooking ware. Unlike other Pueblo ceramic, it is undecorated or simply incised. Some of this pottery is old and blackened from cooking fires, but new pots can be bought, often with instructions not to pour undiluted detergent directly into the item, which is also noted to be dishwasher-safe.

Almost every smallish American city has a restaurant on which the national snob-food magazines and chicken-tourist bibles—*Gourmet, Food and Wine,* the Mobil guides—lay their most florid commercial laurels. The Compound, on Santa Fe's gallery-laden Canyon Road, was voted, among other things, the best place a New Mexican businessman could take another businessman to lunch, according to a plaque on the restaurant's plaque-wall. Since the Compound enjoys so heated a reputation, and since it sits in a gorgeously outfitted adobe house with walls thicker than the girth of any who enter them, we had

310   Jeff Weinstein

our first dinner here. One always hopes, if not for the best, at least for the curious, but four stars told us that this meal would heighten all the rest in town, and indeed it did: at $50 per person, including wine, it was the most expensive, and it was the worst.

Decent and friendly service, appended to ridiculous white gloves, could not offset the salad of undetermined lettuce, one piece each of Belgian endive and radicchio, one olive, one slice kiwi, a chunk of celery, and a slice of canned beet. This salad didn't need to be dressed, it needed to be locked up. Tolerable mushroom broth couldn't compensate for rack of M&M lamb (mushy and muttony) or for gray sliced duck breast fanned around sauce that couldn't have lifted the adjoining flesh even if such fowl were rosy and moist, in the mode of three years ago. One is always offended by a chef's laziness and bad value, but of true interest is the lack of "placement" of this restaurant in ongoing restaurant time; its continuing survival depends upon thoughtless habit and the need for an anglo outpost in an area of culinary contamination.

You will find obsession tempered with true, somewhat nutty, populism in a textbook example of why you not only can but should compare high-rent apples and public oranges: Josie's Casa de Comida (which none of the guidebooks will tell you has moved down the block, to 255 *East* Marcy). Josie's is a diner in a house. Lines of citizens chalk their first names and number on a board and wait on the porch or sidewalk for hours till they're summoned. The food is heaven on earth, although I must say for accuracy's sake that I ate only a few of the offered dishes, which is the case in most of the places in this article. There is only so much time in one stomach.

Lunch is Josie's meal—there is a Josie, who compares well to the painting of her on the wall—and the menu splits into New Mexican and the honest other, which means sandwiches or Southern specials like chicken fried steak. I was pleased with my tamale and red chile (pleased? it was the best I'd had north of you know what Border) as well as with the chile relleno and pinto beans, distinctly not *refritos,* but the apotheosis began with the typical New Mexican side dish of pozole (posole, or posoli), made by adding lime and water to white corn (unsplit hominy made from green corn is called *pozole de chicos*) and boiling until the skins peel and the ruptured pellets are left. The hominy is then stewed with red chile, some kind of pork and rind, salt, and often garlic, onion, and oregano—recipes are different, which is why cooking delights. This stew, somewhat heavy but fluffy at the same time, has its components twist and turn so that nothing becomes predominant, allowing it to satisfy as accompaniment or main squeeze both.

The trip upward ends with Josie's desserts, because she is so clearly a baker. Apples are local fruit, and many restaurants offer careful apple pie. Josie's cobbler was bottomed with a sugary brandy syrup and topped with unusually substantial and dairysome whipped cream; apples and crust did very well in between. Almost better than this (lunch, remember?) was the cool lemon souffle, really a kind of baked fool, in which the citrus flavor intensifies as the dense center of the deceptively frivolous item is reached. Santa Fe cannot be called a large city, and Josie's isn't more than 15 minutes from most of it.

Some of Santa Fe's Mexican restaurants set themselves up "family style," with long tables and cheaper prices (full dinner about $8 per person) for parties of four or more. Maria Ysabel recently moved to a site on the commercial strip, at 2821 Cerrillos Road, and there serves its specialties: the echt-New Mexican pork dish of carne adovada, and capirotada—hot, sweet bread pudding with cinnamon, raisins, fat, and, hold onto your hat, drizzled melted yellow cheese. We ate the famous carne adovada at the rural and romantic Rancho de Chimayo, an old hacienda on the older High Road to Taos, which offers a cocktail made of local apple juice and tequila so fragrant, so inevitable, that I couldn't be disappointed with the remainder of the meal. Carne adovada differs widely; sometimes the pork is dried after it's marinated, sometimes not. The Rancho's was a monotonous and slightly gritty version of the one at Maria Ysabel's, and even though I'm a newcomer to this food, I think the latter was objectively superior: full of rich red chiles and other spices sunk deep into the meat, with an unexpected resemblance to fiery pork curry.

Contemporary sensibility walks these foodways. In Santa Fe, the newborn Old Mexico Grill, one of many storefronts at the College Plaza shopping center, eliminates tacky decor, opens up the beautifully tiled grilling area to customers' hungry eyes, and serves what we would call unusual sopes (cornmeal tartlets filled with cheese, guacamole, etc.) and average fajitas, the cowboy food so well-popularized in New York. Periscope (221 Shelby Street) has been in the city longer and from my one, absolutely superb lunch (dinner on Saturdays only) we could see how they incorporate native—mostly Mexican-style—cooking into a delicate eclectic menu: using vibrant but not overwhelming green chile, roasted red chile, and tomatillo salsas to bring the gentle pork and veal *farce* of three albondigas (Mexican meatballs) on corn-studded and scented rice to a skillfully balanced head, or complementing spicy boudin blanc with an earthy dollop of well-fired beans, whipped to a hint. The rest of the meal included sourdoughish rolls, artichoke soup, okra vinaigrette, and rose petal ice cream (breath of pink) with strawberries (blood red), at no more than $30 per person.

Wonderful Taos, some Taosenos admit, needs a wonderful restaurant. By this they mean it needs something other than their Mexican ones, which anyone else would praise to the skies. Perhaps you notice that I've left blue corn, cultivated in Arizona and New Mexico, to the end, even though we bought two bags of blue corn tortilla chips at the Safeway in Santa Fe (they look like indigo spilled on slate). Recipes with blue corn come closer to Indian cooking, and although there has been a thorough mixing of Indian and Spanish influence in the cuisine termed New Mexican, most Pueblo recipes are considered "historical." When I asked folks if they knew of any restaurants that served Indian dishes, they simply could not imagine what I meant. Taos pueblo bread, a flat, circular, thickly crusted pillow with a large, white crumb, is still baked in adobe ovens; many tourists try slices fried in lard. I have often imagined a restaurant of Indian food, and one has just opened on Columbus (!) Avenue in New York. Unfortunately it has not yet been able to realize more than a fifth of its projected multi-tribe menu.

Taos should have a Pueblo restaurant, one that might "retraditionalize" corn pudding, bean loaf, piñon soup, or *tiswin,* a drink made from fermented corn, orange, cinnamon, and cloves. In the meantime I can tell the Taosenos that they already possess an almost wonderful eatery within the renovated Taos Inn, a resort which, though intimate and luxurious in the adobe viga-and-weaving manner, is a national landmark. It's named Doc Martin's, after the gent who ran the place, as Hotel Martin, 50 years ago ("Where artists from everywhere gather to paint").

We now know, from my generalizing colleagues, that hotel restaurants can be better than dead roast beef. Doc Martin's, I am sure, would make it anywhere: a brilliant wine list (including New Mexico's $10 finest) and a brainy combo of anglo crowd pleasers (grilled meats and "fresh" -flown fish, or pasta specials such as lemoned fettucine with confit of duck, basil, and pimentos) and items we may not be quite used to. I admit that blue corn pancakes with maple syrup, for breakfast, takes localism to a curio pitch. However, consider the fried blue corn polenta: squares of wildly nutty cereal essence arranged in Navaho geometry alongside sliced grilled chicken breast, chicken sausage, and fresh tomato relish. Where does this synthetic cooking come from, and who among the eaters, local and free-ranging, can be entirely familiar with the colors, textures, and flavors, or entirely at sea?

Little pieces of paper are flying around my desk, reminding me of how much I've left out. One is sometimes fortunate to avoid a synthesis of landscape, history, and food in New York—when the building is crummy, the air conditioner on, and the oysters a world in themselves. New Mexico, though, will not allow you to forget where you are. So my lost horizons are these:

A bath in iron water, 104 degress, at Ojo Caliente, hot springs first described and named by a Spanish explorer in the 1500s. Then, the inhabitants bathed in an opening to the underworld; *now, in the transparent light, a young woman in sandals fills her plastic jug from the tap labeled "Lithia."*

One pays a dollar to the clerk at Taos's La Fonda hotel and she unlocks an office door, behind which are sexually graphic paintings by D.H. Lawrence. These are surrounded and partially covered by calendars, snapshots, and framed letters (one from Albert Einstein), ostensibly belonging to the absent occupant of the room. *There's a line, on the floor, of carefully shined men's shoes.*

I am eating a steak, aptly, at an isolated restaurant called the Stakeout, eight miles south of Taos, in a high plains desert overlooking the Rio Grande Gorge and just short of the mountains called Sangre de Christo. We took a table outside; most folks were indoors. The steak tastes like Holiday Inn, but the sun has just set, the air is cooling, and *the new dew extracts dual fragrances, from the rosebushes planted in back of us, and from the sagebrush everywhere around. All food disappears.*

(7/22/1986)

Yuppie Falls, Hits Bottom

I can't remember disliking a restaurant more. New York's Cadillac Bar treats customers like children by converting them into children. It equates booze and booze alone with enjoyment. It takes an already fictional Tex-Mex culture and grinds it into dust. Everything about the place is fake and soulless and greedy. It will probably consider this review "publicity."

The food, I hasten to say, isn't bad: it's not a factor at all. The Mexican stuff is garbage, but that's nothing new in this town. Sometimes the marinated beef fajitas are tasty (when not mushy), even rolled in the flavorless flour tortillas; the pork fajitas are so fibrous you can hardly cut 'em. The splayed quail, mesquited or fried, have some snap. But the margaritas—the margaritas, Marge!—are watery jokes; I ordered one straight up and the server tried to get me to order a pitcher because a single marg, he confided, was "awfully small." He seemed genuinely relieved when I backed it up with a beer. (Would they have docked his tips?) When one of our party ordered club soda, he actually inquired if she were on medication. This is disgusting behavior, but all our servers were the worst, the *worst,* as if they had never been trained. Usually I blame management, but it takes two to screw up this badly.

Well, you're now saying, I am probably a prude and I must have been in *such* a mood. Not so, kiddo. Let me see if I can give you a feel for the Cadillac experience. Enter on time, and you will be kept waiting. Twice at the door I was knocked into by drunken young men in suspenders, who laughed. There's a front room of tables, and a bar back and to the right covered attractively with a giant hood made of brown and green beer bottles, through which light pours down on the upright crowd. A row of tables lines a hall to the back, with a second row overhead, on a balcony. The large rear room opening on 22nd Street has been empty, with nothing but a calculator on a makeshift table in full view. The calculator gets its use.

Walls are covered with graffiti. Who did it? They're graffiti without a cause (the restaurant's only a month old). Whom did they pay to scrawl? I've not seen anyone write on the walls. Do you know what it's like to read graffiti that are insincere? Even the *Voice* bathrooms have real graffiti, mostly about a performance artist who sticks yams up her rear and about how awful Pete Hamill would be as an editor.

Who comes here, I asked a waiter, and he said: "B and Ts. That's why I can't do my job right." "B and T" means Bridge and Tunnel, or those folks from the boroughs and Jersey, but I don't think that's fair, or correct. The night after a *Times* plug appeared—its critic was delighted because his tortillas weren't hard and cracked—suited men over 40 and their colleagues, even their mates, took tables and stewed in puzzlement. The next week a tunnel was dug from Wall Street for the apprentice brogue set, who have heard that no one will mind if they throw food or throw up. Taxis are onto the situation, for at 7 p.m. they treat 21st Street as if it were La Guardia, lining up to drop them off.

One of these business fellows, in gray flannel, climbed

over the second-story railing, attempting to reach the bathroom without using the stairs. Instead he fell on his ass; hurt, dazed, he got up, almost knocking the Flaming Mexican Flag (a "unique" after-dinner drink) off a waiter's tray. A voice above offered five dollars if he'd do it again. The Sunday after, I noticed that the balcony was closed; a server agreed that yes, it might be because too many eaters fell down the night before. Waiters are now accustomed to beefy young males dropping from the skies, and hold their trays accordingly.

How does the clientele become so Zorroesque? It's the result of employees called "shooters," women dressed in black, rigged out in leather bandoliers studded with "shot" glasses (get it?) and holsters pregnant with bottles of tequila and 7-Up. Their presence explains the previously inexplicable series of tepid or elongated yells that punctuate the din every three minutes, like clockwork. A shooter serves the "slammer." She coolly sizes up the table and, if the group seems pliant, pours full shots of the mixture ("7-Up is better than lime, also it takes the edge off") and says that as soon she bangs the glasses on the table three times, you are all supposed to yell and gulp your drink "jus' as fast as you can." She collects four bucks a sugary shot, plus a dollar tip per pour, which is obviously expected; she draws no wage.

A friend's reaction to this vision of dark liquorers carefully working the floor was profound: "They're systematically injecting the customers with alcohol, and most of them don't even know what they're drinking." And those of you who think the slammer is a quaint, butch Texas ritual, think again.

There is indeed an original Cadillac bar in Nuevo Laredo, on the Tex-Mex border; every fraud has an original. The Laredo Cadillac (along with a dozen other dives across the country) is said to have invented that Southern brunch staple, the Ramos Gin Fizz. Cessnas would fly to the Cadillac for lunch, and you can't get more Texas than that. But six years ago Edward Gregg Wallace and Carol Wallace opened a mesquite grill in Houston and called it the Cadillac, no relation to the real thing. Everyone agreed, it was fake-funky, but frat rats loved it, at least until it was taken over by insurance agents and their clients. The food, my mole tells me, is the same variable output as here.

The Houston Cadillac, however, didn't boast shooters until just a few years ago. The shooter is pure bull, bull with a cash register through its nose, and the pay-for howls are insulting perversions of the Mexican "rebel yell" or *grito,* whose impulse is typically inebriate but inherently spontaneous. Another meaning of *grito* has political, revolutionary implications south of our border, but awareness of that would be too, too much to ask.

The New York Cadillac is crowded now, and will remain so for a time. I don't mean to romanticize New Yorkers, especially the Cadillac's Julietless Romeos on their way down, but I'd like to think that "we" will catch on to this venture that calls itself a restaurant. Even if the fakery is acceptable, as a form of fun, we'll get bored. New Yorkers, B and Ts included, get bored awfully fast.

(8/19/1986)

Crimes Against Dining

Restaurants and their customers are finally at war. Mutual martial blood courses through anterooms and between the legs of tables; truces called reservations are broken as often as they're made. No longer civilians, we no longer employ civility, so when I phoned Palio restaurant, in the recently new Equitable Building, to request a table on Thursday for dinner at 8, it was de rigueur to be answered, "You'll take a table at nine o'clock." I will? No hint of a question mark in the corporal's reply, just a rifle's report, bang, dead.

War breeds war crimes, crimes against dining, all the rudenesses, idiocies, and avoidable disappointments that blight one's pleasure and the other's profit. Some of the obvious violations have been denounced by my colleagues, and I need not repeat their lists; chances are good that reader-eaters and restaurateurs know what these are without being told. However, I wish to limn the more touchy, personal crimes that curdle the very liaison of trust between host and guest.

"Host and guest"—what a sad joke, what a throwback to a golden age. Was there ever a golden age of dining out, you might ask? Weren't *garçons* always offhand and nasty, tavernkeepers greedy, customers drunken and gross? Yes, that's what gives eating out its, uh, historical continuity. But it's the myth of hospitality, and the ritual of service, that stands up to the egregious historicity of sneers, and my crimes are crimes against myth.

Twice in two weeks a waiter touched me. Not the same waiter, and in different restaurants. They were both young males, and both times I was utterly infuriated and embarrassed. When calm, I was amazed at how quickly I responded, acting not thoughtfully but from my gut. Am I too fastidious? No one has called me so before, and I don't particularly dislike being touched, by young males or anyone else. So what was going on?

The waiter at the first place was a well-meaning nincompoop. He forgot bread and water (the jailhouse syndrome) and had no clue to the menu: where anything came from, how it was cooked, if it had nuts on top—you get the picture. One wanted to shoot him, but one also looked for excuses, like maybe it's his first night. But when his bumbling worsened, he tried to cover up his ignorance with pompous familiarity. We joked back a little, to help him and to ease the strain, but at that point he spilled his first dish (more to come). No cleanup. And finally, when I asked him about a proffered pasta that should have been squid, *he put his hand on my shoulder.* I turned involuntarily and stared at the hand. His hand was on me. He realized what he was doing, mumbled something, and almost ran away.

There's less a story to the second waiter: he seemed more expert. Our annoyance was with the posings of this expensive vacation restaurant, not with him. But he was amused that we should request salad dressing ("it's our house dressing; it's also our only dressing") on the side, and when he brought it out, and I thanked him, *he patted me on the back.* My table partner cringed, but the waiter half laughed, half shrugged, and sauntered away.

I knew when I set out to talk about this that I would risk sounding like a snob, that I would, in fact, have to convince you that being touched by a waiter was indeed a crime. Take my word for it: it is. Your mother or father may kiss your brow when serving giblets at Thanksgiving, your lover may nuzzle the back of your neck as he or she takes away your plate, but a waiter cannot even so much as place a finger on your person while you are at the restaurant's table. By the way, you, a customer, can't touch a waiter, either. Women who wait are pinched black and blue (some men are too); this is sexual harassment. But the other kind of touching, the kind I am decrying, is almost as bad and just as shocking, as I found out when, in a crowded dining room, I tried to get a helpful waiter's attention (to thank her) by tapping her on the shoulder. She turned around with the same look on her face I imagine I had, when touched, on mine.

The rule is there, but why? It is not simply because the waiter is traditionally considered a servant, although it is easy to see the no-touch rule as a theatrical realization of "keeping one's place." All restauranting is rules; you break one, you break them all. What if I, a stranger, arose and took your chop, your oyster, from your plate? What if I walked into the kitchen and turned up the flame? What if I sat down at your table and started to croon? But touching and eating forbid each other on every course: there was a milky time when eating *was* touching, and adults are supposed to be beyond that. We are extremely vulnerable at table, in a position of civilized physical trust, a trust the waiter is employed to mediate as neutrally as possible.

Who was knifed in the back while eating, while being served?
    She turned around so fast, so mad.

(9/9/1986)

Cold buffet, Paris, 1920s.

Paris, New York

A thousand cliches, wrapped in a Hermes scarf. A bread baton in every hand, but "he handles you like a loaf of bread," said one Frenchman, about an American's kneading embrace. The embroidered poodle, the iron tower that invented semiotics, the Arc de Triomphe, askew. Coffee is time, wine is talk, champagne is love. It's a city meant for walking; it's a city meant for sitting. They all, even the poorest, have one perfect suit. In that suit, they stare down Americans who have not wiped croissant crumbs from their lips, flaccid, uncolored lips numbed by unaccustomed butter. Trumpets resound, the crowd is hushed, the herald proclaims: "You cannot have a bad meal in Paris."

I'd be surprised if impressionable Americans could avoid seeing Paris through a movie's eyes. This has nothing to do with work, friends, politics, or the Roland Barthes you've read; it has to do with Paris's role in the screenplay, its wide and willing arms. Parisians will pardon me for saying it, but since their popular advertising culture imagines cowboys on the Hudson (neo-bolos are big this year), ours will be excused for Leslie Caron. If I must report on Paris, let it be in parallel columns, or, perhaps more apt, in bundled ribbons that curl. For example, the red ribbon would go: the battles of Algiers; the ramparts of 1968; the failure of Mitterrand; a terror-conscious

325

city where the mayor is also head of state; the greatest disparity between the haves and have-nots in the Common Market. You trail this along with the blue ribbons of couture, cuisine, and all the other fine arts, retrograde and not. You are a tourist, with a tourist's perennial first impressions. You are an expert, on intimate terms with generalization. You are genuinely surprised by unexpected passion. You are from New York.

The first meal? I want the typical meal, I told Bill, over and over, no three-star Michelin feeds for me. How does the working Parisian eat out? (Bill—an American, pronounced "Beel"—turns up, again and again, as helper and guide. Thanks Bill, and Hervé, and François, and also Yanou, who got me those reservations for big-M tables I wasn't supposed to want.) The question made no sense; so Bill smiled and took me to his neighborhood example of why France is better, called Au Pied De Fouet. Can a place that seats a dozen not be crowded? We grabbed paper mats, four glasses (for two), set our places, then ourselves. Beel bantered with the woman who obviously set down, with hips and tongue, the laws of the restaurant. Suited diplomats (from surrounding embassies) bent to her preference, suitable students to her remarks. "When I arrive in Paris," Beel told me, "I come here and order oeufs mayonnaise, and then I'm sure I'm back." And so I ordered them, hoping they would presage my return.

I was shaking with jet palsy. There was no objectivity: the eggs mayonnaise tasted like nostalgia without memory. Chicken livers, mashed potatoes for me, rabbit and boiled potatoes for him. "By the way, don't think this is usual,

people come to this hole in the wall from all over the city."
Oh, great. "Especially for the baking, some of the best in
Paris." I liked the look of the lemon tart. Lemon tarts often
fight tartness with sugar. This one had solved that problem, concentrating the lemon flavor neutrally so it could
move on to texture and crust. Pockets of denser yellow
were suspended in an airy pastel whip. The result was heterogeneous as well as light and dry, a lemon-tart first for
me. Perfect sturdy crust, a container and an end. Geographic riddle: where is a lemon tart a madeleine? Beel's
dark-chocolate gateau concentrated in the same manner
the essence of the drug in a vehicle neither too dry nor too
sweet, a wallop that would at once keep you awake and put
you to sleep. So much of Paris eating felt like that, the
body a battlefield on which opposing impulses struggled.
You were exhausted, yet had never moved.

When you attain an impossible reservation at a three-
star restaurant, you take it, said the devil in my head.
These stars are not like the schoolmarm stickers we have
in the States: these are supposed to indicate, at least, con-
sistency and a respectable balance between fussy tradition
and badboy innovation. So what if it's my first night, I had
wanted to eat Joël Robuchon's racy neonouvelle cooking
since I read about it. The French work late and eat at nine.
Jamin's *menu dégustation* costs 530 francs per person; 6.4
francs equaled one dollar, that day. When will this moment
come again?

The success of Robuchon's meal did not come into focus until I had eaten many others in the following week, so
I will recount his menu of the season further in this article.

This is the memory I use to recall the dinner. After six courses, a cheese board is tabled. The selections divide into five groups, I think, such as hard, blued, runny; all the types we know, with names we may have thought we understood. Cantal Saint-Nectaire, Reblochon, and a Camembert de Chèvre. A what? These were my four, with another of Robuchon's famous crusty rolls or slightly sour pain au levain. I began with the goat Camembert, took a forkful, watching the pearl pretend to liquefy but actually stay put, and glided it onto my bread. I took them, not it, into my mouth, and involuntarily inhaled the flavors—yeast, mold, grass—as vinophiles, in reflex, inhale wine.

And understood that wine heightens cheese, not cheese wine. And decided that Pasteur should be shot—poor New York. And watched myself taste the cheese; rather, watched it taste me. There was no will involved in this experience, for some foods dictate the grounds on which they are proven. The cheese rumor I've heard all my life is true. My eyes swelled. Cool, randy, glandular flavor repeated and rolled into its previous instant of flavor, cumulatively. I burst into tears. It had been a long day.

Beel, who had run with many a Camembert, the next day pointed out that he had become misty, too, so I could trust my instinct that this had been great, not just unfamiliar, cheese. I was beginning to feel the parameters of the workweek: my innocence against my experience, the thrill of novelty against the judgment of possible verification. These characteristics weren't mutually exclusive; whatever happiness and knowledge this trip afforded depended upon their simultaneity. What could be brought back? I risked embarrassing readers with pâtisserie gush. The solution came midway, for everything in France spoke to New York, my New York.

Sit at the table for hours, in a neighborhood of fashion, with a *salade niçoise* and orange *pressé,* as you have been advised to do for the last 30 years. Women? Smartly coiffed and superbly shod, not a hair or heel out of place. Stockings and makeup necessary, hair longish, colored, "up." Not so many of those promised suits, but very few jeans or slacks among professionals (and professional shoppers). The men in the street, however, have been given permission by Americans not to wear ties during the week, but they haven't—and probably won't—shed their jackets so the look is dowdy, going to dandy in a pinch, sometimes with hair color that looks as if it would smear in the rain. Men take their wristwatches seriously; this is where those diamond-crusted Rolexes are *proper.* Most men's windows push heavy wing tips and button-downs, just like the U.S. in its move from Italian to English four or five years ago; a garden event at a chateau outside Paris was, according to a canny observer, *"Quel Burberry."* The kids and intelligentsia who could afford it dressed MTV but with the color knob turned slightly down; racial uniformity (de facto segregation), a mood of temporary political quiet resulting from fear of numerous sentried *flics,* and that ever-present Parisian respect for the continuous past result in duller boys and girls: compare to London. Youth must grow into standard elegance.

Dinner taken in the only restaurant of chic that felt even a bit Manhattan: Maison Blanche, with a chef from Portu-

gal (Parisians exclaim here), José Lampreia. This is quite
informal compared to Jamin; sports clothes are found, the
crowd is gabbing but still polite (and stares en masse when
a foursome with a slightly less "invested" look walks in).
The merit of the meal, which was obvious, springs from
the nerve of the chef: he dares to flirt with his home cooking; he even uses olive oil! (This in puréed potatoes with a
texture like hot cloud and the smell of a tree). Yet we're in
Paree: sleek blond wood trim on the otherwise severe gridded glass room, footloose Persian rugs (red: daddy's private library). The food most easy to love: an aperitif of
effervescent peach-colored wine made from . . . peaches;
beef marrow wrapped in crenellated emerald cabbage;
lotte, with a texture like lobster, over minijuliennes of carrot and courgette seasoned with coriander seed—an "ori-
ental" touch popular in Paris right now—and seated in a
quarter-inch of olive-fragrant broth; pigeon ("from the
center of France," the chef told Beel), its body splayed and
little legs twisted into a Kama Sutra invention, roasted
with fresh dates; tiny peaches "from the vine," scarlet
fleshed; also an interesting rhubarb tart, with sugar apparent only in the crunchy-gooey caramel grid drizzled over
the top, so it comes together in the chew. We drank a San-
cerre. Total, 652 francs for two, comparable to Manhattan
moneywise although in no other important way.

I had a few more fancy meals from which to generalize.
Not all of them were so delightful, and a few were sunk,
even when the cooking was ambitious and accurate, by the
weight of their conceit. Two two-star restaurants served
unripe berries. The much touted light touch of chef Guy

Savoy, at the restaurant of the same name, resulted in no discoveries beyond his and his staff's utter ease with simple fish and meat—and a vanilla ice cream made to order that takes its place in my slowly melting pantheon. One would have to live in France to understand the ripples a first course called "castanet of vegetables" (or the like) could create. A big secret: no matter what impression you get from the markets, Parisian restaurants rarely offer vegetables, except as salad or footstool to the fish.

Parisians complained about the decline in their quality of pleasure. Fresh fish was harder to find: fewer and fewer restaurants possessed the "feel" my informants associate with the joys of their youth. Bread, wine, butter: none of it is what it was, although it's not yet reached the point that anyone's "rediscovering" honest French ingredients or, to my knowledge, fast-fooding the old cuisine *à la bonne femme.*

I replied: in none of the restaurants I visited, good and less good, did I ever question that I would be served what I ordered, question that I would be treated by staff as an expected part of the day and not as an emergency, question that some skilled effort would be made to take my satisfaction as a matter of course. In New York, every new restaurant is a puzzle to be figured, a gauntlet to be run, a war to be survived. You must compete for your portion of hospitality and competence under a general shadow of doubt. This doubt, I think, has increased over the last five years with the restaurant world's idiotic dance to fame and profit, and now blights the humanity inherent in eating out, the acknowledgment that easeful pleasure can and should be taken in public.

In Paris, I learned this about New York. I blanched over there, when I saw a great chef's cookbook displayed behind a glass door in this restaurant's foyer, or advertised by a grin and a toque on a card set between the candles of an otherwise perfect table. Had American hype hit Paris? No, for France invented the Famous Chef; luckily, its food will survive his fame.

SOME FANCY RESTAURANTS, BISTROS, AND BRASSERIES I GENERALIZED FROM

AU PIED DE FOUET
   45, rue de Babylone (three courses and wine, about $12 per person)

JAMIN JOËL ROBUCHON
32, rue de Longchamps (the $85 set menu, as
   written):
caviar jelly with cauliflower cream
braised langoustine with coriander
white bass cooked in its skin, sauce "verjutée"
calf's sweetbread ravioli with mushrooms
pigeon breast and foie gras with cabbage
"little rustic salad" [with pigeon legs]
cheeses, fresh and ripe
*"choice of desserts" [no choice—you're expected to
   eat all three]*
espresso with "dainties"

MAISON BLANCHE
82, boulevard Lefebvre, J.L. Poujauran supplies
   bread ($50 per person)

MICHEL ROSTANG
20, rue Rennequin (don't ask, but the single fried
   baby Mediterranean red mullet was almost worth
   it)

GUY SAVOY
28, rue Duret ($65 per person)

LES MINISTERES
30, rue de Bac (average "fake" brasserie, $20 per
   person)

VAUDEVILLE
29, rue Vivienne (the real 1925 thing, $30 per
   person)

AU DUC DE RICHELIEU
rue de Richelieu ($25 per person)

We do love New York for its vertical energy and bou-
quets of different flowers. Paris's biggest Jewish deli—
with bullet holes in the window, circled in yellow to
memorialize those who died in the terrorist attack—has
food that Beel found inedible. I am staying in New York,
for I live here. This is where I learned—and continue to
learn—to eat. Can the two cities come together?

Not all the pictures came out. There's the sign, *Au Duc de Richelieu, le coeur du beaujolais, Restaurant, Bar.* Photos never mesh with how you felt; for example, these look dark, whereas, over our three-hour lunch, light filled the room. I never imagined how much rillettes—potted pork, seasoned, fatted, and pounded to shreds—resemble tuna. "This is what it should be, now I know." We ate, nodded, ate *and* nodded, until we tried the 90-franc carafe, a 1976 Fleurie. We laughed, in the middle of the afternoon. Marinated white fish, a 30 percent foie gras *delice*—oh dear, who would need 100 percent? Grilled and sliced beef—simple?—with pommes frites, lettuce salad with parsley and puckering mustard, to remind us of the meat we had dispatched. Here's the owner, 76 years old. He just finished his lunch, is offering us a marc. How can these men drink so much? I don't believe it's five o'clock.

"This is almost the last of its kind in Paris," said Hervé. "That can't be," I said.

Just like New York, the last and best of New York. Home?

(11/11/1986)

Sans Bell-Bottoms

In Paris, the only New York restaurant I was asked about was Revolution, the present incarnation at 1 University Place, a barnlike, unwholesome site once occupied by the late art-restaurateur Mickey Ruskin's final money generators (serially called One University Place—Mickey's—and Chinese Chance). I was amused by this curiosity but not surprised. Any restaurant named Revolution should pique French interest, so fond is that country of working-class uprisings that consolidate the power of the bourgeoisie. But don't get the wrong idea; Revolution is not another Paris Commune (a restaurant on Bleecker Street). A small mural under the sign, and the lettering of the name itself, places this revolution not near the Bastille, 1789, but smack dab in Berkeley, 1968.

That this happens to be New York University territory, 1986, probably works against the intended effect. These kids don't even look up at the sign as they walk in (if they walk in—business ain't so hot). The most shocking thing I ever heard may explain this. Five years ago, a college teacher in Southern California asked his class to discuss Marilyn Monroe as a cultural icon. He couldn't get them started; he prodded and cajoled, until one of the more helpful students suggested that maybe he should first tell them who Marilyn Monroe might be.

Perhaps Revolution would do better on the Upper West Side, where those of us in our late thirties would get all teary comparing marches and in doing so not worry about the awful food—wretched pork chops and wimpy chili. As it stands, the restaurant is a failure, for its ill-conceived and worse-executed Jimi Hendrixy murals don't even come close to the graphic style of the period it proposes to evoke. In fact, Revolution is like the '60s seen through alien eyes, proximate in intention but distinctly off, as if it were the set of a parallel planet's counterculture, a la *Star Trek.* Is recent history nothing but distorted style?

Right now, the East Village contains at least three stores that carry '60s clothing, furniture, and objets d'kitsch. L.A. has some, and San Francisco must as well (although the difference between past and present in that city is not so distinct). The market for both vintage and neovintage products of the '60s seems to be out there, but I wonder who that market is. Certainly, no one who has lived with inflatable chairs and daisy decals would suffer them again so soon, when we're still having nightmares in which they serve as active props. Most '60s clothing has resisted recycling (used, tight polyester shirts stink in the seams), although a few cues of the period, such as leather minis and hippie fringe, have settled in for a long run as suggestive short subjects.

What must the decently young think of the events of the immediate past? Some evidence suggests that most are doing everything in their power to ignore them. Of course, no past is homogenous, or even stable, and it's ridiculous to imagine that all youth of the '60s were card-carrying members of a counterculture. "Counterculture," if I remember correctly, was a term used predominantly by the media. I have a powerful urge to argue that the superficial objects of that counterculture—my wide-wale hip huggers and American-flag shirt, for instance—in some way stood for the ideals through which that counterculture (and this very newspaper!) best remembers itself: ideals that were antiwar, antiracist, antisexist, progay. But that's garbage. Did the cast of *Laugh-In* agree about Vietnam? What was Edie Sedgwick's stand on the Black Panthers? Did everyone who first bought Kleenex Boutique Tissues ("Ho-hum tissues are out, luv") smoke dope?

In these times, '60s ephemera have only a faint aroma of revolution left on them. They are being asked, as it were, to fill the cracks of memory, even to displace, via chic objectness, now-dim emotions or actions of those old enough to have felt or initiated them. At the same time, leavings of the '60s have the power to jolt us back to their time. Revolution the restaurant, however debased its costume, has flung me into a vale of pamphlets, marches, and humane possibilities, not all of which have been entirely lost. This double duty describes the paradox, the dialectic, of retro style.

It isn't so strange that a restaurant attempts to cash in on collegiate fascination with a neutered past. College youth have money. And it's not so awful that the restaurant doesn't know how the '60s looked; after all, the '60s cannibalized itself, stylewise, to oblivion. Never had a material culture been so self-aware, so chameleonic, so eager to please. If music, clothes, and attitude could symbolize politics—for this was the thrill, the promise, of the streets—then these same spoor of fashion could be—must be!—turned on themselves and vitiated. Markets for such attractive products had to be made to grow beyond the radical fringe. I am glad to recall that those who resisted our role in Vietnam weren't exactly a minority . . . but now we're in the '70s, a time for populist regroupment and assimilation. Its restaurant—McDonald's—has been waiting in the wings.

How soon will the '70s be remembered? And what of the '80s will we have to recycle, to forget?

(11/25/1986)

Cloy to the World

You can see homeless men and women from restaurants with windows. When the window is decorated with holly and tinsel, the frame becomes even more poignant. We who are inside go on with dinner, but the nature of our meal is changed, even for those who possess the fortitude to shrug off that most constant image of history: humans eating in the presence of others who cannot.

This year is not appreciably different from the last: a few thousand more ill and homeless folks, a medium-cooling of restaurant fever. Some lucky consumers become slightly less permeable to the disparities. How could they go on if not? Anyone looking back to our time would wonder how the cautiously solvent among us did not simply go mad. Our safety valves—the dime dropped in a shaking cup—are less and less effective. Dreams of permanent change are limited to a very few, and even these visionaries are not immune to the discontinuity of pleasure that was once called guilt.

The holidays enthrone this discontinuity through charity, and in doing so attempt to make the world right again. What would a world without "Christmas" be like? It would be like a world without sugar.

No single stuff has materialized so fully as sugar the payment some have made for others' pointed enjoyment. I am hardly the first to say this: Sidney W. Mintz, in his recent book *Sweetness and Power,* describes the creation of the slavery that enabled cane sugar's production, the creation of the eating habits that built its market, and the creation of meaning that made sugar a food necessary to millions instead of a condiment or medicine proper to a few. Mintz does not confuse sugar with sweetness; milk is sweet, honey is sweet, revenge is sweet. But sugar entails power. Refined cane sugar, until recently, usurped all other Western sweetness; it brought imperialism and capitalism together in a powerful shake of hands. Africa was raided, the Caribbean raped, shipping fortunes made as the new industrial working classes traded whole wheat bread and ale for a cuppa and a lump with white bread, plus treacle, jam, pudding. It follows that in the late 19th century, "dessert" became a course, and a symbol.

Cane sugar use is falling, but sugar has not given over its crown. High-fructose corn syrup or HFCS, now in Coca-Cola as well as other industrial edibles, appeals to the American cornbelt, but it remains invisible as an *image* of sweetness. Any ingredient designated by initials has trouble entering the consuming imagination. Only sugar crystals glow hard and clear, turning any bakery window into a micro-Tiffany. White sugar will mean sweetness even if its production withers in an economy of ever-cheaper replacement.

Sugar is unique too in that it is perceived by most simultaneously as a necessity and a pleasure. Conspicuous desserts still have the power to evoke childish "ahs," and adults of demonstrable sophistication melt at the sight of a chocolate confection they know looks better than it will taste. Sugar taps a giant reservoir of fluffy anticipation, which at mealtime is a kind of renewal: I ate all those salty, peppery, difficult things that remind me of work, but now I will be young again.

The need for the cheer of sugar was clear during World War II; England especially felt its shortage. But the sugar industry is fighting its rivals and substitutes with campaigns based not on delectable wickedness but on health. Of course they're doomed to failure. No one likes to see sweetness linked to health. The teenager who needs the "energy" from a Snickers bar to finish his game must be a jerk, for candy is supposed to be distracting; Gatorade tastes like— should taste like—the tonic he asks for. The cane sugar people needn't worry, for when pleasure becomes addictive, as it obviously has, it becomes necessary. Annual sucrose use in America remains a strong 100 pounds per capita, more if other HFCS and beet sugars are included. This is a lot of calories dedicated only to fun.

Many would be disgusted if they remembered, at table, the wrenching, tortuous work that produces the sugar that goes into dessert. Should we stop eating sugar because of it? (And would that be right? Haitian cane cutters, the poorest in the world, are forced to leave the country for work because the new government is closing plantations.)

No one will stop. Especially not now, during the holidays, when we are asked to, and most need to, believe in the inevitability of the necessary pleasure. We have time. The new year comes all too fast.

(12/23/1986)